Fanny Burney And Her Friends: Select Passages From Her Diary And Other Writings

Fanny Burney, Leonard Benton Seeley

FANNY BURNEY

AND HER FRIENDS

FANNY BURNEY

AND HER FRIENDS

Frances Burney.

FANNY BURNEY

AND HER FRIENDS

SELECT PASSAGES FROM HER DIARY AND
OTHER WRITINGS

EDITED BY

L. B. SEELEY, M.A.

Late Fellow of Trinity College, Cambridge

AUTHOR OF

"HORACE WALPOLE AND HIS WORLD"

WITH NINE ILLUSTRATIONS AFTER
REYNOLDS, GAINSBOROUGH, COPLEY, AND WEST

FOURTH EDITION

NEW YORK
CHARLES SCRIBNER'S SONS
743-745 BROADWAY
1892

-14665-

CONTENTS.

CHAPTER I.

CHAPTER II.

CHAPTER XI.

CHAPTER XII.

CHAPTER XIII.

LIST OF ILLUSTRATIONS.

Fanny Burney and her Friends.

CHAPTER I.

FRANCES BURNEY was born at King's Lynn on the 13th
of June, 1752. She was the second daughter, and third
child, of Dr. Charles Burney, author of the well-known
' History of Music,' by Esther Sleepe, his first wife.

It has been stated,* we know not on what authority,
that Dr. Burney was a descendant in the fifth degree of
James Macburney, a native of Scotland, who attended
King James I. when he left that country to take possession of the English throne. The doctor himself was
certainly unacquainted with this fact, if fact it be. His
grandfather and father were each named James Macburney,

* Owen and Blakeway's ' History of Shrewsbury,' vol. ii., p. 388.

I

but they were both born at the village of Great Hanwood, in Shropshire, where the former inherited a considerable estate ; there was no trace in their connections of Celtic extraction ; and Charles has recorded that he could never find at what period any of his ancestors lived in Scotland or Ireland.   Doubtless it was the adventures of the two historical James Macburneys which led Macaulay to conclude that the family was of Irish origin.   James the younger offended his father by eloping with an actress from the Goodman's Fields Theatre.   'The old gentle-man could devise no more judicious mode of wreaking vengeance on his undutiful boy than by marrying the cook.'   He married some sort of domestic, at any rate, who brought him a son, named Joseph, to whom he left all his property.   Joseph, however, soon ran through his fortune, and was reduced to earn his bread as a dancing-master in Norfolk.   His elder brother James survived the actress, and though a poor widower with a swarm of children, gained the hand of Miss Ann Cooper, an heiress and beauty, who had refused the addresses of the celebrated Wycherley.   After his second marriage, James followed the profession of a portrait-painter, first at Shrewsbury, and later at Chester.   The number of his children rose to twenty-two ; the youngest being Charles, afterwards Dr. Burney, and a twin sister, Susannah, who were born and baptized at Shrewsbury on the 12th of April, 1726 ; at which date their father still retained the name of Macburney.   When and why the Mac was dropped we are not informed, but by the time Charles attained to manhood, the family in all its branches— uncles and cousins, as well as brothers and sisters—had concurred in adopting the more compact form of Burney.

The musical talents of Charles Burney showed them-selves at an early age.   In his eighteenth year, the proficiency he had acquired under his eldest half-brother, James Burney, organist of St. Mary's, Shrewsbury, recommended him to the notice of Dr. Arne, the composer of 'Rule, Britannia,' who offered to take him as a pupil. In 1744, accordingly, Charles was articled to the most famous English musician of that day, and went to live in London. At the house of the no less famous Mrs. Cibber,* who was sister of Dr. Arne, he had opportunities of mixing with most of the persons then distinguished by their writings or their performances in connection with the orchestra and the stage. At the end of his third year with Arne, Burney acquired a still more useful patron. Among the leaders of *ton* in the middle of last century was Fulk Greville, a descendant of the favourite of Queen Elizabeth and friend of Sir Philip Sidney. To a passion for field sports, horse-racing, and gaming, this fine gentleman united an equally strong taste for more refined pleasures, and his ample possessions enabled him to gratify every inclination to the utmost. Greville met Burney at the shop of Kirkman, the harpsichord-maker, and was so captivated with his playing and lively conversation, that he paid Arne £300 to cancel the young man's articles, and took him to live with himself as a sort of musical companion. The high-bred society to which he was now introduced prepared Burney to take rank in later years as the most fashionable professor of music, and one of the most polished wits of his time. In Greville's town circle, and at his country seat, Wilbury House, near Andover, his dependent constantly encountered peers, statesmen, diplomatists, macaronis, to whose various humours this son of a provincial portrait-painter seems to have adapted

---

* Actress and singer; married Theophilus Cibber, son of Colley Cibber. She was a special favourite with Handel, who wrote much of his contralto music for her. In the latter part of her career she was associated with Garrick at Drury Lane. Born, 1714; died, 1766.

himself as readily as if he had been to the manner born. So firm a hold did he gain on his protector, that neither the marriage of the latter, nor his own, appears in any degree to have weakened his favour. When Greville chose to make a stolen match with Miss Frances Macartney,* or, as the lady's father expressed it, 'to take a wife out of the window whom he might just as well have taken out of the door,' Burney was employed to give the bride away. When Burney himself became a benedict, Mr. and Mrs. Greville cordially approved both the act and his choice, and Mrs. Greville subsequently stood as god-mother to Frances Burney.

It was in 1749 that Charles Burney took to wife the lady before mentioned, who, on her mother's side, was of French origin, and grandchild of a Huguenot refugee named Dubois. Esther Sleepe, herself was bred in the City of London, and her future husband first saw her at the house of his elder brother, Richard Burney, in Hatton Garden. To his fashionable friends the marriage must have seemed an imprudent one, for Miss Sleepe had no fortune to compensate for her obscure parentage. From the 'Memoirs of Dr. Burney,'† we learn that her father was a man of ill conduct; but Fanny everywhere speaks with enthusiasm of her mother's mother. Somewhat strangely, this lady herself adhered to the Roman Catholic creed, though she was the child of a man exiled by the revocation of the Edict of Nantes, and though she suffered her own daughter Esther to be brought up in the Anglican Communion. In view of the union which Frances Burney afterwards' contracted, it is as well to bear in mind that one of her parents was partly of French extraction. In

---

*This lady wrote verses, and acquired some repute by a poem entitled ' A Prayer for Indifference.'
† 'Memoirs of Dr. Burney, by his Daughter, Madame d'Arblay,' 1832.

consequence of his wife's connections, Charles Burney on his marriage hired a house in the City. He was presently elected organist of St. Dionis Backchurch, produced several pieces of music, and laid himself out to obtain pupils. These flocked to him from all sides. The Grevilles had gone abroad shortly after he left them, but he could still count on their influence, and that of the friends they had procured him, while he found new supporters daily among the merchants and bankers east of Temple Bar. His wife bore him a first-born son, who was baptized James, according to the immemorial usage of the Burney race, and then a daughter, who received her mother's name of Esther. But when all things looked fair and promising, the sky suddenly became overcast. The young father's health broke down: a violent attack of fever was succeeded by a train of symptoms threatening consumption; and, as a last resource, he was ordered by his medical adviser, the poet-physician Armstrong,* to throw up his employments in London and go to live in the country.

In this emergency, Burney was offered and accepted the place of organist at Lynn, whither he removed in 1751, and where he spent the nine following years. His stipend was fixed at £100 a year, a handsome sum for those days, and he largely added to it by giving music lessons in the town, and in many of the great houses of Norfolk. The qualities which had stood him in good stead in London proved equally acceptable to the country gentlemen of East Anglia. 'He scarcely ever entered one of their houses upon terms of business without leaving it on terms of intimacy.' His journeys to Houghton, Holkham, Kimberley, Rainham and Felbrig were performed on the back of his mare Peggy, who leisurely padded along the

* Author of a didactic poem, 'The Art of Preserving Health.'

sandy cross-roads, while the rider studied a volume of
Italian poetry with the aid of a dictionary which he carried
in his pocket. As Burney's income grew, his family also
increased. After his third child, Frances, came another
daughter, Susanna ; next a second son, who was called
Charles, and then a fourth daughter, Charlotte. The
keen breezes from the Wash helped to brace his spare
person, and though constant riding about the country in
winter was not desirable exercise, Burney gradually recon-
ciled himself to his provincial lot, which he enlivened by
laying plans for his ' History of Music,' corresponding with
the Grevilles and other old friends, and commencing an
acquaintance by letter with Dr. Johnson. In 1759, however, he gained some general reputation by his musical
setting of an ode for St. Cecilia's Day, which was performed
with much applause at Ranelagh Gardens ; and, stimulated
by the exhortations which reached him from various
quarters, he prepared to resume his career in the capital.
Foremost in urging the step was Samuel Crisp, whom he
had met and taken for his mentor at Wilbury House,
and of whom we shall have more to say presently. To
settle for life among the foggy aldermen of Lynn, wrote
Crisp, would be to plant his youth, genius, hopes and
fortune against a north wall. Burney took the warning,
and in 1760, having sufficiently recruited his constitution,
he returned to London with his wife and family.

He established himself in Poland Street, which, from
having been in high fashion, was then lapsing by degrees
to the professional and the less wealthy mercantile classes,
though it still boasted among its inhabitants the Duke of
Chandos, besides several lesser personages whose names
were written in the peerage. This was the very situation
for an ambitious music-master of slender means but good
connections. In a very short time, we are told, Burney

'had hardly an hour that was not appropriated to some fair disciple.' He began his round of lessons as early as seven o'clock in the morning, and sometimes did not finish it till eleven at night. He often dined in a hackney coach on the contents of a sandwich-box and a flask of sherry and water, which he carried in his pocket. The care of his six little ones of necessity devolved wholly on their mother, who was well worthy of the charge. In talents and accomplishments Mrs. Burney appears to have been at least the equal of her husband. While she lived, a certain touch of Huguenot decision in her added strength to his less strenuous nature; and her French blood undoubtedly contributed its full share to the quick and lively parts that in different degrees distinguished their children. These, as they grew out of infancy, composed a group which, on every view that we get of it, presents an extremely pleasant picture. In most cases, their minds blossomed at an early period. The eldest daughter, Esther, inherited her father's musical genius; when only eight years of age she performed with surprising skill on the harpsichord. James, the eldest son, appears to have been a lad of spirit and vivacity. Beginning as 'a nominal midshipman' at the age of ten, he chose the navy for his profession, sailed twice round the world with Captain Cook, rose to the rank of rear-admiral, and lived to have his 'flashes of wild wit' celebrated by Charles Lamb in one of the essays of 'Elia.' Susanna, the favourite and special friend of our Fanny, has left letters worthy of being printed on the same page with those of her famous sister, and her power of writing showed itself sooner than did Fanny's. Finally, Charles,* the second son, though for some reason he quitted Cambridge with-

* Born at Lynn, December 4, 1756; LL.D. Aberdeen, 1792; vicar of Deptford, prebendary of Lincoln, chaplain to the King; died 1817.

out taking a degree, made his mark in Greek criticism before completing his twenty-fifth year; in that department of study, so speedy a harvest affords sufficient proof of a forward spring. The fame of the younger Dr. Charles Burney is now somewhat faded: in his prime, he was classed with Porson and Parr as one of the three chief representatives of English scholarship; and on his death his library was purchased by the nation and placed in the British Museum.

The one marked exception to the rule of early development in the Burney family was noted in the case of the daughter who was destined to be its principal ornament. We are told that the most remarkable features of Frances Burney's childhood were her extreme shyness and her backwardness at learning. At eight years of age, she did not even know her letters; and her elder brother, who had a sailor's love of practical jokes, used to pretend to teach her to read, and give her the book upside down, which, he said, she never found out. An officious acquaintance of her mother suggested that the application of the little dunce might be quickened by the rod, but the wiser parent replied that 'she had no fear about Fanny.' Mrs. Burney, it is clear, favoured no forcing methods in education. She was laid aside by illness shortly after the family's return to London, and, so long as her health lasted, seems to have given regular teaching to the eldest of her daughters only, whose taste for reading she very early began to form. "I perfectly recollect," wrote Fanny to Esther many years later, "child as I was, and never of the party, this part of your education. At that very juvenile period, the difference even of months makes a marked distinction in bestowing and receiving instruction. I, also, was so peculiarly backward that even our Susan stood before me; she could read when I knew not my letters. But, though so sluggish to learn, I was always observant. Do you remember Mr. Seaton denominating me at fifteen, the *silent, observant Miss Fanny?* Well I recollect your reading with our dear mother all Pope's works and Pitt's ' Æneid.' I recollect, also, your spouting passages from Pope, that I learned from hearing you recite them, before—many years before—I read them myself."

Mrs. Burney died at the end of September, 1761. Towards the close of her illness, Fanny and Susan, with their brother Charles, had been sent to board with a Mrs. Sheeles, who kept a school in Queen Square, that they might be out of the way; and this experienced judge of children was greatly struck by the intensity of Fanny's grief at a loss which girls of nine are apt to realize very imperfectly.

The truth seems to be that Fanny's backwardness and apparent dulness were simply due to the numbing influence of nervousness and extreme diffidence. Her father, the less indulgent to shyness in others because he had experienced it in himself, for a long time did her very imperfect justice. Looking back in later years, he could remember that her talent for observing and representing points of character, her lively invention, even her turn for composition, had shown themselves before she had learnt to spell her way through the pages of a fairy tale. A magician more potent than any books helped to call forth the germs of her latent powers. Among the friends most intimate in Poland Street during the months following Mrs. Burney's death were David Garrick and his engaging wife, La Violetta. While exerting themselves to console the widower, this brilliant and kindly couple did not neglect his motherless family. ' Garrick, who was passionately fond of children, never withheld his visits on account of

the absence of the master of the house.' If Mr. Burney
was not at home, the great actor, keenly alive to his own
gift of bestowing pleasure, would devote himself to entertaining the little ones. The rapture with which his entrance
was greeted by that small audience charmed him as much
as the familiar applause of Drury Lane. The prince of
comedians and mimics was content to lavish all the resources of his art on a handful of girls and boys. When
he left them, they spent the rest of the day in recalling the
sallies of his humour, and the irresistible gestures which
had set them off. So Fanny tells us, the least noticed,
probably, yet the most attentive and observant member
of the whole group. On many a happy night, the elder
ones, in charge of some suitable guardian, were permitted
to occupy Mrs. Garrick's private box at the theatre.
There they beheld 'the incomparable Roscius' take the
stage, and followed him with eyes of such eager admiration, that it seemed—so their amused father told his
friend—

> 'They did, as was their duty,
> Worship the shadow of his shoe-tie!'

Burney relates of Fanny that ' she used, after having seen
a play in Mrs. Garrick's box, to take the actors off, and
compose speeches for their characters, for she could not
read them.' But, he continues, in company or before
strangers, she was silent, backward, and timid, even to
sheepishness; and, from her shyness, had such profound
gravity and composure of features, that those of Dr.
Burney's friends who went often to his home, and entered into the different humours of the children, never
called Fanny by any other name, from the time she had
reached her eleventh year, than 'the old lady.'

Yet the shyest children will now and then forget their
shyness. This seems to be the moral of a story which

the worthy doctor goes on to tell in his rather prolix and pompous style. " There lived next door to me, at that time, in Poland Street, and in a private house, a capital hair-merchant, who furnished perukes to the judges and gentlemen of the law. The hair-merchant's female children and mine used to play together in the little garden behind the house ; and, unfortunately, one day, the door of the wig-magazine being left open, they each of them put on one of those dignified ornaments of the head, and danced and jumped about in a thousand antics, laughing till they screamed at their own ridiculous figures. Unfortunately, in their vagaries, one of the flaxen wigs, said by the proprietor to be worth upwards of ten guineas—in those days an enormous price—fell into a tub of water, placed for shrubs in the little garden, and lost all its gorgon buckle,* and was declared by the owner to be totally spoilt. He was extremely angry, and chid very severely his own children, when my little daughter, ' the old lady,' then ten years of age, advancing to him, as I was informed, with great gravity and composure, sedately said, ' What signifies talking so much about an accident ? The wig is wet, to be sure ; and the wig was a good wig, to be sure : but 'tis of no use to speak of it any more, because *what's done can't be undone.*' "

Meanwhile, little was done on any regular plan for Fanny's education. She had not been suffered to remain at the school in which she was temporarily placed during her mother's last illness, nor was she sent to any other. When, after the lapse of two or three years, Burney found himself in a position to put two of his girls to school at

* The writer seems to have had in view the lines of Pope :
    'That live-long wig, which Gorgon's self might own,
      Eternal buckle takes in Parian stone.'
By the buckle of a wig was meant its stiff curl when in trim condition.

Paris, he selected the third, Susanna, rather than Fanny, to accompany the eldest sister, proposing to send Fanny and Charlotte together at a future time. Two reasons were assigned for this arrangement. One was the notion that Susanna, who inherited her father's consumptive habit, required change of climate more than the second daughter. The other was a fear lest Fanny's deep reverence for her Roman Catholic grandmother might incline her to adopt the same form of faith, and thus render her perversion easy, if, when so young, she fell within the influence of some enterprising French chaplain. We cannot help suspecting, however, that the true cause of Fanny being passed over on this occasion was an impression that Susanna was a girl of brighter parts, and better fitted to benefit by the teaching of a Paris *pension*.

From whatever motive, Fanny was left behind, nor was any instructor provided for her at home. The widower disliked the idea of introducing a governess into his house, though he had no time to spare even for directing his daughter's studies. She was thus entirely self-educated, and had no other spur to exertion than her unbounded affection for her father, who excused himself for his neglect of her training by the reflection that ' she had a natural simplicity and probity about her which wanted no teaching.' In her eleventh year she had learned to read, and began to scribble little poems and works of invention, though in a character that was illegible to everyone but herself. ' Her love of reading,' we are told, ' did not display itself till two or three years later.' Her father had a good library, over which she was allowed to range at will ; and in course of time she became acquainted with a fair portion of its lighter contents. The solitary child kept a careful account of the authors she studied, making extracts from them, and adding remarks which, we are assured, showed that her mind was riper than her knowledge. Yet she never developed any strong or decided taste for literature. She never became even a devourer of books. Indeed, it may be doubted whether she did not always derive more pleasure from her own compositions than from those of the greatest writers. Plying her pen without an effort, the leisure which most intellectual persons give to reading, Fanny devoted in great part to producing manuscripts of her own. Childish epics, dramas, and romances, were not the only ventures of her youth : she began keeping a diary at the age of fifteen, and, in addition to her published novels and sundry plays which have perished, journals, memoirs, and letters, of which a small proportion only have seen the light, occupied most of the vacant hours in her active womanhood.

During this period of self-education, the person from whom Fanny received most notice and attention appears to have been her father's old friend, Samuel Crisp. This gentleman had gone abroad while the Burneys were in Norfolk, and had taken up his abode at Rome, where he passed several years, improving his taste in music, painting, and sculpture, and forgetting for a while the young English professor who had interested him under Greville's roof. Having at length returned to England, he, some time after Mrs. Burney's death, met Burney by accident at the house of a common acquaintance. The casual encounter immediately revived the old intimacy. Crisp at once found his way to the house in Poland Street, and, like Garrick, was attracted by the group of children there. As the two eldest of these and the lively Susanna were soon afterwards removed to a distance, the chief share in his regard naturally fell to the lot of Fanny. Hence, while all the children came to look upon him with a sort of filial feeling, he was in a special manner appropriated by Fanny as 'her dearest daddy.' And there were points in Crisp's temperament which harmonized well with the girl's shy yet aspiring character. Both, in their turn, set their hearts on the attainment of literary renown; both had the same tendency to shrink into themselves. Success changed Fanny from a silent domestic drudge into a social celebrity; failure helped to change Crisp from a shining man of fashion into a moody recluse.

The story of this strange man has been sketched by Macaulay, but it has so close a bearing on our heroine's life, that we cannot avoid shortly retracing it here. A handsome person, dignified manners, excellent talents, and an accomplished taste procured for Crisp, in his prime, acceptance and favour, not only with Fulk Greville and his set, but also with a large number of other persons distinguished in the great world. Thus, he was admitted to the acquaintance of the highly descended and wealthy Margaret Cavendish Harley, then Duchess Dowager of Portland, whom we mention here because through her Crisp became known to Mrs. Delany, by whom Fanny was afterwards introduced to the Royal Family. Another of his friends was Mrs. Montagu, who then, as he used to say, was 'peering at fame,' and gradually rising to the rank of a lady patroness of letters. And among the most intimate of his associates was the Earl of Coventry, at the time when that 'grave young lord,' as Walpole calls him, after long dangling, married the most beautiful of the beautiful Gunnings. Now, about the date when our Fanny first saw the light, it was buzzed abroad in the coterie of Crisp's admirers that their hero had finished a tragedy on the story of Virginia. A lively expectation was at once awakened. But Garrick, though a personal friend of the author, hesitated and delayed to gratify the public with the rich feast which was believed to be in store for it.

The utmost efforts were employed to overcome his reluctance. The great Mr. Pitt was prevailed on to read the
play, and to pronounce in its favour. Lord Coventry
exerted all his influence with the coy manager. Yet not
until Lady Coventry herself had joined her solicitations
to those of her husband was 'Virginia' put in rehearsal at
Drury Lane. The piece was produced in February, 1754,
and ran several nights, buoyed up by the acting and
popularity of Garrick, who contributed a remarkably good
epilogue.* But no patronage or support could keep alive
a drama which, in truth, had neither poetical merit nor
the qualities of a good acting play to recommend it.
'Virginia' was very soon withdrawn, and, as usual, the
writer, while cruelly mortified by his failure, attributed it
to every cause but the right one. Lord Coventry advised
alterations, which Crisp hastened to execute, but Garrick,
though civil, was determined that so ineffective a muse
should not again cumber his stage. His firmness, of
course, cost him the friendship of the ungrateful Crisp,
who, conscious of considerable powers, and unable to
perceive that he had mistaken their proper application,
inveighed with equal bitterness against manager, performers, and the public, and in sore dudgeon betook
himself across the sea to Italy. Macaulay, indeed, will
have it that his disappointment ruined his temper and
spirits, and turned him into 'a cynic, and a hater of mankind.' But in this, as in too many of the essayist's
trenchant statements, something of accuracy is sacrificed
for the sake of effect. Crisp appears to have enjoyed
himself not a little in Italy, and on his return, though he
did not again settle in London, he fixed his first abode as
near to it as the courtly village of Hampton, where he
furnished a small house, filling it with pictures, statuary,

* Walpole to Bentley, March 6, 1754.

and musical instruments, as became a man of taste. Far from shunning society in this luxurious retreat, he entertained so many guests there that his hospitality in a short time made a serious inroad on his small fortune. Chagrin at his imprudence brought on a severe attack of gout; and then it was that, broken alike in health and finances, he resolved on secluding himself from the world. Having sold his villa and its contents, he removed a few miles off to a solitary mansion belonging to an old friend, Christopher Hamilton, who, like himself, had lost the battle of life, and desired to be considered as dead to mankind.

Chesington Hall, which thenceforth became the joint residence of this pair of hermits, stood on an eminence rising from a wide and nearly desolate common, about midway between the towns of Epsom and Kingston; the neglected buildings were crumbling to pieces from age, having been begun in the same year in which Wolsey laid the first stone of Hampton Court; and the homestead was surrounded by fields, that for a long period had been so ploughed up as to leave no road or even regular footpath open across them. In this hiding-place Crisp fixed his abode for the rest of his life. So isolated was the spot that strangers could not reach it without a guide. But the inhabitants desired to have as few visitors as possible. Only as the spring of each year came round would Crisp, while his strength allowed, quit his refuge for a few weeks, to amuse himself with the picture-shows and concerts of the London season.

It seems to have been during one of these excursions that Burney met Crisp again after their long separation. The revival of their friendship gave the solitary man one more connecting link with the outside world. Down to that time Crisp's only visitor in his retreat seems to have been his sister, Mrs. Sophia Gast, of Burford, in Oxfordshire. Now to Burney also was entrusted the clue for a safe route across the wild common to Chesington Hall, while from all others, including Mr. Greville, it was still stead-fastly withheld. There is no reason to suppose that the acquaintances whom Crisp thus relinquished were more faithless than a poor man's great friends usually are. He had been flattered with hopes of obtaining some public appointment through their interest; but his health had failed before the value of the promises made to him could be fairly tested. When restored strength might have rendered seclusion irksome, and employment acceptable, his pride rebelled against further solicitation, and fixed him in the solitude where his poverty and lack of energy alike escaped reproach. Charles Burney alone, from whom he had nothing to expect, and who had always looked up to him, was admitted where others were excluded.

The modern village of Chesington lies about two miles to the north-west of the railway-station at Ewell. Some patches of heathy common still remain. Though not so solitary a place as in the days of which we write, Chesington has still a lonely look.*

Crisp, in his sanctuary, and his occasional secret journeys to London, resumed his office of mentor to Burney, and became also the confidential adviser of Burney's daughters. For such trust he was eminently qualified; since, to borrow the words of Macaulay, though he was a bad poet, he was a scholar, a thinker, and an excellent counsellor. He surpassed his younger friend, Charles, in general knowledge and force of mind, as much as he was surpassed by Charles in social tact and pliability of temper. And Burney was

* Thorne's 'Environs of London.' The name is now written Chessington, but we retain the spelling which was always used by Fanny Burney and her friends.

2

far from resenting or grudging the influence which Crisp acquired in his family; for Burney was a sweet-natured as well as a sensible man. No pitiful vanity or treacherous jealousy lay hid under his genial and gracious exterior. Conscious, apparently, that both from too great easiness of disposition, and from his manifold engagements, he was ill-fitted to discharge all the duties devolving on him as sole surviving parent, he cordially welcomed the assistance of his old and valued friend. Mrs. Thrale afterwards complained that Dr. Burney liked to keep his hold on his children; but the engrossing lady patroness seems to have meant only that he objected, as well he might, to have Fanny disposed of for months or years at a time without regard to his wishes or convenience. He was never disturbed by unworthy alarms lest some interloping well-wisher should steal away the hearts of his children from himself. He stooped to no paltry manœuvres to prevent them from becoming too much attached to this or that friend. He certainly did not interfere to check the warmth of his daughters' regard for the rugged old cynic of Chesington, nor put any restraint on the correspondence which grew up between Fanny and her 'dearest daddy.' And he reaped the full reward of his unselfishness, or, we should rather say, of his straightforward good sense. No son or daughter was ever estranged from him by the feeling that his jealousy had robbed them of a useful connection or appreciative ally. Fanny's fondness for her adopted father, as might have been expected, did not in the least diminish her love for her natural parent. 'She had always a great affection for me,' wrote Dr. Burney at the close of his life. The latter was, indeed, the standard by which she generally tried the claims of any other person to be considered admirable or charming. In her twenty-sixth year she expressed her enthusiasm for her newly-made friend, Mrs. Thrale, by saying: 'I never before saw a person who so strongly resembles my dear father.' At forty-one, she described her husband as being 'so very like my beloved father in disposition, humour, and taste, that the day never passes in which I do not exclaim: "How you remind me of my father!"'

Crisp himself, at the time when Fanny made his acquaintance, had no pretension to gentle manners or a graceful address; but, like many other disappointed men who assume the character of misanthropes, he possessed at bottom a warm, and even tender, heart, and was particularly fond of young persons. In his intimate intercourse with the Burney family, all ceremony was discarded; towards the junior members he adopted a plain, rough style of speech, which, being unmistakably playful, left them always quite at home with him. Very soon the death of Crisp's companion in retirement rendered the society of the Burneys more indispensable to the survivor, while it placed him in a better position for receiving these visits. The male line of the Hamiltons ended in Christopher, and his dilapidated estate descended to a maiden sister, Mrs. Sarah Hamilton. Rather than sell the property, this ancient lady, under Crisp's advice, divided the capacious old Hall between herself and Farmer Woodhatch, who rented and cultivated what remained of the lands. To assist her in keeping up the residence she still retained, Mrs. Hamilton called in as 'lady help' a rustic niece, named Kitty Cooke, and Crisp became her lodger, securing to his own use 'a favourite apartment, with a light and pleasant closet at the end of a long corridor.' In this closet a great part of Burney's 'History of Music' was written. There was a larger scheme, also, at this time, for turning the whole suite of rooms into a boarding establishment, but applicants for accommodation in so remote and obscure an abode were likely to be few in number. Mrs. Gast, however, came thither from time to time, and Frances Burney and her sisters were often there. We shall see, in due course, how the animated scenes of the famous novel, 'Cecilia,' or most of them, were elaborated within those mouldering walls. To the end of her life the author's thoughts wandered back with delight to the quaint old place. Her memory let nothing slip: "not a nook or corner; nor a dark passage 'leading to nothing'; nor a hanging tapestry of prim demoiselles and grim cavaliers; nor a tall canopied bed tied up to the ceiling; nor japan cabinets of two or three hundred drawers of different dimensions; nor an oaken corner-cupboard, carved with heads, thrown in every direction, save such as might let them fall on men's shoulders; nor a window stuck in some angle close to the ceiling of a lofty slip of a room; nor a quarter of a staircase, leading to some quaint unfrequented apartment; nor a wooden chimney-piece, cut in diamonds, squares, and round knobs, surmounting another of blue and white tiles, representing, *vis-à-vis*, a dog and a cat, as symbols of married life and harmony."*

The time arrived when, in accordance with their father's original design, Frances and Charlotte Burney should have been placed at school in Paris in succession to Esther and Susanna. Burney presently made another journey to the French capital to bring back the pair of sisters who had completed the term of two years assigned for their education there, but he was not accompanied by either of his other daughters. He was not deterred from taking them by any misgiving as to the results of his first experiment, which, we are assured, had fully answered

* 'Memoirs of Dr. Burney,' vol. ii., p. 185.

his expectations, but rather by some uncertainty of means and plans, connected, perhaps, in part with his approaching second marriage. Some lines from the pen of Susanna have been preserved, which are said to have been written shortly after her return, and which, if the date ascribed to them be correct, would show that the writer, who was then barely fourteen, was a remarkably forward girl of her age. As this short composition sketches in contrast Susanna's two elder sisters, we give it entire:

" Hetty seems a good deal more lively than she used to appear at Paris; whether it is that her spirits are better, or that the great liveliness of the inhabitants made her appear grave there by comparison, I know not: but she was there remarkable for being *sérieuse*, and is here for being gay and lively. She is a most sweet girl. My sister Fanny is unlike her in almost everything, yet both are very amiable, and love each other as sincerely as ever sisters did. The characteristics of Hetty seem to be wit, generosity and openness of heart: Fanny's—sense, sensibility, and bashfulness, and even a degree of prudery. Her understanding is superior, but her diffidence gives her a bashfulness before company with whom she is not intimate, which is a disadvantage to her. My eldest sister shines in conversation, because, though very modest, she is totally free from any *mauvaise honte:* were Fanny equally so, I am persuaded she would shine no less. I am afraid that my eldest sister is too communicative, and that my sister Fanny is too reserved. They are both charming girls—*des filles comme il y en a peu.*"

Burney's second marriage took place not long after the return of Esther and Susanna from Paris. His choice on this occasion was an intimate friend of the first Mrs. Burney, whom she succeeded after an interval of six years. This lady was the widow of Mr. Stèphen Allen, a merchant of Lynn, and by him the parent of several children. The young Allens had been playmates of the young Burneys. If not equal in mind or person to the adored Esther Sleepe, Mrs. Allen was a handsome and well-instructed woman, and proved an excellent stepmother to Fanny and her sisters, as well as an admirable wife to their father. For some reason or other, the nature of which does not very clearly appear, it was judged desirable that not only the engagement between the widow and widower should be kept secret, but that their wedding should be celebrated in private. They were married some time in the spring of 1768, at St. James's, Piccadilly, by the curate, an old acquaintance of the bridegroom, their intention being confided to three other friends only. Crisp, who was one of these, had clearly no mind that Burney's new connection should put an end to their alliance, or deprive himself of the relief which the visits of the widower and his children had afforded to the monotony of his retirement. The freshly married couple carried their secret and their happiness 'to the obscure skirts of the then pathless, and nearly uninhabited Chesington Common, where Mr. Crisp had engaged for them a rural and fragrant retreat, at a small farm-house in a little hamlet a mile or two from Chesington Hall.'

The secret, we are further told, as usual in matrimonial concealments, was faithfully preserved for a time by careful vigilance, and then escaped through accident. Betrayed by the loss of a letter, Mrs. Burney came openly to town to be introduced to her husband's circle, and presently took her place at the head of his household in Poland Street. The young people on both sides accepted their new relationships with pleasure. The long-deferred scheme of sending Fanny and her youngest sister to Paris was now finally abandoned. Susanna undertook to instruct Fanny in French, and Charlotte was put to school in Norfolk. For some years the united families spent their summer holidays at Lynn, where Mrs. Burney had a dower-house. But, whether in town or country, Frances and Susanna were specially devoted to each other. Susan alone was Fanny's confidante in her literary attempts.

As the latter's age increased, her passion for writing became more confirmed. Every scrap of white paper that could be seized upon without question or notice was at once covered with her manuscript. She was not long in finding out that her turn was mainly for story-telling and humorous description. The two girls laughed and cried together over the creations of the elder's fancy, but the native timidity of the young author, and still more, perhaps, her father's low estimate of her capacity, made her apprehend nothing but ridicule if what she scribbled were disclosed to others. She worked then under the rose, imposing the strictest silence on her faithful accomplice. When in London, she plied her pen in a closet up two pair of stairs, that was appropriated to the younger children as a play-room. At Lynn, she would shut herself up to write in a summer-house, which went by the name of 'The Cabin.' Yet all her simple precautions could not long elude the suspicion of her sharp-sighted stepmother. The second Mrs. Burney was a bustling, sociable person, who did not approve of young ladies creeping out of sight to study; though herself fond of books, and, as we learn, a particular admirer of Sterne's 'Sentimental Journey,' then recently published, she was a matron of the period, and could not tolerate the idea of a young woman under her control venturing on the disesteemed career of literature. The culprit, therefore, was seriously and frequently admonished to check her scribbling propensity. Some morsels of her compositions, falling into the hands of Mrs. Burney, appear to have added point to the censor's remarks. Fanny was warned not to waste time and thought over idle inventions; and she was further cautioned, and not unreasonably, according to the prevailing notions of the day, as to the discredit she would incur if she came before the public as a female novelist. The future author of ' Cecilia ' was only too ready to assent to this view, and to cry *peccavi*. She bowed before her stepmother's rebukes, and prepared herself inwardly for a great act of sacrifice. Seizing an opportunity when her father was at Chesington, and Mrs. Burney was in Norfolk, ' she made over to a bonfire, in a paved play-court, her whole stock ' of prose manuscripts.

The fact of the *auto da fé* rests on the authority of the penitent herself: her niece and biographer, Mrs. Barrett, adds that Susanna stood by, weeping at the pathetic spectacle ; but this is perhaps only a legendary accretion to the tale. It seems certain that Fanny fell into error, when, long years afterwards, she wrote of the incident as having occurred on her fifteenth birthday.* Fanny was never very careful about her dates, and she was unquestionably more than fifteen when her father's second marriage took place. In spite of this, we are not warranted in questioning Mrs. Barrett's express statement that her aunt's famous Diary was commenced at the age of fifteen. Though of that portion of the Diary which belongs to the years preceding the publication of ' Evelina,' only the opening passages have been printed, and though the style of these•may seem to betoken a more advanced age than that mentioned, the whole was before the biographer when she wrote, and the contents must have spoken for themselves.

Frances Burney had burned her papers with the full intention of breaking off altogether the baneful habit of

* Preface to the ' Wanderer.'

authorship. Doubtless, however, she did not consider that her resolution of total abstinence debarred her from keeping a journal; and she was not long in discovering that, however steadfastly she might resist the impulses of her fancy, its wings were always pluming themselves for a flight. The latest-born of her literary bantlings committed to the flames had been a tale setting forth the fortunes and fate of Caroline Evelyn, who was feigned to be the daughter of a gentleman by a low-bred wife, and, after the death of her father, to contract a clandestine marriage with a faithless baronet, and then to survive her husband's desertion of her just long enough to give birth to a female child. The closing incident of this tragic and tragically-destroyed production left a lively impression on the mind of the writer. Her imagination dwelt on the singular situations to which the infant, as she grew up, would be exposed by the lot that placed her between the rival claims of her vulgar grandmother and her mother's more refined connections, and on the social contrasts and collisions, at once unusual and natural, which the supposed circumstances might be expected to occasion. In this way, from the ashes of the ' History of Caroline Evelyn' sprang Frances Burney's first published work, 'Evelina; or, A Young Lady's Entrance into the World.' We do not know how long a time expired from the burning of her manuscripts before Fanny relapsed into the sin of fiction-scribbling; but the flood of her invention probably rose the faster for being pent up. Irresistibly and almost unconsciously, she tells us, the whole story of ' Evelina ' was laid up in her memory before a paragraph had been committed to paper. Even when her conscience had ceased to struggle, her opportunities for jotting down the ideas which haunted her were few and far between. She had to write in stolen moments, for she was under the eye of her stepmother. The demands on her time, too, became greater than they had been when Caroline Evelyn was her heroine. Her Diary occupied a large part of her leisure, and her hours of regular employment were presently lengthened by the work of transcribing for her father.

Charles Burney was now rising to eminence in his profession. To be Master of the King's Band was the highest honour then within the reach of a musician, and Burney had been promised this appointment, though the promise was broken in favour of a candidate supported by the Duke of York.* In the summer of 176ς, the Duke of Grafton was to be installed as Chancellor of the University of Cambridge. The poet Gray wrote the Installation Ode. Burney proposed to set it to music, and to conduct the performance at the ceremony, intending, at the same time, to take the degree of Doctor of Music at Cambridge. The Chancellor Elect accepted his offer as one which the composer's rank well entitled him to make; but it soon appeared that the ideas of the two men as to the relative value of money and music were widely different. His Grace would consent to allow for the expense of singers and orchestra only one-half the amount which the conductor considered due to the occasion and his own importance. Burney in disgust threw up his commission, and, without loss of time, repaired to the sister University for his doctorate, which was conferred on him in June, 1769; the exercise produced by him as his qualification was so highly thought of that it was repeated three years successively at choral meetings in Oxford, and was afterwards performed at Hamburg under C. P. E. Bach.

Dr. Burney's new title did not appear on his door-plate till a facetious friend exhorted him to brazen it. But,

* Edward, brother of King George III.

retiring as he was, the constitutional diffidence which his second daughter inherited was now giving way in him before the consciousness of ability and attainments, and the irresistible desire to establish a lasting reputation. In the latter part of the same year, he ventured anonymously into print with his first literary production. Ten years earlier, the return of Halley's Comet at the time predicted seems to have given him an interest in astronomy, which he retained through life. There was again a comet visible in 1769, and this drew from him an Essay on Comets, to which he prefixed a translation from the pen of his first wife, Esther, of a letter by Maupertuis.* But this pamphlet was only an experiment, and being obviously the work of an amateur, attracted little notice. Having once tried his 'prentice hand at authorship, he fixed his attention on his proper subject, and devoted himself to his long-projected ' History of Music.'

He had for many years kept a commonplace book, in which he laid up notes, extracts, abridgments, criticisms, as the matter presented itself. So large was the collection thus accumulated that it seemed to his family ' as if he had merely to methodize his manuscripts, and entrust them to a copyist, for completing his purpose.' The copyist was at hand in his daughter Frances, who became his principal secretary and librarian. But, as the enterprise proceeded, the views of the historian expanded. Much information that would now be readily supplied by public journals or correspondence was then only to be

* The title-page runs : ' An Essay towards the history of the principal Comets that have appeared since 1742 ; with remarks and reflections upon the present Comet ; to which is prefixed a Letter,' etc. London, 1759. It is a curious instance of Madame d'Arblay's inaccuracy in the matter of dates, that she writes in detail of this little tract, the title of which she misquotes, as having been produced when ' the comet of the immortal Halley ' was being awaited. (' Memoirs of Dr. Burney,' vol. i., pp. 214-217.) But it was in 1759, not 1769, that Halley's Comet returned. For notices of the comet of 1769, see the *Gentleman's Magazine* of that year.

obtained by personal investigation on the spot. Early in
1770, Dr. Burney had determined that it would be needful
for him to undertake a musical tour through France and
Italy. He started on this expedition in June of that year,
and did not return until the following January. His
absence gave Fanny a considerable increase of leisure
and opportunity for indulging her own literary dreams
and occupations. Her stepmother, as well as her father,
seems to have left her at liberty, for during part of
this interval, at least, the attention of Mrs. Burney was
engaged in providing a better habitation for her husband.

The house in Poland Street had been found too small
to accommodate the combined families. In addition to the
children of their former marriages, there had been born to
the parents a son, who was baptized Richard Thomas, and
a daughter to whom they gave the name of Sarah Harriet.
Mrs. Burney now found, and having found, proceeded to
purchase and furnish, a large house in the upper part of
Queen Square, Bloomsbury, which then enjoyed an uninterrupted view of the Hampstead and Highgate Hills.
The new abode had once belonged to Alderman Barber,
the friend of Dean Swift; and the Burneys pleased themselves with the thought that there the great saturnine
humourist had been wont sometimes to set the table in a
roar. The removal was effected while the Doctor was still
on the Continent. On his arrival in London, he was
welcomed to the new home by his wife and children, and
by the never-failing Mr. Crisp. We hear, however, but
little of this house in Queen Square, and even less of
Fanny's doings there. Her father had scarcely time to
become acquainted with it before he was off to Chesington,
where he occupied himself for several weeks in preparing
the journal of his tour for the press. All his daughters
were pressed into the service of copying and recopying

his manuscript, but the chief share of this labour fell upon the scribbling Fanny. The book, which was called 'The Present State of Music in France and Italy,' appeared in the season of 1771. Thenceforth his friend Crisp's retreat became Burney's constant resort when he had literary work in hand. A further production of his pen, dealing with a matter of 'musical technique, came forth before the close of the same year. At the beginning of July, 1772, he set out on another tour, with the same object of collecting materials for his history, his route being now through Germany and the Netherlands. During this second pilgrimage, his family spent their time partly at Lynn, partly at Chesington; and Fanny, as we are told, —apparently on the authority of her unpublished Diaries —profiting by the opportunities which these visits afforded, then " gradually arranged and connected the disjointed scraps and fragments in which ' Evelina ' had been originally written." But, careful to avoid offence, " she never indulged herself with reading or writing except in the afternoon; always scrupulously devoting her time to needlework till after dinner."

The traveller's absence lasted five months : he reached Calais on his return in a December so boisterous that for nine days no vessel could cross the Channel; and Fanny relates that, when at length the passage was effected, he was too much exhausted by sea-sickness to quit his berth, and, falling asleep, was carried back to France to encounter another stormy voyage, and a repetition of his sea-sickness, before he finally landed at Dover. The fatigues and hardships of his homeward journey brought on a severe attack of rheumatism, to which he was subject. Fanny and her sisters nursed him, sitting by his bedside, pen in hand, to set down the narrative of his German tour as his sufferings allowed of his dictating it. As soon as he was sufficiently recovered, he went down to Chesington not forgetting to carry his secretaries with him.

During this illness, or a relapse which followed it, the house in Queen Square had to be relinquished from difficulties respecting the title; and Mrs. Burney purchased and fitted up another in a central situation, which was at once more convenient for her husband's teaching engagements, and more agreeable to him as being nearer to the opera, the theatres, and the clubs. St. Martin's Street, Leicester Fields, to which the family removed, is now among the most dingy, not to say the most squalid, of London streets; even in 1773, 'its unpleasant site, its confined air, and its shabby immediate neighbourhood,' are spoken of as drawbacks requiring compensation on an exchange from the fair and open view of the northern heights, crowned with Caen Woods, which had faced the windows in Bloomsbury. But, apart from the practical advantages before mentioned, the new home was invested with a strong attraction for the incomers in having been once inhabited by a personage whom our astronomical Doctor revered, and taught his children to revere, as 'the pride of human nature.' The belief that the house in Queen Square had occasionally been visited by Dean Swift was nothing compared with the certain knowledge that No. 1, St. Martin's Street, had been the dwelling of Sir Isaac Newton.* The topmost story was surmounted by an 'observatory,' having a leaden roof, and sides composed entirely of small panes of glass, except such parts as were taken up by a cupboard, fireplace and

* The house is now No. 35. It was occupied by Newton from the time when he became President of the Royal Society down to his death in 1727. He did not actually die there, as has been sometimes stated, but at Orbell's Buildings, Kensington, whither he used to resort for change of air. See *Notes and Queries*, Third Series, i. 29. For the number of the house during Dr. Burney's occupation, see a letter from him to Fanny in her Diary, New Edition, vol. i., 297.

chimney. This structure being much dilapidated when Dr. Burney entered into possession, his first act was to put what he looked on as a special relic of his great predecessor into complete repair. The house itself was sufficiently large for the new tenant's family, as well as for his books, 'which now began to demand nearly equal accommodation.' Having recovered his health, and set his affairs in order, the Doctor next resumed his daily round of lessons, and applied himself to remedy any injury which his professional connection had sustained from his two prolonged absences on the Continent. His pen was laid aside for a time, but the German Tour was published before the end of this year, and proved very successful. About the same time, its author was elected a fellow of the Royal Society. The first volume of his ' History of Music '—in which work the main part of both his Tours was incorporated—did not appear till 1776. We are now arrived at the time when our heroine has attained majority. Her womanhood may be said to have commenced with the removal to St. Martin's Street. In our next chapter we shall see how the first portion of it was spent.

CHAPTER II.

Life in St. Martin's Street—Increase of Fame and Friends—Garrick's First
Call—Confusion—The Hairdresser—'Tag-rag and Bobtail'—The History of
Histories—Imitation of Dr. Johnson—The Great Roscius—Mr. Crisp's Gout
—Correspondence between him and Fanny—Dr. Burney's Concerts—Abys-
sinian Bruce—Supper in St. Martin's Street—Italian Singers—A Musical
Evening—Visit of Count Orloff—His Stature and Jewels—Condescension—
A Matrimonial Duet—The Empress's Miniature—Jemmy Twitcher—Present
State of St. Martin's Street—Mr. and Mrs. Thrale—Dr. Johnson—Visit of
the Thrales and Johnson—Appearance of Dr. Johnson—His Conversation
—His Contempt for Music—Meeting of Dr. Johnson and Mr. Greville—
Mrs. Thrale Defiant—Signor Piozzi.

FRANCES BURNEY's Memoirs of her father, her letters
to Daddy Crisp, and her Diary, together, give us a pretty
distinct idea of her life in the little street south of Leicester Square. From the time when Dr. Burney became
established in that quarter, the circle of his friends and
his reputation steadily widened. In no long time he
made acquaintance with his neighbours, Sir Joshua Reynolds, Miss Reynolds, and their nieces, the Misses
Palmer; with another neighbour, the sculptor Nollekens;
with the painter Barry, Harris of Salisbury,* Mrs. Ord,
Sir Joseph Banks, and Abyssinian Bruce, then just returned from his travels. All these and others were, from
time to time, to be found in the Doctor's modest drawing-
room, together with many old friends, such as the

* James Harris, author of 'Hermes; or a Philosophical Inquiry into
Universal Grammar,' and several other works. Entering Parliament in 1761,
he became a Lord of the Admiralty, and subsequently a Lord of the Treasury,
etc. He died in 1786.

Stranges, Garrick, Colman, Mason, the Hooles, father and son, Twining, and Baretti.

We have, in the 'Memoirs,' an account of David Garrick's first call at the house in St. Martin's Street, which, though written in the author's later style, was no doubt derived from contemporary notes or journals :—It was early morning, and the doorsteps were being washed by a new housemaid, who, not recognising the actor, demurred to his entering unannounced. He brushed past her, ran upstairs, and burst into the Doctor's study. Here he found the master of the house under the hands of his hairdresser; while Susanna was reading a newspaper to him, Charlotte making his tea, and Fanny arranging his books. There was a litter of papers everywhere. Burney would have cleared a chair, but the visitor plumped down into one that was well cushioned with pamphlets, crying: 'Ay, do now, Doctor, be in a little confusion! Whisk your matters all out of their places, and don't know where to find a thing that you want for the rest of the day, and that will make us all comfortable.' The Doctor then, laughing, returned to his place on the stool, that his wig—or, as Madame d'Arblay calls it, the furniture of his head—might go through its proper repairs. David, assuming a solemn air of profound attention, fastened his eyes upon the hairdresser, as if wonderstruck at his amazing skill. The man, highly gratified by such notice from the celebrated Garrick, briskly worked on, frizzing, curling, powdering, and pasting, after the mode of the day, with the utmost importance and self-complacency. Garrick himself had on what he called his scratch wig, which was so uncommonly ill-arranged and frightful that the whole family agreed no one else could have appeared in such a state in the public streets without risk of being hooted at He dropped now all talk with the

Doctor, not even answering what he said, and seemed wholly absorbed in watching what was going on ; putting on, by degrees, with a power like transformation, a little mean face of envy and sadness, such as he wore in repre- senting Abel Drugger, till at length, in the eyes of the spectators, he passed out of himself altogether, and, with his mouth hanging stupidly open, and his features vacant of all expression, he became the likeness of some daubed wooden block in a barber's shop window. The friseur, who at the beginning had felt flattered on seeing his opera- tions so curiously observed, was put out of countenance by this incomprehensible change, became presently so embar- rassed that he hardly knew what he was about, and at last fell into utter consternation.   Scared and confounded, he hastily rolled up the last two curls, and prepared to make his retreat ; but before he could escape, Garrick, lifting his own miserable scratch from his head, and holding it out on his finger and thumb, squeaked out in a whining voice, ' Pray now, sir, do you think, sir, you could touch me up this here old bob a little bit, sir ?'

The hairdresser dismissed, the actor, who could not help acting, proceeded to give further proofs of his versa- tility. ' And so, Doctor,' he began, ' you, with your tag- rag and bobtail there——' Here he pointed to some shelves of shabby books and tracts, which he started up to examine ; the next moment, becoming an auctioneer, he offered for sale these valuable works, each worth a hundred pounds, and proclaimed that they were 'going, going, going, at a penny apiece.' Then, quietly reseat- ing himself : ' And so, Doctor,' he continued, ' you, and tag-rag and bobtail there, shut yourselves up in this snug little bookstall, with all your bright elves around you, to rest your understanding !' There were loud cries of mock indignation from the young people at the idea of papa resting his understanding. Garrick apologized in his best stage manner, and after some further talk, inquired, ' But when, Doctor, shall we have out the History of Histories ? Do let me know in time, that I may prepare to blow the trumpet of fame.' Of course, this was a prelude to his appearing in the character of a cheap-jack, advertising ' the only true History.' Invited to the parlour to breakfast, he excused himself on the plea of being engaged at home to Twiss* and Boswell, whom immediately he took off to the life. Encouraged by the laughter of his audience, this most reprehensible person, who set no bounds to his levity, proceeded to offer an imitation of Dr. Johnson himself. He sincerely honoured and loved Dr. Johnson, he said, but that great man had eccentricities which his most attached admirers were irresistibly impelled to mimic. Arranging, therefore, his dress so as to enlarge his person, in some strange way, several inches beyond its natural size, assuming the voice and authoritative port of the lexicographer, and giving a thundering stamp on the carpet, the devout worshipper of Dr. Johnson delivered, with sundry extraordinary attitudes and gestures, a short dialogue that had passed between them during the preceding week :

" David ! Will you lend me your ' Petrarca ' ?"

" Y—e—s, sir !"

" David, you sigh ?"

" Sir, you shall have it, certainly."

" Accordingly," Garrick continued, " the book—stupendously bound—I sent to him that very evening. But scarcely had he taken the noble quarto in his hands, when, as Boswell tells me, he poured forth a Greek ejaculation, and a couplet or two from Horace ; and then, in one of those fits of enthusiasm which always

* Author of ' Travels in Spain.'

seem to require that he should spread his arms aloft in the air, his haste was so great to debarrass them for that purpose, that he suddenly pounces my poor 'Petrarca' over his head upon the floor—Russia leather, gold border, and all! And then, standing for several minutes erect, lost in abstraction, he forgot, probably, that he had ever seen it, and left my poor dislocated Beauty to the mercy of the housemaid's morning mop!"

This concluded the performance, and the performer presently took his leave. After he had said good-bye, and left the room, he hastily came back, whimsically laughing, and said: 'Here's one of your maids downstairs that I love prodigiously to talk to, because she is so cross! She was washing, and rubbing, and scrubbing, and whitening and brightening your steps this morning, and would hardly let me pass. Egad, sir, she did not know the great Roscius! But I frightened her a little just now: "Child," says I, "you don't guess whom you have the happiness to see! Do you know that I am one of the first geniuses of the age? You would faint away upon the spot if you could only imagine who I am!"'

One familiar face was no longer seen at Burney's house. Mr. Crisp had become subject to such frequent fits of gout that his visits to London were almost given up, and he rarely slept even a single night away from Chesington. But his interest in musical and literary news, and in all that concerned the Burney family, continued unabated. What he could no more take part in himself was duly communicated to him by letter.

How early the correspondence between Frances and the family friend began we are not informed. But it must have commenced long before she was old enough to be admitted to parties such as she had now to describe to her 'daddy.' In a passage written at seventy-two, she has set down " a charge delivered to me by our dear vehement Mr. Crisp at the opening of my juvenile correspondence with him : ' Harkee, you little monkey ! dash away whatever comes uppermost ; if you stop to consider either what you say, or what may be said of you, I would not give one fig for your letters.' " So rough a speech could not have been addressed, even by a professed cynic, to any young lady very far advanced in her teens. In the letters from which we are about to quote, Miss Fanny prattles to the old man with perfect ease and confidence, showing that she felt herself on terms of established familiarity, and was quite free from the shyness and embarrassment that would attend a timid girl's first efforts to entertain him.

For many years Dr. Burney had given informal evening concerts at his house. These entertainments, to which he had been prompted by Crisp, began in Poland Street, were continued in Queen Square, and attained their highest distinction in St. Martin's Street. There was no band, no hired singer, no programme, no admission by ticket. A word from the courteous host was the only invitation needed or expected. But the company, as well as the music, was attractive even to guests accustomed to fashionable society. Before his writings made him famous, Burney's extensive acquaintance brought him visitors whom the curious were anxious to meet. Some came to see Sir Constantine Phipps, afterwards Lord Mulgrave, on his return from his Arctic voyage. Others came for a view of Omai, whom Captain Cook had imported from the South Seas. On one occasion the gentle savage obliged the musical audience with a Tahitian love-song, which proved to be a mere confused rumbling of uncouth sounds. Whatever the incident of the evening, Crisp looked for a full report of it from ' his Fannikin.'

The sense of humour which we may still see brimming over in her portrait was greatly provoked by Bruce, the particular lion of that day. The explorer was reported to have brought home with him drawings of a Theban harp at least three thousand years old, and of an Abyssinian lyre in present use, about which Fanny was evidently more sceptical than her father, who was always ready to welcome materials for his 'History.' 'The Abyssinians have lyres, have they?' said George Selwyn; 'well, they have one less since *he* left their country.' Bruce was a personage of stupendous height and breadth, whose pompous manners were proportioned to his size and fame. 'He is the tallest man you ever saw in your life—at least *gratis*,' wrote the observer. Nevertheless 'the man-mountain' condescended to the Burneys. In the season of his greatest glory, he figured several times at the Doctor's concerts, of which visits faithful accounts were duly despatched to Chesington. On one of these evenings Mr. Bruce even consented to stay supper, "which, you know," says Fanny, "with us is nothing but a permission to sit over a table for chat, and roast potatoes or apples. But now," she continues, "to perfect your acquaintance with this towering Ethiopian, where do you think he will take you during supper? To the source, or sources, you cry, of the Nile? to Thebes? to its temple? to an arietta on the Theban harp? or perhaps to banqueting on hot raw beef in Abyssinia? No such thing, my dear Mr. Crisp—no such thing. Travellers who mean to write their travels are fit for nothing but to represent the gap at your whist-table at Chesington, when you have only three players; for they are dummies. Mr. Bruce left all his exploits, his wanderings, his vanishings, his reappearances, his harps so celestial, and his bullocks so terrestrial, to plant all our entertainment within a hundred yards of our own coterie; namely, at the masquerades at the Haymarket." Then follows a story of a practical jest not worth copying. "To have looked at Mr. Bruce in his glee at this buffoonery, you must really have been amused; though methinks I see, supposing you had been with us, the picturesque rising of your brow, and all the dignity of your Roman nose, while you would have stared at such familiar delight in an active joke as to transport into so merry an *espiègle* the seven-footed loftiness of the haughty and impetuous tourist from the sands of Ethiopia, and the waters of Abyssinia; whom, nevertheless, I have now the honour to portray in his *robe de chambre*, that is, in private society, to my dear Chesington daddy."

But far greater things were to follow this stalking of the African lion. The Continental reputation which Dr. Burney acquired by his tours, and which was extended by the first instalment of his 'History,' 'attracted to his house,' as Macaulay points out, 'the most eminent musical performers of that age. The greatest Italian singers who visited England regarded him as the dispenser of fame in their art, and exerted themselves to obtain his suffrage. Pacchierotti* became his intimate friend. The rapacious Agujari,† who sang for nobody else under fifty pounds an air, sang her best for Dr. Burney without a fee; and in the company of Dr. Burney even the haughty and eccentric Gabrielli‡ constrained herself to behave with civility. It was thus in his power to give, with scarcely any expense, concerts equal to those of the

---

* 'Nothing is fit to be heard but Pacchierotti,' was the general verdict, according to Walpole.

† A celebrated Italian singer, wife of Colla, an Italian composer. She was engaged at the Pantheon to sing two songs nightly, for which she received £100.

‡ A performer of great Continental reputation, whose merits were much controverted in England. 'Is, or has the Gabrielli been, a great singer?' asks Walpole of his Florence correspondent. 'She has, at least, not honoured us but with a most slender low voice.'

aristocracy. On such occasions the quiet street in which he lived was blocked up by coroneted chariots, and his little drawing-room was crowded with peers, peeresses, ministers, and ambassadors.'

The following extract from one of Fanny's letters contains a full description of the most memorable of these musical evenings, though it was one on which no foreign artist performed :

"You reproach me, my dear Mr. Crisp, for not sending you an account of our last two concerts. But the fact is, I have not anything new to tell you. The music has always been the same: the matrimonial duets* are so much *à la mode*, that no other thing in our house is now demanded. But if I can write you nothing new about music, you want, I well know you will say, to hear some conversations.

My dear Mr. Crisp, there is, at this moment, no such thing as conversation. There is only one question asked, meet whom you may, namely : ' How do you like Gabrielli ?' and only two modes, contradictory, to be sure, but very steady, of reply: either, ' Of all things upon earth !' or, ' Not the least bit in the whole world !'

Well, now I will present you with a specimen, beginning with our last concert but one, and arranging the persons of the drama in the order of their actual appearance.

But, imprimis, I should tell you that the motive to this concert was a particular request to my father from Dr. King, our old friend, and the chaplain to the British— something—at St. Petersburg, that he would give a little music to a certain mighty personage, who, somehow or

* Duets between Esther Burney, now married, and her husband, who was also her cousin and a Burney. Esther was the beauty of the family, and became a wife early.

other how, must needs take, transiently at least, a front place in future history, namely, the famed favourite of the Empress Catherine of Russia—Prince* Orloff.

There, my dear Mr. Crisp! what say you to seeing such a doughty personage as that in a private house, at a private party, of a private individual—fresh imported from the Czarina of all the Russias, to sip a cup of tea in St. Martin's Street? I wonder whether future historians will happen to mention this circumstance? I am thinking of sending it to all the keepers of records. But I see your rising eyebrows at this name—your start—your disgust—yet big curiosity.

Well, suppose the family assembled, its honoured chief in the midst—and Tat, tat, tat, tat, at the door.

Enter Dr. Ogle, Dean of Winchester.

Dr. Burney, after the usual ceremonies :—'Did you hear the Gabrielli last night, Mr. Dean?'

The Dean : 'No, Doctor, I made the attempt, but soon retreated, for I hate a crowd—as much as the ladies love it! I beg pardon!' bowing with a sort of civil sneer at us fair sex.

My mother was entering upon a spirited defence, when—Tat, tat, tat.

Enter Dr. King.

He brought the compliments of Prince Orloff, with his Highness's apologies for being so late; but he was obliged to dine at Lord Buckingham's, and thence to show himself at Lady Harrington's.

As nobody thought of inquiring into Dr. King's opinion of La Gabrielli, conversation was at a stand, till—Tat, tat, tat, tat, too, and

---

* Fanny should rather have written, *Count* Orloff.

Enter Lady Edgcumbe.

We were all introduced to her, and she was very chatty, courteous, and entertaining. [Lady Edgcumbe is asked the usual question about Gabrielli, as also are the Honourable Mr. and Mrs. Brudenel, who appear next. Then we are introduced in succession to the Baron Demidoff, Harris of Salisbury, and Lord Bruce.] At length —Tat, tat, tat, tat, tat, tat, tat, tat, too!

Enter his Highness Prince Orloff.

Have you heard the dreadful story of the thumb, by which this terrible Prince is said to have throttled the late Emperor of Russia, Peter, by suddenly pressing his windpipe while he was drinking? I hope it is not true; and Dr. King, of whom, while he resided in Russia, Prince Orloff was the patron, denies the charge. Nevertheless, it is so currently reported, that neither Susan nor I could keep it one moment from our thoughts; and we both shrank from him with secret horror, heartily wishing him in his own Black Sea.

His sight, however, produced a strong sensation, both in those who believed, and those who discredited this disgusting barbarity; for another story, not perhaps of less real, though of less sanguinary guilt, is not a tale of rumour, but a crime of certainty; namely, that he is the first favourite of the cruel, inhuman Empress—if it be true that she connived at this horrible murder.

His Highness was immediately preceded by another Russian nobleman, whose name I have forgot; and followed by a noble Hessian, General Bawr.

Prince Orloff is of stupendous stature, something resembling Mr. Bruce. He is handsome, tall, fat, upright, magnificent. His dress was superb. Besides the blue garter, he had a star of diamonds of prodigious brilliancy, a shoulder-knot of the same lustre and value, and a picture of the Empress hung about his neck, set round with diamonds of such brightness and magnitude that, when near the light, they were too dazzling for the eye. His jewels, Dr. King says, are estimated at one hundred thousand pounds sterling.

His air and address are showy, striking, and assiduously courteous. He had a look that frequently seemed to say, ' I hope you observe that I come from a polished Court ? I hope you take note that I am no Cossack ?' Yet, with all this display of commanding affability, he seems, from his native taste and humour, ' agreeably addicted to pleasantry.' He speaks very little English, but knows French perfectly.

His introduction to my father, in which Dr. King pompously figured, passed in the drawing-room. The library was so crowded that he could only show himself at the door, which was barely high enough not to discompose his prodigious toupee. He bowed to Mr. Chamier,* then my next neighbour, whom he had somewhere met ; but I was so impressed by the shocking rumours of his horrible actions, that involuntarily I drew back even from a bow of vicinity ; murmuring to Mr. Chamier, ' He looks so potent and mighty, I do not like to be near him !'

' He has been less unfortunate,' answered Mr. Chamier archly, ' elsewhere ; such objection has not been made to him by all ladies.'

Lord Bruce, who knew, immediately rose to make way for him, and moved to another end of the room. The Prince instantly held out his vast hand, in which, if he had also held a cambric handkerchief, it must have looked like a white flag on the top of a mast—so much higher than the

---

* Anthony Chamier was member of Parliament for Tamworth, and Under-Secretary of State from 1775 till his death in 1780. He was an original member of the celebrated Literary Club.

most tip-top height of every head in the room was his spread-out arm, as he exclaimed, '*Ah! milord me fuit!*'

His Honour,* then, rising also, with a profound reverence, offered his seat to his Highness; but he positively refused to accept it, and declared that if Mr. Brudenel would not be seated, he would himself retire; and seeing Mr. Brudenel demur, still begging his Highness to take the chair, he cried, with a laugh, but very peremptorily, '*Non, non, monsieur! Je ne le veux pas! Je suis opiniâtre, moi; un peu comme Messieurs les Anglais!*'

Mr. Brudenel then reseated himself; and the corner of a form appearing to be vacant, from the pains taken by poor Susan to shrink away from Mr. Orloff, his Highness suddenly dropped down upon it his immense weight, with a force—notwithstanding a palpable and studied endeavour to avoid doing mischief—that threatened his gigantic person with plumping upon the floor, and terrified all on the opposite side of the form with the danger of visiting the ceiling.

Perceiving Susan strive, though vainly, from want of space, to glide further off from him, and struck, perhaps, by her sweet countenance, '*Ah, ha!*' he cried, '*je tiens ici, je vois, une petite prisonnière!*'

Charlotte, blooming like a budding little Hebe, actually stole into a corner from affright at the whispered history of his thumb ferocity.

Mr. Chamier, who now probably had developed what passed in my mind, contrived, very comically, to disclose his similar sentiment; for, making a quiet way to my ear, he said in a low voice, 'I wish Dr. Burney had invited Omiah here to-night instead of Prince Orloff!'—meaning,

---

* A name by which Mr. Brudenel, afterwards Earl of Cardigan, was known.

no doubt, of the two exotics, he should have preferred the most innocent!

The grand duet of Müthel was now called for, and played; but I can tell you nothing extra of the admiration it excited. Your Hettina looked remarkably pretty; and, added to the applause given to the music, everybody had something to observe upon the singularity of the performers being husband and wife. Prince Orloff was witty quite to facetiousness; sarcastically marking something beyond what he said, by a certain ogling, half-cynical, half-amorous cast of his eyes; and declaring he should take care to initiate all the foreign academies of natural philosophy in the secret of the harmony that might be produced by such nuptial concord.

The Russian nobleman who accompanied Prince Orloff, and who knew English, they told us, so well that he was the best interpreter for his Highness in his visits, gave us now a specimen of his proficiency; for, clapping his fore-finger upon a superfine snuff-box, he exclaimed, when the duet was finished, ' Ma foi, dis is so pretty as never I hear in my life!'

General Bawr also, to whom Mr. Harris directed my attention, was greatly charmed. He is tall, and of stern and martial aspect. 'He is a man,' said Mr. Harris, ' to be looked at, from his courage, conduct, and success during the last Russian war; when, though a Hessian by birth, he was a lieutenant-general in the service of the Empress of Russia, and obtained the two military stars, which you now see him wear on each side, by his valour!' . . . . . .

Then followed, to vary the entertainment, singing by Mrs. Brudenel.

Prince Orloff inquired very particularly of Dr. King who we four young female Burneys were; for we were all dressed alike, on account of our mourning; and when Dr. King answered, 'Dr. Burney's daughters,' he was quite astonished, for he had not thought our dear father, he said, more than thirty years of age, if so much.

Mr. Harris, in a whisper, told me he wished some of the ladies would desire to see the miniature of the Empress a little nearer; the monstrous height of the Prince putting it quite out of view to his old eyes and short figure; and being a man, he could not, he said, presume to ask such an indulgence as that of holding it in his own hands. Delighted to do anything for this excellent Mr. Harris, and quite at my ease with poor prosing Dr. King, I told him the wish of Mr. Harris. Dr. King whispered the desire to M. de Demidoff; M. de Demidoff did the same to General de Bawr; and General de Bawr dauntlessly made the petition to the Prince, in the name of *The Ladies.*

The Prince laughed, rather sardonically; yet with ready good humour complied, telling the General, pretty much *sans ceremonie,* to untie the ribbon round his neck, and give the picture into the possession of *The Ladies.*

He was very gallant and debonnaire upon the occasion, entreating they would by no means hurry themselves; yet his smile, as his eye sharply followed the progress from hand to hand of the miniature, had a suspicious cast of investigating whether it would be worth his while to ask any favour of them in return! and through all the superb magnificence of his display of courtly manners, a little bit of the Cossack, methought, broke out, when he desired to know whether *The Ladies* wished for anything else—declaring, with a smiling bow, and rolling, languishing, yet half-contemptuous eyes, that, if *The Ladies* would issue their commands, they should strip him entirely!

You may suppose, after that, nobody asked for a closer

view of any more of his ornaments! The good, yet
unaffectedly humorous philosopher of Salisbury could not
help laughing, even while actually blushing at it, that his
own curiosity should have involved *The Ladies* in this
supercilious sort of sarcastic homage.

There was hardly any looking at the picture of the
Empress for the glare of the diamonds. One of them, I
really believe, was as big as a nutmeg; though I am
somewhat ashamed to undignify my subject by so culinary
a comparison.

When we were all satisfied, the miniature was restored
by General Bawr to the Prince, who took it with stately
complacency; condescendingly making a smiling bow to
each fair female who had had possession of it, and receiving from her in return a lowly courtesy.

Mr. Harris, who was the most curious to see the
Empress, because his son, Sir James,* was, or is intended
to be, Minister at her Court, had slyly looked over every
shoulder that held her; but would not venture, he archly
whispered, to take the picture in his own hands, lest he
should be included by the Prince amongst *The Ladies*, as
an old woman!

Have you had enough of this concert, my dear Mr.
Crisp? I have given it in detail, for the humour of
letting you see how absorbing of the public voice is La
Gabrielli; and also for describing to you Prince Orloff, a
man who, when time lets out facts, and drives in mys-
teries, must necessarily make a considerable figure, good
or bad—but certainly not indifferent—in European history.
Besides, I want your opinion whether there is not an odd
and striking resemblance in general manners, as well as
in herculean strength and height, in this Siberian Prince
and his Abyssinian Majesty?"

* Afterwards Lord Malmesbury.

On another musical evening, of which Fanny wrote an account, there were present : the French Ambassador, the Count de Guignes, at whose request the concert was given; the Danish Ambassador, Baron Deiden, and his wife; the Groom of the Stole, Lord Ashburnham, 'with his gold key dangling from his pocket;' Lord Barrington from the War Office, and Lord Sandwich, First Lord of the Admiralty. Of this last, the boon-companion and denouncer* of Wilkes, Miss Fanny naïvely asks, "I want to know why he is called Jemmy Twitcher in the newspapers? Do pray tell me that."

Very seldom, in these latter days, does any private carriage, with or without a coronet on its panels, turn into the decayed thoroughfare running down from the bottom of Leicester Square. 'Vulgarly-peopled,' according to Madame d'Arblay, even in her father's time, St. Martin's Street has since fallen many degrees lower yet. The house to which the fashionable world was drawn by the charms of Burney's music stands on the east side, immediately above the chapel at the corner of Orange Street. The glass observatory which Dr. Burney repaired, and which he subsequently rebuilt when it was blown away by a gale of wind, has long since disappeared. It was replaced by a wooden† erection, or what Macaulay

---

* We need scarcely remind our readers that, in 1763, Sandwich had denounced Wilkes in the House of Lords for having composed and printed the 'Essay on Woman,' an indecent parody on Pope's 'Essay on Man.' Society resented the attack, placing the accuser and accused on a par in point of morals. 'The public indignation went so far, that the *Beggar's Opera* being performed at Covent Garden Theatre soon after this event, the whole audience, when Macheath says, "That Jemmy Twitcher should peach, I own surprises me," burst out into an applause of application, and the nickname of "Jemmy Twitcher" stuck by the Earl so as almost to occasion the disuse of his title.'— Walpole's 'Memoirs of George III.,' vol. i., p. 313.

† The observatory in its later form is stated to have been put up in the early years of the present century, by a Frenchman, then tenant of the house, who placed in it some mathematical instruments, which he exhibited as the identical instruments with which the great Newton made his discoveries; and we are told that this ingenious person realized a considerable sum before his imposture was exposed. See 'The Streets of London,' by J. T. Smith, edited by Charles Mackay, 1849, p. 76.

calls 'a square turret,' which, when the essayist wrote, distinguished the house from all the surrounding buildings. This erection also has been removed, but the house itself cannot be mistaken by any passer-by who cares to see it. A tablet on the front bears the inscription: 'Sir Isaac Newton, philosopher, lived here.' The house is at present the quarters of the United Service Warrant Officers' Club. No great effort is required to imagine the plain, silent Newton passing in and out of that slender doorway. The movements of the man *qui genus humanum ingenio superavit* were without noise and ostentation. We may let half a century go by in thought, and with equal ease picture to ourselves David Garrick tripping up the steps before breakfast; Samuel Johnson rolling up them for a call, on his way to dine with Mrs. Montagu; pleasant Dr. Burney briskly setting out on his daily round of lessons; and demure Miss Fanny sallying forth to seek an interview *incognita* with her publisher. But how call up the scene, when the lacqueys of Count Orloff—Orloff the Big, Walpole calls him—thundered at the knocker, or when officers of the Household, displaying the ensigns of their rank, peers with stars and orders, and great ladies arrayed in brocaded silks and immense head-dresses, followed one another up a confined staircase* into a couple of small and crowded reception-rooms? Standing opposite to the club where our gallant petty officers of to-day congregate, and noticing that to the left of it, on the other side of Long's Court, there is now a cheap lodging-house for working men, and that a little further to the left, at the entrance from the Square, the roadway narrows, as we

* There is some account both of the inside and outside of Newton's house in the *Gentleman's Magazine* for 1814. At that date, we learn among other things, the original chimney-piece in the observatory remained, though the room itself had undergone a change. The house appears to have been built about 1692.

4

learn from the " Memoirs " that it did in Burney's time, till there is barely room for a single vehicle of moderate size to pass, we recognise the limitations of the human fancy. It is difficult to conceive of a great aristocratic crowd assembling in such a place. We can understand the pride with which Fanny set down the prolonged *rat-tat-tat-tat-too* that announced the arrival of each titled and decorated visitor. We may observe the pains she took to draw and colour for her country correspondent groups of dazzling figures such as had never been seen in the more spacious area of Queen Square. But they are gone, and in presence of the dirt and squalor which have made St. Martin's Street little better than an East-End slum, their shadows will not revisit the glimpses of the moon. *Sic transit gloria mundi.*

Somewhat later, Dr. Burney formed a new connection which had an important influence on the life of his second daughter. He was invited to Streatham by Mr. and Mrs. Thrale to give lessons in music to their eldest daughter, familiarly called Queeny, who afterwards became Viscountess Keith. There, besides winning the regard of the Thrales, he renewed his acquaintance with Dr. Johnson, to whom he had made himself known by letter twenty-two years before. Johnson, who had no ear, despised music, and was wont to speak slightingly of its professors, but he conceived a strong liking for Burney. In bringing out the 'Tour to the Hebrides,' the author confessed that he had kept his friend's Musical Tours in view. At this time, Richard, the youngest son of Dr. Burney, born of his second marriage, was preparing for Winchester School, whither his father proposed conveying him in person. Johnson, who was a friend of Dr. Warton, the headmaster, volunteered to accompany them, and introduce the new pupil. This joint expedition of Johnson and

Burney was followed by a similar one to Oxford, and their intercourse became so cordial that Mrs. Thrale and Johnson arranged to meet in St. Martin's Street, there to make acquaintance with Burney's family, to look over his library, and to see Newton's house. Fanny, who had just come up from Chesington, wrote an account of this visit to her daddy:

"MY DEAREST MR. CRISP,

My father seemed well pleased at my returning to my time; so that is no small consolation and pleasure to me for the pain of quitting you. So now to our Thursday morning and Dr. Johnson, according to my promise.

We were all—by we, I mean Suzette, Charlotte, and I —for my mother had seen him before, as had my sister Burney; but we three were all in a twitter from violent expectation and curiosity for the sight of this monarch of books and authors.

Mrs. and Miss Thrale, Miss Owen, and Mr. Seward,* came long before Lexiphanes. Mrs. Thrale is a pretty woman still, though she has some defect in the mouth that looks like a cut or scar; but her nose is very hand-some, her complexion very fair; she has the *embonpoint charmant*, and her eyes are blue and lustrous. She is extremely lively and chatty, and showed none of the supercilious or pedantic airs so freely, or rather so scoffingly, attributed by you envious lords of the creation to women of learning or celebrity; on the contrary, she is full of sport, remarkably gay, and excessively agree-able. I liked her in everything except her entrance into the room, which was rather florid and flourishing, as who should say, 'It's I!—no less a person than Mrs. Thrale!' However, all that ostentation wore out in the course of

* William Seward, afterwards author of 'Anecdotes of Distinguished Persons,' and 'Biographiana,' a sequel to the same.

the visit, which lasted the whole morning; and you could not have helped liking her, she is so very entertaining— though not simple enough, I believe, for quite winning your heart . . . .

The conversation was supported with a great deal of vivacity, as usual when il Signor Padrone is at home; but I can write you none of it, as I was still in the same twitter, twitter, twitter, I have acknowledged, to see Dr. Johnson. Nothing could have heightened my impatience —unless Pope could have been brought to life again—or, perhaps, Shakespeare !

This confab was broken up by a duet between your Hettina and, for the first time to company-listeners, Suzette; who, however, escaped much fright, for she soon found she had no musical critics to encounter in Mrs. Thrale and Mr. Seward, or Miss Owen, who know not a flat from a sharp, nor a crotchet from a quaver. But every knowledge is not given to everybody—except to two gentle wights of my acquaintance : the one commonly hight il Padre, and the other il Dadda. Do you know any such sort of people, sir ? Well, in the midst of this performance, and before the second movement was come to a close, Dr. Johnson was announced !

Now, my dear Mr. Crisp, if you like a description of emotions and sensations—but I know you treat them all as burlesque; so let's proceed.

Everybody rose to do him honour, and he returned the attention with the most formal courtesy. My father then, having welcomed him with the warmest respect, whispered to him that music was going forward, which he would not, my father thinks, have found out; and, placing him on the best seat vacant, told his daughters to go on with the duet; while Dr. Johnson, intently rolling towards them one eye—for they say he does

Sir J. Reynolds.   A. Dawson Ph. f.   W. Doughty

Dr. Johnson.

not see with the other—made a grave nod, and gave a
dignified motion with one hand, in silent approvance of
the proceeding.

But now, my dear Mr. Crisp, I am mortified to own
—what you, who always smile at my enthusiasm, will hear
without caring a straw for—that he is, indeed, very ill-
favoured. Yet he has naturally a noble figure; tall, stout,
grand, and authoritative: but he stoops horribly; his
back is quite round : his mouth is continually opening
and shutting, as if he were chewing something; he has a
singular method of twirling his fingers, and twisting his
hands: his vast body is in constant agitation, see-sawing
backwards and forwards : his feet are never a moment
quiet; and his whole person looked often as if it were going
to roll itself, quite voluntarily, from his chair to the floor.

Since such is his appearance to a person so prejudiced
in his favour as I am, how I must more than ever
reverence his abilities, when I tell you that, upon asking
my father why he had not prepared us for such uncouth,
untoward strangeness, he laughed heartily, and said he
had entirely forgotten that the same impression had been,
at first, made upon himself, but had been lost even on
the second interview—how I long to see him again, to
lose it, too!—for knowing the value of what would come
out when he spoke, he ceased to observe the defects that
were out while he was silent.

But you always charge me to write without reserve or
reservation, and so I obey, as usual. Else, I should be
ashamed to acknowledge having remarked such exterior
blemishes in so exalted a character.

His dress, considering the times, and that he had
meant to put on all his best *becomes*—for he was engaged
to dine with a very fine party at Mrs. Montagu's—was as
much out of the common road as his figure. He had a

large, full, bushy wig, a snuff-colour coat, with gold buttons (or, peradventure, brass), but no ruffles to his doughty fists; and not, I suppose, to be taken for a Blue, though going to the Blue Queen, he had on very coarse black worsted stockings.

He is shockingly near-sighted; a thousand times more so than either my Padre or myself. He did not even know Mrs. Thrale, till she held out her hand to him, which she did very engagingly. After the first few minutes, he drew his chair close to the pianoforte, and then bent down his nose quite over the keys, to examine them, and the four hands at work upon them; till poor Hetty and Susan hardly knew how to play on, for fear of touching his phiz; or, which was harder still, how to keep their countenances; and the less, as Mr. Seward, who seems to be very droll and shrewd, and was much diverted, ogled them slyly, with a provoking expression of arch enjoyment of their apprehensions.

When the duet was finished, my father introduced your Hettina to him, as an old acquaintance, to whom, when she was a little girl, he had presented his Idler.

His answer to this was imprinting on her pretty face— not a half touch of a courtly salute—but a good, real, substantial, and very loud kiss.

Everybody was obliged to stroke their chins, that they might hide their mouths.

Beyond this chaste embrace, his attention was not to be drawn off two minutes longer from the books, to which he now strided his way; for we had left the drawing-room for the library, on account of the pianoforte. He pored over them, shelf by shelf, almost brushing them with his eyelashes from near examination. At last, fixing upon something that happened to hit his fancy, he took it down; and, standing aloof from the company, which he seemed clean and clear to forget, he began, without further ceremony, and very composedly, to read to himself; and as intently as if he had been alone in his own study.

We were all excessively provoked: for we were languishing, fretting, expiring to hear him talk—not to see him read! What could that do for us?

My sister then played another duet, accompanied by my father, to which Miss Thrale seemed very attentive; and all the rest quietly resigned. But Dr. Johnson had opened a volume of the British Encyclopædia, and was so deeply engaged, that the music, probably, never reached his ears.

When it was over, Mrs. Thrale, in a laughing manner, said: ' Pray, Dr. Burney, will you be so good as to tell me what that song was, and whose, which Savoi sang last night at Bach's* concert, and which you did not hear?'

My father confessed himself by no means so able a diviner, not having had time to consult the stars, though he lived in the house of Sir Isaac Newton. But, anxious to draw Dr. Johnson into conversation, he ventured to interrupt him with Mrs. Thrale's conjuring request relative to Bach's concert.

The Doctor, comprehending his drift, good-naturedly put away his book, and, see-sawing, with a very humorous smile, drolly repeated: 'Bach, sir?—Bach's concert? And pray, sir, who is Bach? Is he a piper?'

You may imagine what exclamations followed such a question.

Mrs. Thrale gave a detailed account of the nature of the concert, and the fame of Mr. Bach, and the many charming performances she had heard, with all their varieties, in his rooms.

When there was a pause, ' Pray, madam,' said he, with the calmest gravity, 'what is the expense for all this?'

---

* John Christian Bach, sometimes called Bach of Berlin, who for many years was established in England.

'Oh,' answered she, 'the expense is much trouble and solicitation to obtain a subscriber's ticket—or else, half a guinea!'

'Trouble and solicitation,' he replied, 'I will have nothing to do with; but, if it be so fine, I would be willing to give'—he hesitated, and then finished with—'eighteen-pence.'

Ha! ha! Chocolate being then brought, we returned to the drawing-room; and Dr. Johnson, when drawn away from the books, freely, and with social good-humour, gave himself up to conversation.

The intended dinner of Mrs. Montagu being mentioned, Dr. Johnson laughingly told us that he had received the most flattering note that he had ever read, or that anybody else had ever read, of invitation from that lady.

'So have I, too!' cried Mrs. Thrale. 'So, if a note from Mrs. Montagu is to be boasted of, I beg mine may not be forgotten.'

'Your note, madam,' cried Dr. Johnson, smiling, 'can bear no comparison with mine; for I am at the head of all the philosophers—she says.'

'And I,' returned Mrs. Thrale, 'have all the Muses in my train.'

'A fair battle!' cried my father. 'Come, compliment for compliment, and see who will hold out longest!'

'I am afraid for Mrs. Thrale,' said Mr. Seward; 'for I know that Mrs. Montagu exerts all her forces when she sings the praises of Dr. Johnson.'

'Oh yes,' cried Mrs. Thrale, 'she has often praised him till he has been ready to faint.'

'Well,' said my father, 'you two ladies must get him fairly between you to-day, and see which can lay on the paint the thickest—Mrs. Montagu or Mrs. Thrale.'

'I had rather,' said the Doctor very composedly, 'go to Bach's concert!'"

Not long after the morning call described in our last extract, Johnson spent an evening in St. Martin's Street, for the purpose of being introduced to Mr. and Mrs. Greville. The Doctor came with Mr. and Mrs. Thrale. Signor Piozzi was there, invited to amuse the company by his musical skill. But the account of the second visit reads much less pleasantly than that of the first. This is due in great part to the different behaviour of the principal guests. Burney's old patron, Greville, had for years been going steadily down hill, through indulgence in play and other extravagances. The loss of his fortune, perhaps, inclined him to assert more stiffly the claims of his rank. At any rate, in presence of the Thrales and Johnson, he thought it necessary to appear superior to the brewer's wealth and the author's fame. Johnson seems to have only half perceived his disdain; but the Doctor was not in a mood for talking, and Greville made no attempt to draw him out. Nor are the actors only changed on this subsequent occasion; the narrator is changed also. Instead of a letter by Fanny Burney, dashed off in the hey-day of youth and spirits, we have a formal account by her later self, Madame d'Arblay, composed in the peculiar style which makes a great part of the 'Memoirs' such difficult reading. However, as this account records Mrs. Thrale's first meeting with the man who was destined to exercise a fatal influence on her after-life, we give a portion of it here:

"Mrs. Thrale, of the whole coterie, was alone at her ease. She feared not Dr. Johnson; for fear made no part of her composition; and with Mrs. Greville, as a fair rival genius, she would have been glad, from curiosity, to have had the honour of a little tilt, in full carelessness of its event; for though triumphant when victorious, she had spirits so volatile, and such utter exemption from envy or spleen, that she was gaily free from mortification when vanquished. But she knew the meeting to have been fabricated for Dr. Johnson, and, therefore, though not without difficulty, constrained herself to be passive.

" When, however, she observed the sardonic disposition of Mr. Greville to stare around him at the whole company in curious silence, she felt a defiance against his aristocracy beat in every pulse; for, however grandly he might look back to the long ancestry of the Brookes and the Grevilles, she had a glowing consciousness that her own blood, rapid and fluent, flowed in her veins from Adam of Saltsburg;* and, at length, provoked by the dulness of a taciturnity that, in the midst of such renowned interlocutors, produced as narcotic a torpor as could have been caused by a dearth the most barren of human faculties, she grew tired of the music, and yet more tired of remaining, what as little suited her inclinations as her abilities, a mere cipher in the company; and, holding such a position, and all its concomitants, to be ridiculous, her spirits rose rebelliously above her control, and, in a fit of utter recklessness of what might be thought of her by her fine new acquaintance, she suddenly but softly arose, and stealing on tip-toe behind Signor Piozzi, who was accompanying himself on the pianoforte to an animated *aria parlante*, with his back to the company, and his face to the wall, she ludicrously began imitating him by squaring her elbows, elevating them with ecstatic shrugs of the shoulders, and casting up her eyes, while

---

* Hester Lynch Salusbury (Mrs. Thrale) claimed to be lineally descended from Adam of Saltsburg, who came over to England with the Conqueror.

languishingly reclining her head, as if she were not less enthusiastically, though somewhat more suddenly, struck with the transports of harmony than himself.

"This grotesque ebullition of ungovernable gaiety was not perceived by Dr. Johnson, who faced the fire, with his back to the performer and the instrument. But the amusement which such an unlooked-for exhibition caused to the party was momentary; for Dr. Burney, shocked lest the poor Signor should observe, and be hurt by this mimicry, glided gently round to Mrs. Thrale, and, with something between pleasantry and severity, whispered to her, 'Because, madam, you have no ear yourself for music, will you destroy the attention of all who, in that one point, are otherwise gifted?'

"It was now that shone the brightest attribute of Mrs. Thrale, sweetness of temper. She took this rebuke with a candour, and a sense of its justice the most amiable; she nodded her approbation of the admonition; and, returning to her chair, quietly sat down, as she afterwards said, like a pretty little miss, for the remainder of one of the most humdrum evenings that she had ever passed.

"Strange, indeed, strange and most strange, the event considered, was this opening intercourse between Mrs. Thrale and Signor Piozzi. Little could she imagine that the person she was thus called away from holding up to ridicule, would become, but a few years afterwards, the idol of her fancy, and the lord of her destiny! And little did the company present imagine, that this burlesque scene was but the first of a drama the most extraordinary of real life, of which these two persons were to be the hero and heroine; though, when the catastrophe was known, this incident, witnessed by so many, was recollected and repeated from coterie to coterie throughout London, with comments and sarcasms of endless variety."

CHAPTER III.

WE now approach the time when the 'History of Evelina'
was given to the world. There has been much futile controversy as to the date at which this novel was composed.
As the author was unquestionably half-way between twenty-
five and twenty-six when her first book was published, it
has been inferred that she was not much below that age
when she began the story. This inference was put in sharp
contrast with a current report—which cannot be traced
to Frances Burney or her family—that she wrote
'Evelina' at seventeen. Her enemy Croker went so
far as to suggest that she represented herself to have
been ten years younger than she really was at the period
of the publication.* But if we may trust Mrs. Barrett,

---

* 'There was no want of low minds and bad hearts in the generation which
witnessed her first appearance. There was the envious Kenrick and the savage
Wolcot, the asp George Steevens and the polecat John Williams. It did not,
however, occur to them to search the parish register of Lynn, in order that they
might be able to twit a lady with having concealed her age. That truly chival-
rous exploit was reserved for a bad writer of our own time, whose spite she

who had not only the ' Memoirs,' but Fanny's early and still unpublished journals to guide her, the author herself would have been puzzled to say exactly when her tale was written. It was planned in girlhood, worked at by snatches, and occupied long years in growing up. The idea of seeing it in print seems to have been conceived in 1776, shortly after the appearance of the first volume of her father's History, and we are distinctly told by Madame d'Arblay and her biographer, that there was already a manuscript in existence. We gather, however, that this manuscript was imperfect ; and it would manifestly be presuming too much to suppose that its contents remained unaltered, and unimproved, in the transcript which the writer proceeded to make before taking any other step.

Though stimulated by her father's success, and en- couraged by her sisters, whom she took into her con- fidence, Fanny was, nevertheless, determined that, in bringing forward her work, she would keep its authorship unknown. She therefore copied out her manuscript in a feigned upright hand, in order to guard against the possibility of her ordinary writing being recognised by some one who had seen the numerous pages of the paternal books which she had transcribed for the printer. Tiring of her irksome task when she had accomplished enough to fill two volumes, she wrote a letter, without signature, to be sent to some bookseller, offering the fairly-copied portion for immediate publication, and pro-

---

had provoked by not furnishing him with materials for a worthless edition of Boswell's Life of Johnson, some sheets of which our readers have doubtless seen round parcels of better books.'—*Macaulay's Essay.* This passage has been often quoted and admired. Yet is not such writing rather too much in the style of Mr. Bludyer, who, the reader will remember, was reproached with mangling his victims? Compare Macaulay's swashing blow with the deadly thrust of a true master of sarcasm. ' Nobody was stronger in dates than Mr. Rigby ; . . . detail was Mr. Rigby's forte ; . . . *it was thought no one could lash a woman like Rigby.* Rigby's statements were arranged with a formidable array of dates—rarely accurate.'—*Coningsby.*

mising to forward the rest in the following year. This proposal was first directed to Dodsley, who, in answer, declined to look at anything without being previously informed of the author's name. Fanny and her sisters, "after sitting in committee on this lofty reply," addressed another offer, in like terms, to Lowndes, a publisher in Fleet Street. The latter, less exacting than his brother at the West-End, desired to see the manuscript, which—there being no Parcels Delivery Company in those days—was conveyed to him by young Charles Burney, muffled up by his sisters to make him look older than he was. Lowndes read, was pleased, and declared himself willing to purchase and print the work when finished, but he naturally would not hear of publishing an unfinished novel. Disappointed at this second rebuff, the impatient aspirant gave up hope; but, her spirits reviving, after a time, her third volume was completed and copied before the end of the twelvemonth. Meanwhile, a scruple had arisen in her mind. Her correspondence with Lowndes had been carried on without her father's knowledge; the publisher's letters to her being addressed to Mr. Grafton, and sent to the Orange Coffee House, in Orange Street. But she now saw it to be her duty not to rush into print without Dr. Burney's consent. Availing herself of a propitious moment, when he was bidding her good-bye before setting out on a visit to Chesington, she confessed to him, with many blushes, that she had written a little book, and hoped that he would allow her to publish it on condition of not disclosing her name. She assured him that he should not be troubled in the business, which her brother Charles would manage for her, and only begged further that he would not himself ask to see the manuscript. The Doctor was first amazed, then amused, and finally bursting into a laugh, kissed her, and bade her see that

Charles was discreet, thus tacitly granting her petition. The completed work was now forwarded to Lowndes, who without much delay accepted it, and paid the author what seemed to her the magnificent sum of twenty pounds for the copyright.

Much censure has been thrown on Dr. Burney for his conduct in this transaction. He ought, we are told, to have given his daughter serious counsel as to the perils of authorship, to have inquired into the merits of her production, and to have seen that she made the best possible terms with the bookseller. 'Happily,' says Macaulay, 'his inexcusable neglect of duty caused her no worse evil than the loss of twelve or fifteen hundred pounds.' We doubt if it cost her the twelfth part of the smaller sum. It is most unlikely, we think, that an untried and anonymous writer could, with the best assistance, have commanded a hundred pounds for a first attempt at fiction. We are not concerned to defend Dr. Burney, but to us he seems to have failed less in carefulness than in discernment. He could not believe his ears when Frances spoke of having a book ready for the press. He looked on her scheme of publication as an idle fancy, and doubtless was convinced that nothing would come of it. Her motive for concealing her project from him had been merely dread of his ridicule. Until 'Evelina' became an assured success, he had no faith in the ability of his second daughter. 'Poor Fanny'—so he used to call her—was, in his eyes, a dutiful and affectionate child, and a useful amanuensis, and nothing more. So little did he expect ever to hear again of her embryo work, that he did not even ask its title.

At length, in January, 1778, 'Evelina' was published. The author was informed of the event through hearing an advertisement announcing it read aloud by her step-mother at breakfast-time. Those of the party who were in the secret smiled, or blushed; those who were not suspected nothing. Several weeks elapsed before the new novel attracted much attention. Meanwhile the writer was laid up with inflammation of the lungs. On quitting her bedroom, she found that, in the circles known to her, her book was being widely read, with speculations as to its authorship. One acquaintance attributed it to Anstey, then famous for his 'New Bath Guide;' most voices agreed that it could not have proceeded from a woman's pen—a conclusion which, with the usual perversity of her sex, Miss Burney regarded as a high compliment. Then the magazines commenced to speak in its praise. The *London Review* and the *Monthly Review* both gave favourable notices. Thus stimulated, the sale increased, till at the end of the fifth month two editions had been exhausted, and a third was fast being disposed of.* By May, Fanny was sufficiently recovered to leave town, and went on a long visit to Chesington, where, as she 'could hardly walk three yards in a day at first,' she amused herself with reading 'Evelina' to Daddy Crisp, and goading his curiosity by allusions to dark reports about its origin. Crisp, who, of course, suspected some mystery, was guarded in his praise, but gratified his young favourite by betraying a most un-cynical eagerness for the third volume as soon as the first two had been despatched. Before long, exciting letters from home began to pour in on the convalescent at the Hall. She gives the substance of some of them in her Diary:

" I received from Charlotte a letter, the most interesting that could be written to me, for it acquainted me that my

* The first edition consisted of 800 copies, the second of 500, the third of 1,000. A fourth edition, the extent of which was not divulged, followed in the autumn. After the third edition, Lowndes paid the author a further sum of ten pounds in full satisfaction of any claim or expectation which she or her friends might found on the continued success of the book.

dear father was at length reading my book, which has now been published six months. How this has come to pass, I am yet in the dark; but it seems . . . . he desired Charlotte to bring him the *Monthly Review*; she contrived to look over his shoulder as he opened it, which he did at the account of 'Evelina; or, A Young Lady's Entrance into the World.' He read it with great earnestness, then put it down; and presently after snatched it up, and read it again. Doubtless his paternal heart felt some agitation for his girl in reading a review of her publication!—how he got at the name I cannot imagine. Soon after, he turned to Charlotte, and bidding her come close to him, he put his finger on the word 'Evelina,' and saying *she knew what it was*, bade her write down the name, and send the man to Lowndes', as if for herself. This she did, and away went William. When William returned, he took the book from him, and the moment he was gone, opened the first volume—and opened it upon the *Ode!*"

Prefixed to Evelina was an inscription in verse to the writer's father, much more remarkable for tenderness of feeling than for poetical merit.

" How great must have been his astonishment at seeing himself so addressed! Indeed, Charlotte says he looked all amazement, read a line or two with great eagerness, and then, stopping short, he seemed quite affected, and the tears started into his eyes. Dear soul! I am sure they did into mine; nay, I even sobbed as I read the account.

I believe he was obliged to go out before he advanced much further. But the next day I had a letter from Susan, in which I heard that he had begun reading it with Lady Hales and Miss Coussmaker, and that they liked it vastly! Lady Hales spoke of it very innocently, in the

5

highest terms, declaring she was sure it was written by somebody in high life, and that it had all the marks of real genius! She added, 'He must be a man of great abilities.'"

Dr. Burney's opinion was expressed with even greater simplicity than this. From an unbeliever he had been suddenly changed into a worshipper, and in the first glow of his conversion, he pronounced the new novel to be the best he had met with, excepting Fielding's, and in some respects better than *his!* A proselyte himself, he was at once full of schemes for spreading the knowledge of the true faith. He would begin by telling Mrs. Thrale, as the centre of a large literary circle. Before he could broach the subject, he heard his daughter's book celebrated at the Streatham tea-table. " Madam," cried Dr. Johnson, see-sawing on his chair, " Mrs. Cholmondeley was talking to me last night of a new novel, which, she says, has a very uncommon share of merit—'Evelina.' She says that she has not been so entertained this great while as in reading it, and that she shall go all over London to discover the author." Mrs. Cholmondeley was a sister of Peg Woffing-ton, the actress, and had married Captain Cholmondeley, second son of the Earl of Cholmondeley, and a nephew of Horace Walpole. Her husband afterwards quitted the army, and took orders; and at this time the *salon* of the witty and eccentric Mrs. Cholmondeley was in high repute. Besides recommending Evelina to Johnson, she had engaged Burke and Reynolds to get it, and announced her intention of keeping it on her table the whole summer to make it as widely known as possible. All this made it necessary for her friend and rival, Mrs. Thrale, not to be left in the background. There was but one thing to be done : the lady of Streatham lost no time in procuring and reading this new success ; fell into a rapture over it;

bepraised it with her usual vivacity, and passed it on to Johnson. The great man took to it immensely. When he had finished one volume, he was as impatient as Crisp had been for the next, protesting that *he could not get rid of the rogue;* and his judgment was that there were passages in the book that might do honour to Richardson. The packet of letters in which this compliment was transmitted to Fanny reported also that Sir Joshua Reynolds had forgotten his dinner while engrossed with her story, and that Burke had sat up all night to finish it; and Dr. Burney added an enclosure, in which he said: 'Thou hast made thy old father laugh and cry at thy pleasure.'

If Mrs. Cholmondeley could claim to have introduced Evelina to the polite world, to Mrs. Thrale fell the distinction of making known its author. After ratifying the general opinion of the work, Mrs. Thrale asked, in Burney's presence, whether Mrs. Cholmondeley had yet found out the writer, 'because,' said the speaker, 'I long to know him of all things.' This inquiry produced an avowal, which the Doctor had obtained his daughter's permission to make; and shortly afterwards he appeared at Chesington to carry her to Streatham, and present her, by appointment, to the Thrales—and to Dr. Johnson.

Many surprising successes are recorded in the annals of literature; but there have been few quite like this. Lately the least noticed member of her father's household, Frances Burney was now elevated far above its head. Other writers before their rise have been insignificant; the author of Evelina was despised. Proud and happy man though he was, Dr. Burney could not at once break off the habit of calling her *poor Fanny.* "Do you breathe, my dear Fanny?" asks Susan in a letter, after recounting part of the wonders above mentioned. "It took away my breath," adds the writer, "and then made me skip about

like a mad creature." "My dearest Susy," responds
Fanny, "don't you think there must be some wager
depending among the little curled imps who hover over
us mortals, of how much flummery goes to turn the head
of an authoress? Your last communication very near did
my business, for, meeting Mr. Crisp ere I had composed
myself, I 'tipt him such a touch of the heroics' as he
has not seen since the time when I was so much celebrated
for dancing 'Nancy Dawson.'* I absolutely longed to
treat him with one of Captain Mirvan's† frolics, and to
fling his wig out of the window. I restrained myself,
however, from the apprehension that they would imagine I
had a universal spite to that harmless piece of goods, which
I have already been known to treat with no little indignity.
He would fain have discovered the reason of my skittish-
ness; but as I could not tell it him, I was obliged to
assure him it would be lost time to inquire further into
my flights." Refraining from the wig, Fanny darted out
of the room, and, as she tells us elsewhere,‡ performed a
sort of jig round an old mulberry-tree that stood on the
lawn before the house. She related this incident many
years afterwards to Sir Walter Scott, who has recorded
it in his journal.§

It will be gathered from our last extract that Mr. Crisp
was not yet in possession of the great secret. Fanny
dreaded the edge of his criticism, even more than she had
dreaded the chill of her father's contempt. Dr. Burney

---

* Mr. Crisp to Miss Burney, January, 1779: "Do you remember, about a
dozen years ago, how you used to dance 'Nancy Dawson' on the grass-plot,
with your cap on the ground, and your long hair streaming down your back,
one shoe off, and throwing about your head like a mad thing!"
† The sea-captain in 'Evelina.'
‡ Diary, i., p. 18; Memoirs, ii., p. 149.
§ Lockhart's 'Life of Scott,' vi., p. 388. There seems to be some trifling
discrepancy between the different accounts, both as to the date and the exact
occasion of this incident.

arrived at the Hall to fetch away his daughter on the first
Saturday in August, and it was agreed between them that
a disclosure could no longer be deferred. " My dear
father," says the Diary, " desired to take upon himself the
communication to my Daddy Crisp, and as it is now in so
many hands that it is possible accident might discover it
to him, I readily consented. Sunday evening, as I was
going into my father's room, I heard him say, ' The
variety of characters, the variety of scenes, and the
language—why, she has had very little education but what
she has given herself—less than any of the others !' and
Mr. Crisp exclaimed, ' Wonderful ! it's wonderful !' I
now found what was going forward, and therefore deemed
it most fitting to decamp. About an hour after, as I was
passing through the hall, I met my Daddy Crisp. His
face was all animation and archness ; he doubled his fist
at me, and would have stopped me, but I ran past him
into the parlour. Before supper, however, I again met
him, and he would not suffer me to escape ; he caught
both my hands, and looked as if he would have looked me
through, and then exclaimed, ' Why, you little hussy,
ain't you ashamed to look me in the face, you ' Evelina,'
you ! Why, what a dance have you led me about it !
Young friend, indeed ! Oh, you little hussy, what tricks
have you served me !' I was obliged to allow of his
running on with these gentle appellations for I know not
how long, ere he could sufficiently compose himself, after
his great surprise, to ask or hear any particulars; and
then he broke out every three instants with exclamations
of astonishment at how I had found time to write so
much unsuspected, and how and where I had picked up
such various materials ; and not a few times did he, with
me, as he had with my father, exclaim, ' Wonderful !'
He has since made me read him all my letters upon this

subject. He said Lowndes would have made an estate, had he given me £1,000 for it, and that he ought not to have given less. 'You have nothing to do now,' continued he, 'but to take your pen in hand, for your fame and reputation are made, and any bookseller will snap at what you write.'"

A day or two after this conversation, Fanny and her father left Liberty Hall, as Mr. Crisp was pleased to designate his retreat. Arrived at the verge of our own heroine's entrance into the world, we shall not stop to discuss the question how far she was entitled to the fame she had so rapidly won, nor shall we engage in any criticism of the work by which she had acquired it. We may assent to the admission of an admirer that the society depicted in Evelina is made up of unreal beings. What else could be expected from a fiction designed in immature youth, executed, like patchwork, at intervals, and put together, at last, without advice from any experienced person? Real or unreal, however, the characters in the novel were vivid enough to interest strongly those of the writer's contemporaries who were most familiar with the world and human nature.

In the conversations which we are about to extract will be found numerous allusions to personages who, though fictitious, are, at any rate, as substantial for us as most of the talkers, who have long since passed into the region of shadows. We may leave to Miss Burney the task of introducing her friends; she mentions the creations of her brain without a word of explanation, because she knew that the few eyes and ears for which her Diary was intended were as well acquainted with them as herself It therefore devolves on us to indicate the chief actors in Evelina to our readers. We have the honour to present: Madame Duval, Evelina's low-bred grandmother from Paris, interlarding her illiterate English with an incessant *Ma foi !* and other French interjections; Captain Mirvan, a fair specimen of the coarse naval officer of that time;* the Branghtons, a vulgar family living on Snow Hill; Mr. Smith, a Holborn beau, lodging with the B-anghtons. Add to these, Lord Orville, the hero, and Sir Clement Willoughby, the villain of the piece; Mr. Lovel, a fop; Lady Louisa, a languishing dame of quality; Sir John Belmont, the heroine's father; M. Du Bois, a Frenchman in attendance on Madame Duval; and Mr. Macartney, a starving Scotch poet. Of the last two, the author conferred on the former the maiden name of her grandmother; on the latter, the maiden-name of her god-mother, Mrs. Greville.

We will give Fanny's account of her first dinner at Streatham in the words of her Diary:

"When we were summoned to dinner, Mrs. Thrale made my father and me sit on each side of her. I said that I hoped I did not take Dr. Johnson's place;—for he had not yet appeared.

'No,' answered Mrs. Thrale, 'he will sit by you, which I am sure will give him great pleasure.'

Soon after we were seated, this great man entered. I have so true a veneration for him, that the very sight of him inspires me with delight and reverence, notwithstanding the cruel infirmities to which he is subject; for he has almost perpetual convulsive movements, either of his hands, lips, feet, or knees, and sometimes of all together.

---

* 'I have this to comfort me : that, the more I see of sea-captains, the less reason I have to be ashamed of Captain Mirvan ; for they have all so irresistible a propensity to wanton mischief, to roasting beaux and detesting old women, that I quite rejoice I showed the book to no one ere printed, lest I should have been prevailed upon to soften his character.'—Diary, May 28, 1780.

Mrs. Thrale introduced me to him, and he took his place. We had a noble dinner, and a most elegant dessert. Dr. Johnson, in the middle of dinner, asked Mrs. Thrale what was in some little pies that were near him.

'Mutton,' answered she; 'so I don't ask you to eat any, because I know you despise it.'

'No, madam, no,' cried he; 'I despise nothing that is good of its sort; but I am too proud now to eat of it. Sitting by Miss Burney makes me very proud to-day!'

'Miss Burney,' said Mrs. Thrale, laughing, 'you must take great care of your heart if Dr. Johnson attacks it; for I assure you he is not often successless.'

'What's that you say, madam?' cried he; 'are you making mischief between the young lady and me already?'

A little while after he drank Miss Thrale's health and mine, and then added:

''Tis a terrible thing that we cannot wish young ladies well without wishing them to become old women!'

'But some people,' said Mr. Seward, 'are old and young at the same time, for they wear so well that they never look old.'

'No, sir, no,' cried the doctor, laughing; 'that never yet was; you might as well say they are at the same time tall and short. I remember an epitaph to that purpose, which is in——'

(I have quite forgot what,—and also the name it was made upon, but the rest I recollect exactly:)

'—— lies buried here;
So early wise, so lasting fair,
That none, unless her years you told,
Thought her a child, or thought her old.'

Mrs. Thrale then repeated some lines in French, and Dr. Johnson some more in Latin. An epilogue of Mr.

Garrick's to 'Bonduca' was then mentioned, and Dr. Johnson said it was a miserable performance, and everybody agreed it was the worst he had ever made.

'And yet,' said Mr. Seward, 'it has been very much admired : but it is in praise of English valour, and so I suppose the subject made it popular.'

'I don't know, sir,' said Dr. Johnson, 'anything about the subject, for I could not read on till I came to it ; I got through half a dozen lines, but I could observe no other subject than eternal dulness. I don't know what is the matter with David ; I am afraid he is grown superannuated, for his prologues and epilogues used to be incomparable.'

'Nothing is so fatiguing,' said Mrs. Thrale, 'as the life of a wit ; he and Wilkes are the two oldest men of their ages I know, for they have both worn themselves out by being eternally on the rack to give entertainment to others.'

'David, madam,' said the doctor, 'looks much older than he is ; for his face has had double the business of any other man's ; it is never at rest ; when he speaks one minute, he has quite a different countenance to what he assumes the next. I don't believe he ever kept the same look for half an hour together in the whole course of his life ; and such an eternal, restless, fatiguing play of the muscles must certainly wear out a man's face before its real time.'

'O yes,' cried Mrs. Thrale ; 'we must certainly make some allowance for such wear and tear of a man's face.'

The next name that was started was that of Sir John Hawkins, and Mrs. Thrale said :

'Why now, Dr. Johnson, he is another of those whom you suffer nobody to abuse but yourself; Garrick is one, too; for if any other person speaks against him, you browbeat him in a minute!'

'Why, madam,' answered he, 'they don't know when to abuse him, and when to praise him; I will allow no man to speak ill of David that he does not deserve; and as to Sir John, why really I believe him to be an honest man at the bottom: but to be sure he is penurious, and he is mean, and it must be owned he has a degree of brutality, and a tendency to savageness, that cannot easily be defended.'

We all laughed, as he meant we should, at this curious manner of speaking in his favour, and he then related an anecdote that he said he knew to be true in regard to his meanness. He said that Sir John and he once belonged to the same club, but that as he ate no supper after the first night of his admission, he desired to be excused paying his share.

'And was he excused?'

'O yes; for no man is angry at another for being inferior to himself! we all scorned him, and admitted his plea. For my part, I was such a fool as to pay my share for wine, though I never tasted any. But Sir John was a most *unclubbable* man!'

'And this,' continued he, 'reminds me of a gentleman and lady with whom I travelled once; I suppose I must call them gentleman and lady, according to form, because they travelled in their own coach and four horses. But at the first inn where we stopped, the lady called for —a pint of ale! and when it came, quarrelled with the waiter for not giving full measure. Now, Madame Duval could not have done a grosser thing.'

Oh, how everybody laughed! and to be sure I did not glow at all, nor munch fast, nor look on my plate, nor lose any part of my usual composure! But how grateful

do I feel to this dear Dr. Johnson, for never naming me
and the book as belonging one to the other, and yet
making an allusion that showed his thoughts led to it,
and, at the same time, that seemed to justify the character
as being natural! But, indeed, the delicacy I met with
from him, and from all the Thrales, was yet more flattering to me than the praise with which I have heard they
have honoured my book.

After dinner, when Mrs. Thrale and I left the gentlemen, we had a conversation that to me could not but be
delightful, as she was all good-humour, spirits, sense, and
agreeability. Surely I may make words, when at a loss, if
Dr. Johnson does.

We left Streatham at about eight o'clock, and Mr.
Seward, who handed me into the chaise, added his interest to the rest, that my father would not fail to bring
me again next week to stay with them for some time. In
short, I was loaded with civilities from them all. And
my ride home was equally happy with the rest of the
day, for my kind and most beloved father was so happy
in *my* happiness, and congratulated me so sweetly, that
he could, like myself, think on no other subject.

Yet my honours stopped not here; for Hetty, who,
with her *sposo*, was here to receive us, told me she had
lately met Mrs. Reynolds, sister of Sir Joshua; and that
she talked very much and very highly of a new novel
called 'Evelina;' though without a shadow of suspicion
as to the scribbler. . . .

Sir Joshua, it seems, vows he would give fifty pounds
to know the author! I have also heard, by the means of
Charles, that other persons have declared they *will* find
him out!

This intelligence determined me upon going myself
to Mr. Lowndes, and discovering what sort of answers

he made to such curious inquirers as I found were likely to address him.   But as I did not dare trust myself to speak, for I felt that I should not be able to act my part well, I asked my mother to accompany me.

We introduced ourselves by buying the book, for which I had a commission from Mrs. G——.   Fortunately Mr. Lowndes himself was in the shop ; as we found by his air of consequence and authority, as well as his age ; for I never saw him before.

The moment he had given my mother the book, she asked if he could tell her who wrote it.

'No,' he answered : 'I don't know myself.'

'Pho, pho,' said she ; 'you mayn't choose to tell, but you must know.'

'I don't, indeed, ma'am,' answered he ; 'I have no honour in keeping the secret, for I have never been trusted.   All I know of the matter is, that it is a gentleman of the other end of the town.'

My mother made a thousand other inquiries, to which his answers were to the following effect : that for a great while, he did not know if it was a man or a woman ; but now, he knew that much, and that he was a master of his subject, and well versed in the manners of the times."

A few days after this, Mrs. Thrale called in St. Martin's Street, and carried her new acquaintance down to Streatham :

"At night, Mrs. Thrale asked if I would have anything? I answered, 'No ;' but Dr. Johnson said,—

'Yes : she is used, madam, to suppers ; she would like an egg or two, and a few slices of ham, or a rasher—a rasher, I believe, would please her better.'

How ridiculous !   However, nothing could persuade

Mrs. Thrale not to have the cloth laid ; and Dr. Johnson was so facetious, that he challenged Mr. Thrale to get drunk !

'I wish,' said he, 'my master would say to me, Johnson, if you will oblige me, you will call for a bottle of Toulon, and then we will set to it, glass for glass, till it is done; and after that I will say, Thrale, if you will oblige me, you will call for another bottle of Toulon, and then we will set to it, glass for glass, till that is done : and by the time we should have drunk the two bottles we should be so happy, and such good friends, that we should fly into each other's arms, and both together call for the third !'

I ate nothing, that they might not again use such a ceremony with me. Indeed, their late dinners forbid suppers, especially as Dr. Johnson made me eat cake at tea; for he held it till I took it, with an odd or absent complaisance.

He was extremely comical after supper, and would not suffer Mrs. Thrale and me to go to bed for near an hour after we made the motion. . . .

Now for this morning's breakfast.

Dr. Johnson, as usual, came last into the library; he was in high spirits, and full of mirth and sport. I had the honour of sitting next to him: and now, all at once, he flung aside his reserve, thinking, perhaps, that it was time I should fling aside mine.

Mrs. Thrale told him that she intended taking me to Mr. T——'s.

'So you ought, madam,' cried he; ''tis your business to be cicerone to her.'

Then suddenly he snatched my hand, and kissing it,

'Ah!' he added, 'they will little think what a tartar you carry to them !'

'No, that they won't!' cried Mrs. Thrale; 'Miss Burney looks so meek and so quiet, nobody would suspect what a comical girl she is; but I believe she has a great deal of malice at heart.'

'Oh, she's a toad!' cried the doctor, laughing—'a sly young rogue! with her Smiths and her Branghtons!'

'Why, Dr. Johnson,' said Mrs. Thrale, 'I hope you are very well this morning! If one may judge by your spirits and good-humour, the fever you threatened us with is gone off.'

He had complained that he was going to be ill last night.

'Why, no, madam, no,' answered he, 'I am not yet well; I could not sleep at all; there I lay, restless and uneasy, and thinking all the time of Miss Burney. Perhaps I have offended her, thought I; perhaps she is angry; I have seen her but once, and I talked to her of a rasher! —Were you angry?'

I think I need not tell you my answer.

'I have been endeavouring to find some excuse,' continued he, 'and, as I could not sleep, I got up, and looked for some authority for the word; and I find, madam, it is used by Dryden: in one of his prologues he says—"And snatch a homely rasher from the coals." So you must not mind me, madam; I say strange things, but I mean no harm.'

I was almost afraid he thought I was really idiot enough to have taken him seriously; but, a few minutes after, he put his hand on my arm, and shaking his head, exclaimed:

'Oh, you are a sly little rogue!—what a Holborn beau have you drawn!'

'Ay, Miss Burney,' said Mrs. Thrale, 'the Holborn beau is Dr. Johnson's favourite; and we have all your

characters by heart, from Mr. Smith up to Lady
Louisa.'

'Oh, Mr. Smith, Mr. Smith is the man!' cried he,
laughing violently. 'Harry Fielding never drew so good
a character!—such a fine varnish of low politeness!—such
a struggle to appear a gentleman! Madam, there is no
character better drawn anywhere—in any book, or by any
author.'

I almost poked myself under the table. Never did I
feel so delicious a confusion since I was born! But he
added a great deal more, only I cannot recollect his exact
words, and I do not choose to give him mine.

'Come, come,' cried Mrs. Thrale, 'we'll torment her
no more about her book, for I see it really plagues
her. I own I thought for awhile it was only affectation,
for I'm sure if the book were mine I should wish to hear
of nothing else. But we shall teach her in time how
proud she ought to be of such a performance.'

'Ah, madam,' cried the Doctor, 'be in no haste to
teach her that; she'll speak no more to us when she
knows her own weight.' . . . .

Some time after the Doctor began laughing to himself,
and then, suddenly turning to me, he called out, 'Only
think, Polly! Miss has danced with a lord!'

'Ah, poor Evelina!' cried Mrs. Thrale, 'I see her
now in Kensington Gardens. What she must have
suffered! Poor girl! what fidgets she must have been in!
And I know Mr. Smith, too, very well; I always have
him before me at the Hampstead Ball, dressed in a white
coat, and a tambour waistcoat, worked in green silk.
Poor Mr. Seward! Mr. Johnson made him so mad
t'other day! "Why, Seward," said he, "how smart you
are dressed! Why you only want a tambour waistcoat,
to look like Mr. Smith!" But I am very fond of Lady

Louisa. I think her as well drawn as any character in the book—so fine, so affected, so languishing, and, at the same time, so insolent!' . . . .

As I have always heard from my father that every individual at Streatham spends the morning alone, I took the first opportunity of absconding to my own room, and amused myself in writing till I tired. About noon, when I went into the library, book-hunting, Mrs. Thrale came to me.

We had a very nice confab about various books, and exchanged opinions and imitations of Baretti ; she told me many excellent tales of him, and I, in return, related my stories.

She gave me a long and very interesting account of Dr. Goldsmith, who was intimately known here ; but in speaking of ' The Good-natured Man,' when I extolled my favourite Croaker, I found that admirable character was a downright theft from Dr. Johnson. Look at the ' Rambler,' and you will find Suspirius is the man, and that not merely the idea, but the particulars of the character are all stolen thence !*

While we were yet reading this ' Rambler,' Dr. Johnson came in : we told him what we were about.

' Ah, madam !' cried he, ' Goldsmith was not scrupulous ; but he would have been a great man had he known the real value of his own internal resources.'

' Miss Burney,' said Mrs. Thrale, ' is fond of his " Vicar of Wakefield," and so am I ; don't you like it, sir ?'

' No, madam ; it is very faulty. There is nothing of real life in it, and very little of nature. It is a mere fanciful performance.'

---

* Suspirius the Screech Owl. See ' Rambler' for Tuesday, October 9, 1750.

He then seated himself upon a sofa, and calling to me, said: 'Come, Evelina—come, and sit by me.'

I obeyed, and he took me almost in his arms—that is, one of his arms, for one would go three times, at least, round me—and, half-laughing, half-serious, he charged me to 'be a good girl.'

'But, my dear,' continued he with a very droll look, 'what makes you so fond of the Scotch? I don't like you for that; I hate these Scotch, and so must you. I wish Branghton had sent the dog to jail—that Scotch dog, Macartney!'

'Why, sir,' said Mrs. Thrale, 'don't you remember he says he would, but that he should get nothing by it?'

'Why, ay, true,' cried the Doctor, see-sawing very solemnly, 'that, indeed, is some palliation for his forbearance. But I must not have you so fond of the Scotch, my little Burney; make your hero what you will but a Scotchman. Besides, you write Scotch—you say, "the one." My dear, that's not English—never use that phrase again.'

'Perhaps,' said Mrs. Thrale, 'it may be used in Macartney's letter, and then it will be a propriety.'

'No, madam, no!' cried he; 'you can't make a beauty of it; it is in the third volume; put it in Macartney's letter, and welcome!—that, or anything that is nonsense.'

'Why, surely,' cried I, 'the poor man is used ill enough by the Branghtons!'

'But Branghton,' said he, 'only hates him because of his wretchedness, poor fellow! But, my dear love, how should he ever have eaten a good dinner before he came to England?'

And then he laughed violently at young Branghton's idea.

'Well,' said Mrs. Thrale, 'I always liked Macartney; he is a very pretty character, and I took to him, as the folks say.'

'Why, madam,' answered he, 'I liked Macartney myself. Yes, poor fellow, I liked the man, but I love not the nation.'"

Miss Burney's visit on this occasion lasted several days, and it was speedily followed by another and another. Mrs. Thrale, having discovered a fresh attraction for her country house, hastened to turn it to the best account. The friendship between her and the new authoress developed with the rapid growth peculiar to feminine attachments. And Fanny enjoyed her life at Streatham. Dr. Johnson was nearly always there; she liked the family; and the opulent establishment, with its well-kept gardens, hot-houses, shrubberies, and paddock, had all the charm of novelty to a young woman, whose time had long been divided between the smoky atmosphere of Leicester Fields and the desolation of Liberty Hall. The great Doctor, whose affection for her increased daily, took an early opportunity of saying to her: 'These are as good people as you can be with; you can go to no better house; they are all good-nature; nothing makes them angry.' She found no cause to complain of Mr. Thrale's curt speech, or the eldest daughter's cold manner, or the roughness of Ursa Major, though she has reported Mrs. Thrale's quick answer to Johnson when he asked the motive of his hostess's excessive complaisance: 'Why, I'll tell you, sir; when I am with you, and Mr. Thrale, and Queeny, I am obliged to be civil for four.'

If Mrs. Thrale engrossed a large share of her novice's time this autumn, she took pains to make her talk a little in company, and prepared her, in some degree, for the ordeal that awaited her during the ensuing winter in London.

Numerous visitors were invited to Streatham to become acquainted with the timid young writer, who, though accustomed to society, had never yet learned to make her voice heard in a circle of listeners. One afternoon Sir Joshua Reynolds and his nieces came down, and on their arrival, the conversation being turned to the subject of Evelina, they were informed that they should meet the author at dinner. After a good deal of guessing, the suspicions of the guests settled on the lady of the house, who sportively assumed a conscious air, but before the close of the day, the secret was allowed to transpire, and when the party broke up, Sir Joshua, approaching Miss Burney, with his most courtly bow, hoped that as soon as she left Streatham he should have the honour of seeing her in Leicester Square.

"The joke is," writes Fanny, "the people speak as if they were afraid of me, instead of my being afraid of them. . . . . Next morning, Mrs. Thrale asked me if I did not want to see Mrs. Montagu? I truly said, I should be the most insensible of animals not to like to see our sex's glory." A note was despatched accordingly, and the glory of her sex graciously accepted. On hearing of this, "Dr. Johnson began to see-saw, with a countenance strongly expressive of inward fun, and after enjoying it some time in silence, he suddenly, and with great animation, turned to me, and cried: 'Down with her, Burney!—down with her!—spare her not!—attack her, fight her, and down with her at once! You are a rising wit, and she is at the top; and when I was beginning the world, and was nothing and nobody, the joy of my life was to fire at all the established wits! and then everybody loved to halloo me on. But there is no game now; everybody would be glad to see me conquered: but then, when I was new, to vanquish the great ones was all the delight of my poor little dear soul! So at her, Burney—at her, and down with her.'" The Queen of the Blue Stockings arrived, attended by her companion, a Miss Gregory; and the usual presentation and disclosure took place. Fanny, of course, had not much to say for herself, but the observant eyes were busy as usual. This is their report of Mrs. Montagu; "She is middle-sized, very thin, and looks infirm; she has a sensible and penetrating countenance, and the air and manner of a woman accustomed to being distinguished, and of great parts. Dr. Johnson, who agrees in this, told us that Mrs. Hervey, of his acquaintance, says she can remember Mrs. Montagu *trying* for this same air and manner. Mr. Crisp has said the same: however, nobody can now impartially see her, and not confess that she has extremely well succeeded." When dinner was upon table, the observer followed the procession, in a tragedy step, as Mr. Thrale would have it, into the dining-room. The conversation was not brilliant, nor is much of it recorded. When Mrs. Montagu's new house* was talked of, Dr. Johnson, in a jocose manner, desired to know if he should be invited to see it. 'Ay, sure,' cried Mrs. Montagu, looking well pleased; 'or else I shan't like it: but I invite you all to a house-warming; I shall hope for the honour of seeing all this company at my new house next Easter-day: I fix the day now that it may be remembered.' "Dr. Johnson," adds Fanny, "who sat next to me, was determined I should be of the party, for he suddenly clapped his hand on my shoulder, and called out aloud: 'Little Burney, you and I will go together.' 'Yes, surely,' cried Mrs. Montagu, 'I shall hope for the pleasure of seeing Evelina.'"

It was at Streatham shortly afterwards that Miss Burney made her first acquaintance with James Boswell.

* She was then building her famous house in Portman Square.

We do not get our account of this meeting direct from the Diary, and have to take it as it stands in the Memoirs, dressed up by the pen of the aged Madame d'Arblay. Boswell, we are told, had a strong Scotch accent, though by no means strong enough to make him unintelligible to an English ear. He had an odd mock solemnity of tone and manner that he had acquired un‐consciously from constantly thinking of, and imitating, Johnson. There was also something slouching in the gait and dress of Mr. Boswell that ridiculously caricatured the same model. His clothes were always too large for him; his hair, or wig, was constantly in a state of negli‐gence; and he never for a moment sat still or upright in his chair. Every look and movement betrayed either in‐tentional or involuntary imitation :

"As Mr. Boswell was at Streatham only upon a morn‐ing visit, a collation was ordered, to which all were as‐sembled. Mr. Boswell was preparing to take a seat that he seemed, by prescription, to consider as his own, next to Dr. Johnson; but Mr. Seward, who was present, waved his hand for Mr. Boswell to move farther on, say‐ing with a smile :

"'Mr. Boswell, that seat is Miss Burney's.'

"He stared, amazed: the asserted claimant was new and unknown to him, and he appeared by no means pleased to resign his prior rights. But after looking round for a minute or two, with an important air of demanding the meaning of the innovation, and receiving no satisfaction, he reluctantly, almost resentfully, got another chair, and placed it at the back of the shoulder of Dr. Johnson; while this new and unheard-of rival quietly seated herself as if not hearing what was passing, for she shrank from the explanation that she feared might ensue, as she saw a smile stealing over every countenance, that of Dr. Johnson himself not excepted, at the discomfiture and surprise of Mr. Boswell.

"Mr. Boswell, however, was so situated as not to remark it in the Doctor; and of everyone else, when in that presence, he was unobservant, if not contemptuous. In truth, when he met with Dr. Johnson, he commonly forbore even answering anything that went forward, lest he should miss the smallest sound from that voice to which he paid such exclusive, though merited, homage. But the moment that voice burst forth, the attention which it excited in Mr. Boswell amounted almost to pain. His eyes goggled with eagerness; he leant his ear almost on the shoulder of the Doctor; and his mouth dropped open to catch every syllable that might be uttered: nay, he seemed not only to dread losing a word, but to be anxious not to miss a breathing; as if hoping from it, latently or mystically, some information.

"But when, in a few minutes, Dr. Johnson, whose eye did not follow him, and who had concluded him to be at the other end of the table, said something gaily and good-humouredly, by the appellation of Bozzy, and discovered, by the sound of the reply, that Bozzy had planted himself, as closely as he could, behind and between the elbows of the new usurper and his own, the Doctor turned angrily round upon him, and, clapping his hand rather loudly upon his knee, said, in a tone of displeasure: 'What do you do there, sir?—Go to the table, sir!'

"Mr. Boswell instantly, and with an air of affright, obeyed; and there was something so unusual in such humble submission to so imperious a command, that another smile gleamed its way across every mouth, except that of the Doctor and of Mr. Boswell, who now, very unwillingly, took a distant seat.

" But, ever restless when not at the side of Dr. Johnson, he presently recollected something that he wished to exhibit; and, hastily rising, was running away in its search, when the Doctor, calling after him, authoritatively said: ' What are you thinking of, sir? Why do you get up before the cloth is removed ?—Come back to your place, sir !'

" Again, and with equal obsequiousness, Mr. Boswell did as he was bid; when the Doctor, pursing his lips not to betray rising risibility, muttered half to himself: ' Running about in the middle of meals ! One would take you for a Branghton !'

" ' A Branghton, sir ?' repeated Mr. Boswell, with earnestness; ' what is a Branghton, sir ?'

" ' Where have you lived, sir ?' cried the Doctor, laughing; 'and what company have you kept, not to know that ?'

" Mr. Boswell now, doubly curious, yet always apprehensive of falling into some disgrace with Dr. Johnson, said, in a low tone, which he knew the Doctor could not hear, to Mrs. Thrale: ' Pray, ma'am, what's a Branghton ? Do me the favour to tell me ! Is it some animal hereabouts ?'

" Mrs. Thrale only heartily laughed, but without answering, as she saw one of her guests uneasily fearful of an explanation. But Mr. Seward cried: ' I'll tell you, Boswell—I'll tell you !—if you will walk with me into the paddock; only let us wait till the table is cleared, or I shall be taken for a Branghton, too !'

" They soon went off together; and Mr. Boswell, no doubt, was fully informed of the road that had led to the usurpation by which he had thus been annoyed. But the Branghton fabricator took care to mount to her chamber ere they returned, and did not come down till Mr. Boswell was gone."

The following December and January Miss Burney

spent at home. She paid her promised visit to Sir Joshua Reynolds:

"We found the Miss Palmers alone. We were, for near an hour, quite easy, chatty, and comfortable; no pointed speech was made, and no starer entered.

"Just then, Mrs. and Miss Horneck were announced . . . .

"Mrs. Horneck, as I found in the course of the evening, is an exceeding sensible, well-bred woman.* Her daughter is very beautiful; but was low-spirited and silent during the whole visit. She was, indeed, very unhappy, as Miss Palmer informed me, upon account of some ill news she had lately heard of the affairs of a gentleman to whom she is shortly to be married.

"Not long after came a whole troop, consisting of Mr. Cholmondeley!—O perilous name!—Miss Cholmondeley, and Miss Fanny Cholmondeley, his daughters, and Miss Forrest. Mrs. Cholmondeley, I found, was engaged elsewhere, but soon expected.

"Now here was a trick of Sir Joshua, to make me meet all these people!

"Mr. Cholmondeley is a clergyman; nothing shining either in person or manners, but rather somewhat grim in the first, and glum in the last. Yet he appears to have humour himself, and to enjoy it much in others . . . .

"Next came my father, all gaiety and spirits. Then Mr. William Burke. Soon after, Sir Joshua returned home. He paid his compliments to everybody, and then brought a chair next mine, and said:

---

* Mrs. Horneck was the wife of General Horneck. Her two daughters, Mrs. Bunbury and Miss Horneck (afterwards Mrs. Gwynn), were celebrated beauties, and their portraits rank among the best productions of Sir Joshua Reynolds's pencil. Mary Horneck was Goldsmith's Jessamy Bride, and became the wife of one of George III.'s equerries; her sister married Harry Bunbury, 'the graceful and humorous amateur artist,' as Thackeray calls him, 'of those days, when Gilray had but just begun to try his powers.'

" ' So you were afraid to come among us ?'

" I don't know if I wrote to you a speech to that purpose, which I made to the Miss Palmers ? and which, I
suppose, they had repeated to him. He went on, saying
I might as well fear hobgoblins, and that I had only to
hold up my head to be above them all.

" After this address, his behaviour was exactly what my
wishes would have dictated to him, for my own ease and
quietness; for he never once even alluded to my book,
but conversed rationally, gaily, and serenely: and so I
became more comfortable than I had been ever since the
first entrance of company . . . .

" Our confab was interrupted by the entrance of Mr.
King; a gentleman who is, it seems, for ever with the
Burkes ; and presently Lord Palmerston* was announced.

" Well, while this was going forward, a violent rapping
bespoke, I was sure, Mrs. Cholmondeley, and I ran from
the standers, and turning my back against the door, looked
over Miss Palmer's cards; for you may well imagine I
was really in a tremor at a meeting which so long has
been in agitation, and with the person who, of all persons,
has been most warm and enthusiastic for my book.

" She had not, however, been in the room half an
instant, ere my father came up to me, and tapping me on
the shoulder, said, ' Fanny, here's a lady who wishes to
speak to you.'

" I curtseyed in silence; she too curtseyed, and fixed
her eyes full on my face, and then tapping me with her
fan, she cried :

" ' Come, come, you must not look grave upon me.'

" Upon this, I te-he'd ; she now looked at me yet more
earnestly, and, after an odd silence, said, abruptly :

* Henry Temple, second Viscount Palmerston, father of the Prime Minister.

" ' But is it true ?'

" ' What, ma'am ?'

" ' It can't be !—tell me, though, is it true ?'

" I could only simper.

" ' Why don't you tell me ?—but it can't be—I don't believe it !—no, you are an impostor !'

" Sir Joshua and Lord Palmerston were both at her side—oh, how notably silly must I look ! She again repeated her question of 'Is it true ?' and I again affected not to understand her ; and then Sir Joshua, taking hold of her arm, attempted to pull her away, saying :

" ' Come, come, Mrs. Cholmondeley, I won't have her overpowered here !'

" I love Sir Joshua much for this. But Mrs. Cholmondeley, turning to him, said, with quickness and vehemence :

" ' Why, I ain't going to kill her ! don't be afraid, I shan't compliment her !—I can't, indeed !' "

Then came a scene in which Mrs. Cholmondeley pursued Fanny across the room, hunted her round the card-table, and finally drove her to take refuge behind a sofa, continually plying her with questions, and receiving her confused replies with exclamations of *Ma foi ! pardie !* and other phrases borrowed from Madame Duval. At length :

" *Mrs. Chol.:* My Lord Palmerston, I was told to-night that nobody could see your lordship for me, for that you supped at my house every night ! Dear, bless me, no ! cried I, not every night ! and I looked as confused as I was able ; but I am afraid I did not blush, though I tried hard for it !

" Then again turning to me :

" ' That Mr. What-d'ye-call-him, in Fleet Street, is a

mighty silly fellow;—perhaps you don't know who I mean ?—one T. Lowndes,—but maybe you don't know such a person ?'

" *F. B.* : No, indeed, I do not !—that I can safely say.

" *Mrs. Chol.* : I could get nothing from him : but I told him I hoped he gave a good price : and he answered me, that he always did things genteel. What trouble and tagging we had ! Mr. —— laid a wager the writer was a man :—I said I was sure it was a woman : but now we are both out; for it's a girl !

" In this comical, queer, flighty, whimsical manner she ran on, till we were summoned to supper. . . . .

" When we broke up to depart, which was not till near two in the morning, Mrs. Cholmondeley went up to my mother, and begged her permission to visit in St. Martin's Street. Then, as she left the room, she said to me, with a droll sort of threatening look :

" ' You have not got rid of me yet : I have been forcing myself into your house.'

" I must own I was not at all displeased at this, as I had very much and very reasonably feared that she would have been by then as sick of me from disappointment, as she was before eager for me from curiosity.

" When we came away, Offy Palmer, laughing, said to me:

" ' I think this will be a breaking-in to you !' "

We have next a visit to the house of the persecutor :

" On Monday last, my father sent a note to Mrs. Cholmondeley, to propose our waiting on her the Wednesday following : she accepted the proposal, and accordingly, on Wednesday evening, my father, mother, and self went to Hertford Street.

" I should have told you that Mrs. Cholmondeley, when my father some time ago called on her, sent me a message.

that if I would go to see her, I should not again be stared at or worried ; and she acknowledged that my visit at Sir Joshua's was a formidable one, and that I was watched the whole evening ; but that upon the whole, the company behaved extremely well, for they only ogled!

"Well, we were received by Mrs. Cholmondeley with great politeness, and in a manner that showed she intended to entirely throw aside Madame Duval, and to conduct herself towards me in a new style.

"Mr. and the Misses Cholmondeley and Miss Forrest were with her ; but who else think you ?—why, Mrs. Sheridan! I was absolutely charmed at the sight of her. I think her quite as beautiful as ever, and even more captivating ; for she has now a look of ease and happiness that animates her whole face.

"Miss Linley was with her ; she is very handsome, but nothing near her sister : the elegance of Mrs. Sheridan's beauty is unequalled by any I ever saw, except Mrs. Crewe.* I was pleased with her in all respects. She is much more lively and agreeable than I had any idea of finding her : she was very gay, and very unaffected,. and totally free from airs of any kind.

"Miss Linley was very much out of spirits ; she did not speak three words the whole evening, and looked wholly unmoved at all that passed. Indeed, she appeared to be heavy and inanimate.

"Mrs. Cholmondeley sat next me. She is determined, I believe, to make me like her : and she will, I believe, have full success; for she is very clever, very entertaining, and very much unlike anybody else.

"The first subject started was the Opera, and all joined in the praise of Pacchierotti. Mrs. Sheridan declared she could not hear him without tears, and that he was

* Daughter of Mr. and Mrs. Greville ; afterwards Lady Crewe.

the first Italian singer who ever affected her to such a degree.

"They then talked of the intended marriage of the Duke of Dorset with Miss Cumberland, and many ridiculous anecdotes were related. The conversation naturally fell upon Mr. Cumberland, and he was finely cut up!

"'What a man is that!' said Mrs. Cholmondeley; 'I cannot bear him—so querulous, so dissatisfied, so determined to like nobody and nothing but himself!'

"'What, Mr. Cumberland?' exclaimed I.

"'Yes,' answered she; 'I hope you don't like him?'

"'I don't know him, ma'am. I have only seen him once, at Mrs. Ord's.'

"'Oh, don't like him for your life! I charge you not! I hope you did not like his looks?'

"'Why,' quoth I, laughing, 'I went prepared and determined to like him; but perhaps, when I see him next, I may go prepared for the contrary.'

"A rat-tat-tat-tat ensued, and the Earl of Harcourt was announced. When he had paid his compliments to Mrs. Cholmondeley—

"'I knew, ma'am,' he said, 'that I should find you at home.'

"'I suppose then, my lord,' said she, 'that you have seen Sir Joshua Reynolds; for he is engaged to be here.'

"'I have,' answered his lordship; 'and heard from him that I should be sure to find you.'

"And then he added some very fine compliment, but I have forgot it.

"'Oh, my lord,' cried she, 'you have the most discernment of anybody! His lordship (turning another way) always says these things to me, and yet he never flatters.'

"Lord Harcourt, speaking of the lady from whose house he was just come, said:

"'Mrs. Vesey* is vastly agreeable, but her fear of ceremony is really troublesome: for her eagerness to break a circle is such, that she insists upon everybody's sitting with their backs one to another; that is, the chairs are drawn into little parties of three together, in a confused manner, all over the room.'

"'Why, then,' said my father, 'they may have the pleasure of caballing and cutting up one another, even in the same room.'

"'Oh, I like the notion of all things,' cried Mrs. Cholmondeley; 'I shall certainly adopt it!'

"And then she drew her chair into the middle of our circle. Lord Harcourt turned his round, and his back to most of us, and my father did the same. You can't imagine a more absurd sight.

"Just then the door opened, and Mr. Sheridan entered.

"Was I not in luck? Not that I believe the meeting was accidental; but I had more wished to meet him and his wife than any people I know not.

"I could not endure my ridiculous situation, but replaced myself in an orderly manner immediately. Mr. Sheridan stared at them all, and Mrs. Cholmondeley said she intended it as a hint for a comedy.

"Mr. Sheridan has a very fine figure, and a good, though I don't think a handsome, face. He is tall, and very upright, and his appearance and address are at once manly

---

* Well known as the founder of the *bas bleu* meetings, and the author of the name. Mr. Edward Stillingfleet, a writer on natural history, who was one of her favourite guests, always wore blue stockings, and a phrase used by her, 'Come in your blue stockings,' or 'We can do nothing without the blue stockings,' caused the *bas bleu* to be adopted as the symbol of her literary parties

and fashionable, without the smallest tincture of foppery or modish graces. In short, I like him vastly, and think him every way worthy his beautiful companion.

" And let me tell you what I know will give you as much pleasure as it gave me—that, by all I could observe in the course of the evening, and we stayed very late, they are extremely happy in each other: he evidently adores her, and she as evidently idolizes him. The world has by no means done him justice.

" When he had paid his compliments to all his acquaint-ance, he went behind the sofa on which Mrs. Sheridan and Miss Cholmondeley were seated, and entered into earnest conversation with them.

" Upon Lord Harcourt's again paying Mrs. Cholmon-deley some compliment, she said :

" ' Well, my lord, after this I shall be quite sublime for some days ! I shan't descend into common life till—till Saturday, and then I shall drop into the vulgar style—I shall be in the *ma foi* way.

" I do really believe she could not resist this, for she had seemed determined to be quiet.

" When next there was a rat-tat, Mrs. Cholmondeley and Lord Harcourt, and my father again, at the command of the former, moved into the middle of the room, and then Sir Joshua Reynolds and Dr. Warton entered.

" No further company came. You may imagine there was a general roar at the breaking of the circle, and when they got into order, Mr. Sheridan seated himself in the place Mrs. Cholmondeley had left, between my father and myself.

" And now I must tell you a little conversation which I did not hear myself till I came home; it was between Mr. Sheridan and my father.

" ' Dr. Burney,' cried the former, ' have you no older

daughters? Can this possibly be the authoress of 'Evelina'?'

"And then he said abundance of fine things, and begged my father to introduce him to me.

"'Why, it will be a very formidable thing to her,' answered he, 'to be introduced to you.'

"'Well, then, by-and-by,' returned he.

"Some time after this, my eyes happening to meet his, he waived the ceremony of introduction, and in a low voice said:

"'I have been telling Dr. Burney that I have long expected to see in Miss Burney a lady of the gravest appearance, with the quickest parts.'

"I was never much more astonished than at this unexpected address, as among all my numerous puffers the name of Sheridan has never reached me, and I did really imagine he had never deigned to look at my trash.

"Of course I could make no verbal answer, and he proceeded then to speak of 'Evelina' in terms of the highest praise; but I was in such a ferment from surprise (not to say pleasure), that I have no recollection of his expressions. I only remember telling him that I was much amazed he had spared time to read it, and that he repeatedly called it a most surprising book; and some time after he added: 'But I hope, Miss Burney, you don't intend to throw away your pen?'

"'You should take care, sir,' said I, 'what you say: for you know not what weight it may have.'

"He wished it might have any, he said; and soon after turned again to my father.

"I protest, since the approbation of the Streathamites, I have met with none so flattering to me as this of Mr. Sheridan, and so very unexpected. . . . .

"Some time after, Sir Joshua returning to his standing-place, entered into confab with Miss Linley and your slave, upon various matters, during which Mr. Sheridan, joining us, said :

"'Sir Joshua, I have been telling Miss Burney that she must not suffer her pen to lie idle.—ought she ?'

"*Sir Joshua :* No, indeed, ought she not.

"*Mr. Sheridan :* Do you then, Sir Joshua, persuade her. But perhaps you have begun something ?   May we ask ? Will you answer a question candidly ?

"*F. B. :* I don't know, but as candidly as *Mrs. Candour* I think I certainly shall.

"*Mr. Sheridan :* What then are you about now ?

"*F. B. :* Why, twirling my fan, I think !

"*Mr. Sheridan :* No, no ; but what are you about at home ?   However, it is not a fair question, so I won't press it.

"Yet he looked very inquisitive ; but I was glad to get off without any downright answer.

"*Sir Joshua :* Anything in the dialogue way, I think, she must succeed in ; and I am sure invention will not be wanting.

"*Mr. Sheridan :* No, indeed ; I think, and say, she should write a comedy.

"*Sir Joshua :* I am sure I think so ; and hope she will.

"I could only answer by incredulous exclamations.

"'Consider,' continued Sir Joshua, 'you have already had all the applause and fame you can have given you in the closet ; but the acclamation of a theatre will be new to you.'

"And then he put down his trumpet, and began a violent clapping of his hands.

"I actually shook from head to foot ! I felt myself already in Drury Lane, amidst the hubbub of a first night.

"'Oh no!' cried I; 'there may be a noise, but it will be just the reverse.'   And I returned his salute with a hissing.

" Mr. Sheridan joined Sir Joshua very warmly.

" Oh, sir!' cried I ; 'you should not run on so—you don't know what mischief you may do !'

" *Mr. Sheridan :* I wish I may—I shall be very glad to be accessory."

We gather from the remarks made by Mrs. Chol-mondeley and Sheridan in the preceding extracts that Miss Burney at this time looked much younger than she really was.   With her low stature, slight figure, and timid air, she did not seem quite the woman.   Probably this youthful appearance may have helped to set afloat the rumour which confounded the age of her heroine with her own.   An unmarried lady of six-and-twenty could hardly be expected to enter a formal plea of not guilty to the charge of being only a girl ; yet we shall see presently that Mrs. Thrale was pretty well informed as to the number of Fanny's years.

Some readers may be tempted to think that, with all her coyness, she was enraptured by the pursuit of her admirers.   This is only to say that she was a woman. We must remember, moreover, that the Diary which betrays her feelings was not written with any design of publication, but consisted of private letters, addressed chiefly to her sister Susan, and intended to be shown to no one out of her own family, save her attached Daddy Crisp.   'If,' says Macaulay very fairly, 'she recorded with minute diligence all the compliments, delicate and coarse, which she heard wherever she turned, she recorded them for the eyes of two or three persons who had loved her from infancy, who had loved her in obscurity, and to whom her fame gave the purest and most exquisite delight. Nothing can be more unjust than to confound these out-pouring of a kind heart, sure of perfect sympathy, with the egotism of a blue stocking, who prates to all who come near her about her own novel or her own volume of sonnets.'

CHAPTER IV.

Return to Streatham—Murphy the Dramatist—A Proposed Comedy—'The Witlings'—Adverse Judgment of Mr. Crisp and Dr. Burney—Fanny to Mr. Crisp—Dr. Johnson on Miss Burney—A Visit to Brighton—Cumberland —An Eccentric Character—Sir Joshua's Prices—Tragedies—Actors and Singers—Regrets for the Comedy—Crisp's Reply—The Lawrence Family at Devizes—Lady Miller's Vase—The Gordon Riots—Precipitate Retreat— Grub Street—Sudden Death of Mr. Thrale—Idleness and Work—A Sister of the Craft—The Mausoleum of Julia—Progress of 'Cecilia' through the Press—Crisp's Judgment on' 'Cecilia'—Johnson and 'Cecilia'—Publica- tion of 'Cecilia'—Burke—His Letter to Miss Burney—Assembly at Miss Monckton's—New Acquaintances—Soame Jenyns—Illness and Death of Crisp—Mrs. Thrale's Struggles—Ill-health of Johnson—Mr. Burney Organist of Chelsea Hospital—Mrs. Thrale marries Piozzi—Last Interview with Johnson—His Death.

IN February, 1779, Miss Burney returned to Streatham. A bedroom was set apart for her exclusive use. She became almost as much a recognised member of the family as Dr. Johnson had for many years been. Nearly all the remainder of 1779 was spent with her new friends, either at Streatham, Tunbridge Wells, or Brighton. Her father could scarcely regain possession of her, even for a few days, without a friendly battle. Johnson always took the side of the resisting party. In one of these contests, when Burney urged that she had been away from home too long: ' Sir,' cried Johnson, seizing both her hands to detain her, ' I do not think it long; I would have her *always* come! and *never* go!' In February, the first new face she saw at Mrs. Thrale's was that of Arthur Murphy,* play-

* 1730-1805. A native of Elphin, in Ireland ; was educated at St. Omer's ; gave up the trade on which he had entered for literature ; published the *Gray's*

wright and translator of Tacitus. Mrs. Thrale charged her to make herself agreeable to this gentleman, whose knowledge of the stage might be of service to her in relation to the comedy which her friends were urging her to write. The exhortation was unneeded, for almost the first words uttered by Murphy in her presence won Fanny's heart. Mrs. Thrale, missing Dr. Burney, who after his weekly lesson had returned to town without taking leave, inveighed against him as a male coquet : he only, she said, gave enough of his company to excite a desire for more. Murphy was ready with his compliment.

'Dr. Burney,' he replied, 'is indeed a most extraordinary man ; I think I don't know such another : he is at home upon all subjects, and upon all so agreeable ! he is a wonderful man.'

Noting down this pretty speech led the diarist to record some words which had passed between Johnson and herself on the same theme :

" 'I love Burney,' said the Doctor ; 'my heart goes out to meet him.'

" 'He is not ungrateful, sir,' cried I : 'for most heartily does he love you.'

" 'Does he, madam ?   I am surprised at that.'

" 'Why, sir ?   Why should you have doubted it ?'

" 'Because, madam, Dr. Burney is a man for all the world to love ; it is but natural to love *him*.'

" I could almost have cried with delight at this cordial, unlaboured *éloge*."

An admirer of her father was a man whom Fanny could trust at once, and she soon had confidences with Murphy,

---

Inn Journal from 1752 to 1754 ; went on the stage, wrote dramas, and engaged in politics ; at last became a barrister, and died a Commissioner of Bankrupts. He produced twenty-three plays, of which the 'Grecian Daughter' was the most popular. His translation of Tacitus had great repute in its day.

as well as with Johnson, on the subject of her projected
play.   In May, the first draft was submitted to the former,
who bestowed on it abundance of flattery.   Mrs. Thrale
also was warm in its praise.   But the piece, when finished,
had to be submitted to critics who felt a deeper interest,
and a stronger sense of responsibility.   The manuscript
was carried by Dr. Burney to Crisp at Chesington, and the
two old friends sat in council on it.   "I should like," wrote
Fanny to Crisp, "that your first reading should have
nothing to do with me—that you should go quick through
it, or let my father read it to you—forgetting all the time,
as much as you can, that Fannikin is the writer, or even
that it is a play in manuscript, and capable of alterations;—
and, then, when you have done, I should like to have three
lines, telling me, as nearly as you can trust my candour,
its general effect.   After that take it to your own desk, and
lash it at your leisure.   Adieu, my dear daddy!   I shall
hope to hear from you very soon, and pray believe me
yours ever and ever."

The comedy was intended to be called 'The Witlings,'
and seems to have borne a strong resemblance to the
Femmes Savantes.   We have not the letter containing
Crisp's judgment, but he told his disciple plainly that
her production would be condemned as a pale copy of
Molière's piece.   We gather also from subsequent correspondence that both he and Dr. Burney felt 'The Witlings,'
to be a failure, even when considered on its own merits.
It was some consolation to Fanny that she had never
read Molière, but she sought no saving for her self-love.
Here is her answer to her daddy :

"Well! 'there are plays that are to be saved, and
plays that are not to be saved!' so good-night, Mr.
Dabbler!—good-night, Lady Smatter,—Mrs. Sapient,—

Mrs. Voluble,—Mrs. Wheedle,—Censor,—Cecilia,—Beaufort,—and you, you great oaf, Bobby !—good-night! goodnight !

And good-morning, Miss Fanny Burney !—I hope now you have opened your eyes for some time, and will not close them in so drowsy a fit again—at least till the full of the moon.

I won't tell you I have been absolutely *ravie* with delight at the fall of the curtain ; but I intend to take the affair in the *tant mieux* manner, and to console myself for your censure by this greatest proof I have ever received of the sincerity, candour, and, let me add, esteem, of my dear daddy. And as I happen to love myself rather more than my play, this consolation is not a very trifling one.

As to all you say of my reputation and so forth, I perceive the kindness of your endeavours to put me in humour with myself, and prevent my taking huff, which if I did, I should deserve to receive, upon any future trial, hollow praise, from you—and the rest from the public.

As to the MS., I am in no hurry for it. Besides, it ought not to come till I have prepared an ovation, and the honours of conquest for it.

The only bad thing in this affair is, that I cannot take the comfort of my poor friend Dabbler, by calling you a crabbed fellow, because you write with almost more kindness than ever; neither can I (though I try hard) persuade myself that you have not a grain of taste in your whole composition.

This, however, seriously I do believe,—that when my two daddies put their heads together to concert for me that hissing, groaning, catcalling epistle they sent me they felt as sorry for poor little Miss Bayes as she could possibly do for herself.

You see I do not attempt to repay your frankness with

the art of pretended carelessness.   But though somewhat disconcerted just now, I will promise not to let my vexation live out another day.   I shall not browse upon it, but, on the contrary, drive it out of my thoughts, by filling them up with things almost as good of other people's.

Our Hettina is much better; but pray don't keep Mr. B. beyond Wednesday, for Mrs. Thrale makes a point of my returning to Streatham on Tuesday, unless, which God forbid, poor Hetty should be worse again.

Adieu, my dear daddy, I won't be mortified, and I won't be *downed*,—but I will be proud to find I have, out of my own family, as well as in it, a friend who loves me well enough to speak plain truth to me.

Always do thus, and always you shall be tried by,
Your much obliged
And most affectionate,
FRANCES BURNEY."

The manuscript comedy does not appear to have been shown to Dr. Johnson. This was not for want of encouragement. He was extremely willing to read it, or have it read to him, but desired that his opinion should be taken before that of Murphy, who was to judge of the stage effect, and as the latter had already offered his services, the scrupulous author felt that this could not be. Fanny continued to grow in favour with Johnson. His expressions of affection became stronger, his eulogy of her novel more unmeasured.

" I know," he said on one occasion, " none like her, nor do I believe there is, or there ever was, a *man* who could write such a book so young."

" I suppose," said Mrs. Thrale, " Pope was no older than Miss Burney when he wrote ' Windsor Forest ;'* and I suppose ' Windsor Forest ' is equal to ' Evelina !' "

* In January, 1779, Mrs. Thrale wrote to Fanny : " You are twenty odd years old, and I am past thirty-six."

'Windsor Forest,' though, according to Pope himself, it was in part written at the age of sixteen, was finished and published when the poet was twenty-five. But Johnson would by no means allow that 'Windsor Forest' was so remarkable a work as 'Evelina.' The latter, he said, seemed a work that should result from long experience and deep and intimate knowledge of the world; yet it had been written without either.

"Miss Burney," added the sage, "is a real wonder. What she is, she is intuitively. Dr. Burney told me she had had the fewest advantages of any of his daughters, from some peculiar circumstances. And such has been her timidity, that he himself had not any suspicion of her powers."

About this time, Johnson began teaching his favourite Latin, an attention with which she would gladly have dispensed, thinking it an injury to be considered a learned lady.

In the autumn of this year, Miss Burney accompanied the Thrales to Tunbridge Wells, and thence to Brighton. Her Diary contains some lively sketches of incidents on the Pantiles and the Steyne, for which we cannot find space. At Brighton she encountered Sir Fretful Plagiary:

" ' It has been,' said Mrs. Thrale warmly, ' all I could do not to affront Mr. Cumberland to-night !'

" 'Oh, I hope not !' cried I; ' I would not have you for the world !'

" 'Why, I have refrained; but with great difficulty !'

"And then she told me the conversation she had just had with him. As soon as I made off, he said, with a spiteful tone of voice:

" 'Oh, that young lady is an author, I hear !'

" ' Yes,' answered Mrs. Thrale, ' author of Evelina !'

" ' Humph—I am told it has some humour !'

" ' Ay, indeed !   Johnson says nothing like it has appeared for years !'

" ' So,' cried he, biting his lips, and waving uneasily in his chair, ' so, so !'

" ' Yes,' continued she ; ' and Sir Joshua Reynolds told Mr. Thrale he would give fifty pounds to know the author !'

" ' So, so—oh, vastly well !' cried he, putting his hand on his forehead.

" ' Nay,' added she, ' Burke himself sat up all night to finish it !'

" This seemed quite too much for him ; he put both his hands to his face, and waving backwards and forwards, said :

" ' Oh, vastly well !—this will do for anything !' with a tone as much as to say, Pray, no more !   Then Mrs. Thrale bid him good-night, longing, she said, to call Miss Thrale first, and say, ' So you won't speak to my daughter? —why, she is no author !' "

At another time, Mrs. Thrale said :

' Let him be tormented, if such things can torment him.   For my part I'd have a starling taught to halloo ' Evelina ' !

At Brighton, also, Miss Burney met with one of those humorous characters which her pen loved to describe :

" I must now have the honour to present to you a new acquaintance, who this day dined here—Mr. B——y, an Irish gentleman, late a commissary in Germany.   He is between sixty and seventy, but means to pass for about thirty ; gallant, complaisant, obsequious, and humble to the fair sex, for whom he has an awful reverence; but when not immediately addressing them, swaggering, blustering, puffing, and domineering. These are his two apparent characters; but the real man is worthy, moral, religious, though conceited and parading.

" He is as fond of quotations as my poor '*Lady Smatter,*' and, like her, knows little beyond a song, and always blunders about the author of that. . . . . His whole conversation consists in little French phrases, picked up during his residence abroad, and in anecdotes and story-telling, which are sure to be re-told daily and daily in the same words. . . . .

" Speaking of the ball in the evening, to which we were all going, 'Ah, madam!' said he to Mrs. Thrale, 'there was a time when—tol-de-rol, tol-de-rol [rising, and dancing and singing], tol-de-rol!—I could dance with the best of them; but, now a man, forty and upwards, as my Lord Ligonier used to say—but—tol-de-rol!—there was a time!'

" 'Ay, so there was, Mr. B——y,' said Mrs. Thrale, 'and I think you and I together made a very venerable appearance!'

" 'Ah! madam, I remember once, at Bath, I was called out to dance with one of the finest young ladies I ever saw. I was just preparing to do my best, when a gentleman of my acquaintance was so cruel as to whisper me— 'B——y! the eyes of all Europe are upon you!'—for that was the phrase of the times. 'B——y!' says he, 'the eyes of all Europe are upon you!'—I vow, ma'am, enough to make a man tremble!—tol-de-rol, tol-de-rol! [dancing] —the eyes of all Europe are upon you!—I declare, ma'am, enough to put a man out of countenance!"

" Dr. Delap, who came here some time after, was speaking of Horace.

" 'Ah! madam,' cried Mr. B——y, 'this Latin—things of that kind—we waste our youth, ma'am, in these vain studies. For my part, I wish I had spent mine in studying French and Spanish—more useful, ma'am. But, bless me, ma'am, what time have I had for that kind of thing? Travelling here, over the ocean, hills and dales, ma'am—reading the great book of the world—poor ignorant mortals, ma'am—no time to do anything.'

" 'Ay, Mr. B——y,' said Mrs. Thrale, 'I remember how you downed Beauclerk and Hamilton, the wits, once at our house, when they talked of ghosts!'

" 'Ah! ma'am, give me a brace of pistols, and I warrant I'll manage a ghost for you! Not but Providence may please to send little spirits—guardian angels, ma'am—to watch us: that I can't speak about. It would be presumptuous, ma'am—for what can a poor, ignorant mortal know?'

" 'Ay, so you told Beauclerk and Hamilton.'

" 'Oh yes, ma'am. Poor human beings can't account for anything—and call themselves *esprits forts*. I vow 'tis presumptuous, ma'am! *Esprits forts*, indeed! they can see no farther than their noses, poor, ignorant mortals! Here's an admiral, and here's a prince, and here's a general, and here's a dipper—and poor Smoker, the bather, ma'am! What's all this strutting about, and that kind of thing? and then they can't account for a blade of grass!'

"After this, Dr. Johnson being mentioned,

" 'Ay,' said he, ' I'm sorry he did not come down with you. I liked him better than those others: not much of a fine gentleman, indeed, but a clever fellow—a deal of knowledge—got a deuced good understanding!' . . . .

" I am absolutely almost ill with laughing. This Mr. B——y half convulses me; yet I cannot make you laugh by writing his speeches, because it is the manner which accompanies them that, more than the matter, renders them so peculiarly ridiculous. His extreme pomposity, the solemn stiffness of his person, the conceited twinkling of his little old eyes, and the quaint importance of his delivery, are so much more like some pragmatical old coxcomb represented on the stage, than like anything in real and common life, that I think, were I a man, I should sometimes be betrayed into clapping him for acting so well. As it is, I am sure no character in any comedy I ever saw has made me laugh more extravagantly.

" He dines and spends the evening here constantly, to my great satisfaction.

" At dinner, when Mrs. Thrale offers him a seat next her, he regularly says :

" ' But where are *les charmantes ?*' meaning Miss T. and me. '.I can do nothing till they are accommodated !'

" And, whenever he drinks a glass of wine, he never fails to touch either Mrs. Thrale's or my glass, with ' *est-il-permis ?*'

" But at the same time that he is so courteous, he is proud to a most sublime excess, and thinks every person to whom he speaks honoured beyond measure by his notice,—nay, he does not even look at anybody without evidently displaying that such notice is more the effect of his benign condescension, than of any pretension on their part to deserve such a mark of his perceiving their exist-ence. But you will think me mad about this man . . . .

" As he is notorious for his contempt of all artists, whom he looks upon with little more respect than upon day-labourers, the other day, when painting was discussed, he spoke of Sir Joshua Reynolds as if he had been upon a level with a carpenter or farrier.

" ' Did you ever,' said Mrs. Thrale, ' see his Nativity ?'

" ' No, madam,—but I know his pictures very well ; I

knew him many years ago, in Minorca; he drew my picture there, and then he knew how to take a moderate price; but now, I vow, ma'am, 'tis scandalous—scandalous indeed! to pay a fellow here seventy guineas for scratching out a head!'

"'Sir!' cried Dr. Delap,* 'you must not run down Sir Joshua Reynolds, because he is Miss Burney's friend.'

"'Sir,' answered he, 'I don't want to run the man down; I like him well enough in his proper place; he is as decent as any man of that sort I ever knew; but for all that, sir, his prices are shameful. Why, he would not [*looking at the poor Doctor with an enraged contempt*]—he would not do *your* head under seventy guineas!'

"'Well,' said Mrs. Thrale, 'he had one portrait at the last Exhibition, that I think hardly could be paid enough for; it was of a Mr. Stuart; I had never done admiring it.'

"'What stuff is this, ma'am!' cried Mr. B——y; 'how can two or three dabs of paint ever be worth such a sum as that?'

"'Sir,' said Mr. Selwyn (always willing to draw him out), 'you know not how much he is improved since you knew him in Minorca; he is now the finest painter, perhaps, in the world.'

"'Pho, pho, sir!' cried he, 'how can you talk so? you, Mr. Selwyn, who have seen so many capital pictures abroad?'

"'Come, come, sir,' said the ever odd Dr. Delap, 'you must not go on so undervaluing him, for, I tell you, he is a friend of Miss Burney's.'

"'Sir,' said Mr. B——y, 'I tell you again I have no objection to the man; I have dined in his company two

* John Delap, D.D. (1725-1812), poet and dramatist. After being curate to Mason, the poet, he held livings in Sussex, and wrote numerous poems and tragedies, all of which have long been forgotten.

SirJ.Reynolds.   A Drawing Profs.   J.R.Smith, fc.

Theophila Palmer.

or three times; a very decent man he is, fit to keep company with gentlemen; but, ma'am, what are all your modern dabblers put together to one ancient? Nothing! —a set of—not a Rubens among them! I vow, ma'am, not a Rubens among them!' . . . .

"Whenever plays are mentioned, we have also a regular speech about them.

"'I never,' he says, 'go to a tragedy,—it's too affecting; tragedy enough in real life: tragedies are only fit for fair females; for my part, I cannot bear to see Othello tearing about in that violent manner;—and fair little Desdemona—ma'am, 'tis too affecting! to see your kings and your princes tearing their pretty locks,—oh, there's no standing it! 'A straw-crown'd monarch,'—what is that, Mrs. Thrale?

'A straw-crown'd monarch in mock majesty.'

I can't recollect now where that is; but for my part, I really cannot bear to see such sights. And then out come the white handkerchiefs, and all their pretty eyes are wiping, and then come poison and daggers, and all that kind of thing,—Oh, ma'am, 'tis too much; but yet the fair tender hearts, the pretty little females, all like it!'

"This speech, word for word, I have already heard from him literally four times.

"When Mr. Garrick was mentioned, he honoured him with much the same style of compliment as he had done Sir Joshua Reynolds.

"'Ay, ay,' said he, 'that Garrick is another of those fellows that people run mad about. Ma'am, 'tis a shame to think of such things! an actor living like a person of quality! scandalous! I vow, scandalous!'

"'Well,—commend me to Mr. B——y!' cried Mrs. Thrale, 'for he is your only man to put down all the people that everybody else sets up.'

" ' Why, ma'am,' answered he, ' I like all these people very well in their proper places; but to see such a set of poor beings living like persons of quality,—'tis preposterous! common sense, madam, common sense is against that kind of thing. As to Garrick, he is a very good mimic, an entertaining fellow enough, and all that kind of thing; but for an actor to live like a person of quality— oh, scandalous !'

" Some time after, the musical tribe was mentioned. He was at cards at the time with Mr. Selwyn, Dr. Delap, and Mr. Thrale, while we ' fair females,' as he always calls us, were speaking of Agujari. He constrained himself from flying out as long as he was able; but upon our mentioning her having fifty pounds a song, he suddenly, in a great rage, called out, ' Catgut and rosin !—ma'am, 'tis scandalous !'

" We all laughed, and Mr. Selwyn, to provoke him on, said :

" ' Why, sir, how shall we part with our money better ?'

" ' Oh fie! fie!' cried he, ' I have not patience to hear of such folly; common sense, sir, common sense is against it. Why, now, there was one of these fellows at Bath last season, a Mr. Rauzzini,*—I vow I longed to cane him every day! such a work made with him! all the fair females sighing for him! enough to make a man sick !' "

At the beginning of 1780, Miss Burney was troubled about her suppressed comedy. She wrote to Mr. Crisp :

" As my play was settled, I entreated my father to call on Mr. Sheridan, in order to prevent his expecting

* An Italian composer and singer. Born at Rome in 1747; came to England in 1774; adopted the profession of singing-master in 1777; settled permanently at Bath in 1787, and died there in 1810. He was the author of several Operas, and counted Braham among his pupils.

anything from me, as he had had a good right to do, from my having sent him a positive message that I should, in compliance with his exhortations at Mrs. Cholmondeley's, try my fortune in the theatrical line, and send him a piece for this winter. My father did call, but found him not at home, neither did he happen to see him till about Christmas. He then acquainted him that what I had written had entirely dissatisfied me, and that I desired to decline for the present all attempts of that sort.

"Mr. Sheridan was pleased to express great concern,— nay, more, to protest he would not accept my refusal. He begged my father to tell me that he could take no denial to seeing what I had done—that I could be no fair judge for myself—that he doubted not but what it would please, but was glad I was not satisfied, as he had much rather see pieces before their authors were contented with them than afterwards, on account of sundry small changes always necessary to be made by the managers, for theatrical purposes, and to which they were loth to submit when their writings were finished to their own approbation. In short, he said so much, that my father, ever easy to be worked upon, began to waver, and told me he wished I would show the play to Sheridan at once."

As the result of this, Fanny conceived a plan for revising and altering her piece, which she submitted to her daddy. Crisp answered:

"The play has wit enough and enough—but the story and the incidents don't appear to me interesting enough to seize and keep hold of the attention and eager expectations of the generality of audiences. This, to me, is its capital defect." He went on to suggest that this fault, being fundamental, admitted of no remedy. And then in

8

reference to a proposed trip to Italy, he added: "They tell me of a delightful tour you are to make this autumn on the other side of the water, with Mr. and Mrs. Thrale, Dr. Johnson, Mr. Murphy, etc. Where will you find such another set? Oh, Fanny, set this down as the happiest period of your life; and when you come to be old and sick, and health and spirits are fled (for the time may come), then live upon remembrance, and think that you have had your share of the good things of this world, and say: For what I have received, the Lord make me thankful!"

The autumnal trip to the Continent did not take place, but in April the Thrales and Miss Burney went by easy stages to Bath:

"The third day we reached Devizes.

"And here, Mrs. Thrale and I were much pleased with our hostess, Mrs. Lawrence, who seemed something above her station in her inn. While we were at cards before supper, we were much surprised by the sound of a pianoforte. I jumped up, and ran to listen whence it proceeded. I found it came from the next room, where the overture to the 'Buona Figliuola' was performing. The playing was very decent, but as the music was not quite new to me, my curiosity was not whole ages in satisfying itself, and therefore I returned to finish the rubber.

"Don't I begin to talk in an old-cattish manner of cards?

"Well, another deal was hardly played, ere we heard the sound of a voice, and out I ran again. The singing, however, detained me not long, and so back I whisked: but the performance, however indifferent in itself, yet surprised us at the Bear at Devizes, and, therefore, Mrs. Thrale determined to know from whom it came. Accordingly, she tapped at the door. A very handsome girl, about thirteen years old, with fine dark hair upon a finely-formed forehead, opened it. Mrs. Thrale made an apology for her intrusion, but the poor girl blushed and retreated into a corner of the room : another girl, however, advanced, and obligingly and gracefully invited us in, and gave us all chairs. She was just sixteen, extremely pretty, and with a countenance better than her features, though those were also very good. Mrs. Thrale made her many compliments, which she received with a mingled modesty and pleasure, both becoming and interesting. She was, indeed, a sweetly-pleasing girl.

"We found they were both daughters of our hostess, and born and bred at Devizes. We were extremely pleased with them, and made them a long visit, which I wished to have been longer. But though those pretty girls struck us so much, the wonder of the family was yet to be produced. This was their brother, a most lovely boy of ten years of age, who seems to be not merely the wonder of their family, but of the times, for his astonishing skill in drawing.* They protest he has never had any instruction, yet showed us some of his productions that were really beautiful. Those that were copies were delightful —those of his own composition amazing, though far inferior. I was equally struck with the boy and his works.

"We found that he had been taken to town, and that all the painters had been very kind to him, and Sir Joshua Reynolds had pronounced him, the mother said, the most promising genius he had ever met with. Mr. Hoare†

---

* This boy was afterwards the celebrated painter, Sir Thomas Lawrence, President of the Royal Academy.

† Mr. C. Prince Hoare. The intended patronage did not take place. The Lawrences left Devizes almost immediately after the date of the above notice, and thenceforth the whole family were supported by the extraordinary talents of the boy artist.

has been so charmed with this sweet boy's drawings that he intends sending him to Italy with his own son.

"This house was full of books, as well as paintings, drawings, and music; and all the family seem not only ingenious and industrious, but amiable; added to which, they are strikingly handsome."

A chief topic of conversation at this time in Bath was Lady Miller's vase at Batheaston. Horace Walpole mentions this vase, and the use to which it was put: 'They hold a Parnassus-fair every Thursday, give out rhymes and themes, and all the flux at Bath contend for the prizes. A Roman vase, dressed with pink ribbons and myrtles, receives the poetry, which is drawn out every festival. Six judges of these Olympic games retire, and select the brightest composition.' Fanny met Lady Miller, whom she describes with her usual candour: 'Lady Miller is a round, plump, coarse-looking dame of about forty, and while all her aim is to appear an elegant woman of fashion, all her success is to seem an ordinary woman in very common life, with fine clothes on. Her habits are bustling, her air is mock-important, and her manners very inelegant.' In the midst of a round of gaieties, the Thrale party attended a reception at Batheaston. The rooms were crowded; but it being now June, the business of the vase was over for that season, and the sacred vessel itself had been removed. On returning to their lodging, they received the news of the Gordon Riots. Next morning Mrs. Thrale had letters acquainting her that her town-house had been three times attacked, but saved by the Guards, with the children, plate, and valuables, which were removed. Streatham had also been threatened and emptied of all its furniture. The same day a

Bath newspaper denounced Mr. Thrale as a papist. The brewer was now in a critical state of health, and it became necessary to remove him without exciting his alarm. Miss Burney was employed to break the matter to him, and obtained his consent to an immediate departure. Arriving at Salisbury on the 11th of June, they were reassured by information that order'had been restored in London, and Lord George Gordon sent to the Tower. In London the friends parted, and Fanny returned to her father's house. Johnson met her at Sir Joshua's a few days after, and mention being made of a house in Grub Street that had been destroyed by the mob, proposed that they should go there together, and visit the seats of their progenitors,

The latter part of this year, and part of 1781, were spent by Miss Burney chiefly in writing 'Cecilia.' While thus occupied she passed most of her time at Chesington. In February, 1781, she writes from that place to Mrs. Thrale: " I think I shall always hate this book, which has kept me so long away from you, as much as I shall always love 'Evelina,' which first *comfortably* introduced me to you." Shortly after the date of this letter, the writer returned home, apparently for the purpose of meeting the Thrales, who were fixed for the winter in Grosvenor Square. She found them engaged in giving parties to half London. In the midst of their entertainments Mr. Thrale died suddenly from a stroke of apoplexy. Fanny could not desert her friend in such trouble. So soon as the widow could bear any society, she summoned her young companion to Streatham, and kept her there, with hardly an interval, till the summer was over. It does not appear that Fanny was at all averse to be detained, but so long a stay was not to her advantage. Her hostess, of course, was much engrossed by the late brewer's affairs. Dr. Johnson, as one of the executors, was similarly employed; and though Miss Burney, from time to time, saw something of him, as well as of his co-executors, Mr. Cator* and Mr. Crutchley,† she met with little in the narrowed and secluded household to compensate her for her loss of time. If she busied herself at all with 'Cecilia' during this period, she seems to have accomplished very little. At any rate, both her fathers became impatient of her inaction. Prompted from Chesington, Dr. Burney would have recalled his daughter, but found himself powerless against the self-willed little lady of Thrale Hall. The more resolute Crisp then took the field in person,‡ and in spite of his infirmities, repaired to Streatham, whence he carried off the captive authoress, and straightway consigned her to what he called the Doctor's Conjuring Closet, at his own abode. There Fanny was held to her task till the beginning of 1782, when she was called home to be present at the marriage of her sister Susan to Captain Phillips; after which Dr. Burney kept her stationary in St. Martin's Street till she had written the word 'Finis' on the last proof-sheet of 'Cecilia.'

However, when the new novel was fairly in the printer's hands, the author was again seen in London society. At a party, given by a Mrs. Paradise, she was introduced to a sister of her craft:

"Mrs. Paradise, leaning over the Kirwans and Charlotte, who hardly got a seat all night for the crowd, said

* M.P. for Ipswich in 1784. Described by Dr. Johnson as having "much good in his character, and much usefulness in his knowledge." Johnson used to visit Mr. Cator at his seat at Beckenham.

† M.P. for Horsham in 1784.

‡ "Memoirs," vol. ii., p. 218.

she begged to speak to me. I squeezed my great person out, and she then said:

"'Miss Burney, Lady Say and Sele desires the honour of being introduced to you.'

"Her ladyship stood by her side. She seems pretty near fifty—at least turned forty; her head was full of feathers, flowers, jewels, and gew-gaws, and as high as Lady Archer's; her dress was trimmed with beads, silver, Persian sashes, and all sort of fine fancies; her face is thin and fiery, and her whole manner spoke a lady all alive.

"'Miss Burney,' cried she, with great quickness, and a look all curiosity, 'I am very happy to see you; I have longed to see you a great while; I have read your performance, and I am quite delighted with it. I think it's the most elegant novel I ever read in my life. Such a style! I am quite surprised at it. I can't think where you got so much invention!'

'You may believe this was a reception not to make me very loquacious. I did not know which way to turn my head.

"'I must introduce you,' continued her ladyship, 'to my sister; she'll be quite delighted to see you. She has written a novel herself; so you are sister authoresses. A most elegant thing it is, I assure you; almost as pretty as yours, only not quite so elegant. She has written two novels, only one is not so pretty as the other. But I shall insist upon your seeing them. One is in letters, like yours, only yours is prettiest; it's called the " Mausoleum of Julia !" '

"What unfeeling things, thought I, are *my* sisters ! I'm sure I never heard them go about thus praising *me !*

"Mrs. Paradise then again came forward, and, taking my hand, led me up to her ladyship's sister, Lady Hawke, saying aloud, and with a courteous smirk, 'Miss Burney, ma'am, authoress of " Evelina."'. . . .

"Lady Hawke arose and curtseyed. She is much younger than her sister, and rather pretty; extremely languishing, delicate, and pathetic; apparently accustomed to be reckoned the genius of her family, and well contented to be looked upon as a creature dropped from the clouds. . . . .

"'My sister intends,' said Lady Say and Sele, 'to print her " Mausoleum," just for her own friends and acquaintances.'

"'Yes,' said Lady Hawke: 'I have never printed yet.' . . . .

"'Well,' cried Lady Say, 'but do repeat that sweet part that I am so fond of—you know what I mean; Miss Burney *must* hear it—out of your novel, you know!'

"*Lady H.:* No, I can't; I have forgot it.

"*Lady S.:* Oh, no! I am sure you have not; I insist upon it.

"*Lady H.:* But I know you can repeat it yourself; you have so fine a memory; I am sure you can repeat it.

"*Lady S.:* Oh, but I should not do it justice! that's all—I should not do it justice!

"Lady Hawke then bent forward, and repeated: 'If, when he made the declaration of his love, the sensibility that beamed in his eyes was felt in his heart, what pleasing sensations and soft alarms might not that tender avowal awaken!'

"'And from what, ma'am,' cried I, astonished, and imagining I had mistaken them, ' is this taken?'

"'From my sister's novel!' answered the delighted Lady Say and Sele, expecting my raptures to be equal to her own; 'it's in the " Mausoleum,"—did not you know that? Well, I can't think how you can write these sweet

novels! And it's all just like that part. Lord Hawke
himself says it's all poetry. For my part, I'm sure I
never could write so. I suppose, Miss Burney, you are
producing another—a'n't you?'

" ' No, ma'am.'

" ' Oh, I dare say you are. I dare say you are writing
one at this very minute!' "

Years afterwards, when Miss Burney had entered the
royal household, Queen Charlotte lent her a presentation
copy of a novel which her Majesty had received from
Lady Hawke. The book proved to be the " Mausoleum
of Julia," then at length given to the public. " It is all
of a piece," laughed Fanny, on reading it—" all love, love,
love, unmixed and unadulterated with any more worldly
materials."

' Cecilia ' was now passing slowly through the press,
amidst the comments and flattering predictions of the
few friends who were permitted to see the manuscript.
Mrs. Thrale and Queeny reddened their eyes over the
pages; Dr. Burney found them more engrossing even
than ' Evelina ;' but the author's only real adviser was
her ' other daddy.' Crisp was a close, but not an overbearing critic; he had great faith in his Fannikin, and
he was restrained, besides, by rankling memories of his
unfortunate ' Virginia.' ' Whomever you think fit to consult,' he wrote, ' let their talents and taste be ever so
great, hear what they say, but never give up, or alter
a tittle, merely on their authority, nor unless it perfectly
accords with your own inward feelings. I can say this to
my sorrow and to my cost. But mum!' And if Crisp
was somewhat dogmatic, he was also a sanguine admirer, declaring that he would insure the rapid and complete success of the novel for half a crown. Miss Burney,

too, though bashful in a drawing-room, had plenty of self-reliance in her study, and was by no means disposed to be often seeking counsel. Macaulay, always confident in his conjectures, will have it that she received assistance from Johnson. But he had before him, in the Diary, a distinct assertion to the contrary, stated to have been made by the Doctor himself some time after the publication. If we may trust Fanny, Johnson said: ' Ay, some people want to make out some credit to me from the little rogue's book. I was told by a gentleman this morning that it was a very fine book if it was all her own. " It is all her own," said I, " for me, I am sure ; for I never saw one word of it before it was printed." '* Macaulay did not mean to emulate Croker; he was betrayed by fancied resemblances of style, than which nothing can be more deceptive. The probability is that the manuscript was not submitted to Johnson, lest he should be held to have written what he only corrected.

' Cecilia ; or, The Memoirs of an heiress,' was published in July, 1782. " We have been informed," says Macaulay, " by persons who remember those days, that no romance of Sir Walter Scott was more impatiently awaited, or more eagerly snatched from the counters of ' the booksellers." The first edition, which was exhausted in the following October, consisted of two thousand copies; and Macaulay was told by some-one, not named, that an equal number of pounds was received by the author for her work. There is no producible authority for the latter statement, and we cannot

---

* Diary, November 4, 1782. The story, which was repeated and believed by Lord Byron, that Johnson superintended ' Cecilia,' was corrected by Moore in his life of the poet, published in 1830. ' Lord Byron is here mistaken. Dr. Johnson never saw " Cecilia " till it was in print. A day or two before publication the young authoress, as I understand, sent three copies to the three persons who had most claim to them—her father, Mrs. Thrale, and Dr. Johnson.'

but think that it is an exaggeration, arising out of some confusion between the amount paid for the copyright, and the number of copies first printed. At any rate, the sum mentioned does not seem to square with some expressions used by Burke, who about this time began to take a personal interest in Miss Burney.

The great statesman was introduced to her, a few days before her second novel appeared, at a dinner given by Sir Joshua in his house on Richmond Hill. At the end of July he addressed her in a letter of congratulation: 'You have crowded,' he wrote, 'into a few small volumes an incredible variety of characters ; most of them well planned, well supported, and well contrasted with each other. If there be any fault in this .respect, it is one in which you are in no great danger of being imitated. Justly as your characters are drawn, perhaps they are too numerous. But I beg pardon ; I fear it is quite in vain to preach economy to those who are come young to excessive and sudden opulence. I might trespass on your delicacy if I should fill my letter to you with what I fill my conversation to others. I should be troublesome to you alone if I should tell you all I feel and think on the natural vein of humour, the tender pathetic, the comprehensive and noble moral, and the sagacious observation, that appear quite throughout that extraordinary performance.' To be addressed in such terms by such a man was enough to turn the head of any young writer ; and this letter may be regarded as marking the topmost point in Fanny's iterary career.

Four months afterwards she encountered Mr. Burke again at Miss Monckton's* assembly. The gathering was

* The Honourable Mary Monckton, daughter of the first Viscount Galway, and wife of the seventh Earl of Cork and Ossory, well known to the readers of Boswell as 'the lively Miss Monckton, who used always to have the finest bit of blue at her parties.' She was born in April, 1746, and died on the 20th of May 1840

a brilliant one : most of the ladies present were going to the Duchess of Cumberland's, and were in full dress, oppressed by the weight of their sacques and ruffles; but as soon as Burke and Sir Joshua Reynolds entered, Frances Burney had no eyes for anyone else. When the knight had paid his compliments, Burke sat down beside her, and a conversation ensued, in which the great man used the words to which we have referred. He began by repeating and amplifying the praises of his letter; and then, not to appear fulsome, proceeded to find fault: the famous masquerade he thought too long, and that something might be spared from Harrel's grand assembly; he did not like Morrice's part at the Pantheon, and he wished the conclusion either more happy or more miserable ; 'for in a work of imagination,' said he, 'there is no medium.' But, he added, there was one further fault more serious than any he had mentioned, and that was the disposal of the book: why had not Mr. Briggs, the city gentleman of the novel, been sent for ? he would have taken care that it should not be parted with so much below par. Had two thousand pounds, or any sum approaching that, been given for the copyright, the price could not have been considered insufficient. We are obliged, therefore, to conclude that the story told to the Edinburgh Reviewer was apocryphal.*

The list of Miss Burney's friends continued to enlarge itself. In the winter of 1782-3, besides being made free of certain fashionable houses, such as Miss Monckton's and Mrs. Walsingham's,† she became known to the two 'old

---

* There is also a letter of Crisp's in which he mentions a promise of Dr. Burney to make up his daughter's gains to even money. A few years later, when her reputation was enhanced by 'Cecilia,' Miss Burney asked for her third novel, 'Camilla,' no more than eleven hundred guineas. On the whole, we are inclined to believe that the sum she received for 'Cecilia' was less than £1,000.

† Daughter of Sir Charles Hanbury Williams.

wits,' Owen Cambridge and Soame Jenyns,* to Erskine, the Wartons, Benjamin West, Jackson of Exeter, William Windham, Dr. Parr, Mrs. Delany, and a host of others, till she began 'to grow most heartily sick of this continual round of visiting, and these eternal new acquaintances.' Soame Jenyns came to meet her at a reception arranged by his special request, and, at seventy-eight, arrayed himself for the occasion in a Court suit of apricot-coloured silk, lined with white satin, making all the slow speed in his power to address her, as she entered, in a studied harangue on the honour, and the pleasure, and the what not, of seeing so celebrated an authoress; while the whole of a large company rose, and stood to listen to his compliments.

But the time was coming when Frances was to learn that life has its trials even for the most favoured children of fortune. In the spring of 1783, Mr. Crisp's old enemy the gout fixed upon his head and chest; and, after an illness of some duration, he sank under the attack. His fits of gout had latterly become so constant that at first the fatal seizure caused little apprehension. In the early part of his sufferings Fanny sent frequent letters to cheer him. 'God bless,' she writes, 'and restore you, my most dear daddy! You know not how kindly I take your thinking of me, and inquiring about me, in an illness that might so well make you forget us all; but Susan assures me your heart is as affectionate as ever to your ever and ever faithful and loving child.' As soon as danger was declared, she hastened to Chesington. She attended the old man throughout his last few days; he called her, at parting, 'the dearest thing to him on

---

* Contributors to "The World." Soame Jenyns was chiefly known by his work "On the Evidences of the Christian Religion." He died in 1877; Cambridge in 1802.

earth;' and her passionate sorrow for his death excited the alarm, though not the jealousy, of her natural father.*

And this loss was not the only trouble of that year. Mrs. Thrale had for some time been meditating her foolish second marriage. As soon as ' Cecilia ' was off her mind, Miss Burney had resumed her visits to Streatham. She at once found that her friend was changed. Mrs. Thrale had become absent, restless, moody. The secret of her attachment to Piozzi was not long in being disclosed to Fanny, who could give her comfort, though not sympathy. The latter remained long enough at Streatham to witness the gradual estrangement of her hostess from Dr. Johnson. One morning the Doctor accompanied his little Burney in the carriage to London : as they turned into Streatham Common, he exclaimed, pointing backwards : ' That house is lost to *me* for ever !' A few weeks later, the house was let to Lord Shelburne. Mrs. Thrale retired to Brighton, and afterwards coming to town, passed the winter in Argyle Street. Frances spent much time with her there. But in the beginning of April the uneasy widow went with her three eldest daughters to take up her abode at Bath, till she could make up her mind to complete the match which all her friends disapproved. Crisp's illness becoming serious shortly afterwards, left Fanny no time at first to grieve over this separation. She felt it all the more on her return to St. Martin's Street after her daddy's death. And in the summer, Dr. Johnson's health, which for some time had been steadily declining, was broken down by a stroke of paralysis. She visited him frequently at his house in Bolt Court. One evening, when she with

* Crisp died April 24, 1783, aged seventy-six. A monument to his memory was put up in the little church at Chesington, with an inscription from the pen of Dr. Burney. His library was sold in the following year.

her father and some others were sitting with him, he turned aside to her, and, grasping her hand, said : ' The blister I have tried for my breath has betrayed some very bad tokens; but I will not terrify myself by talking of them. Ah, *priez Dieu pour moi !'*

One ray of comfort the close of 1783 brought with it. On the day on which the Ministry to which he belonged was dissolved, Mr. Burke appointed Dr. Burney organist of Chelsea Hospital, at the insignificant, though augmented salary of £50 a year, regretting that while he had been Paymaster-General, nothing more worthy of the Doctor's acceptance had fallen to his disposal. About this incident Miss Burney writes : ' You have heard the whole story of Mr. Burke, the Chelsea Hospital, and his most charming letter? To-day he called, and, as my father was out, inquired for me. He made a thousand apologies for breaking in upon me, but said the business was finally settled at the Treasury. Nothing could be more delicate, more elegant than his manner of doing this kindness. I don't know whether he was most polite, or most friendly, in his whole behaviour to me. I could almost have cried when he said, " This is my last act in office." He said it with so manly a cheerfulness, in the midst of undisguised regret. What a man he is !'

The record of 1784 in the Diary is very short. The chief incidents are the marriage of Mrs. Thrale to Piozzi, and the death of Dr. Johnson. Enough, and more than enough, has been written on the subject of the marriage. Most of the lady's contemporaries spoke of it as if it had been some disgraceful offence. Many in later times have adopted the same tone. Dr. Burney had introduced Piozzi to the Thrales, and for this and other reasons, the Doctor and his family were disposed to be more lenient in their judgment. Dr. Burney said : ' No one could blame

Piozzi for accepting a gay rich widow. What could a man do better ?' And the singing-master was a quiet, inoffensive person. Still, as to the lady, it could not be forgotten that she had young daughters, whose prospects she had no right to prejudice by a match so unequal and so generally condemned. It is, therefore, not surprising that when the wedding took place about the middle of this year, and Mrs. Piozzi wrote, demanding cordial congratulations, Miss Burney was unable to reply with warmth enough to satisfy her. The intimate friendship and correspondence of six years, therefore, came to an end. Fanny, who was the last to write, attributed the rupture, at one time, to the cause just mentioned, and, at another, to the resentment of Piozzi, when informed of her constant opposition to the union.

Some months later, Miss Burney had her final interview with Dr. Johnson :

"Last Thursday, Nov. 25th, my father set me down at Bolt Court, while he went on upon business. I was anxious to again see poor Dr. Johnson, who has had terrible health since his return from Lichfield. He let me in, though very ill. He was alone, which I much rejoiced at : for I had a longer and more satisfactory conversation with him than I have had for many months. He was in rather better spirits, too, than I have lately seen him ; but he told me he was going to try what sleeping out of town might do for him.

"'I remember,' said he, 'that my wife, when she was near her end, poor woman, was also advised to sleep out of town ; and when she was carried to the lodgings that had been prepared for her, she complained that the staircase was in very bad condition—for the plaster was beaten off the walls in many places. 'Oh,' said the man of the house, 'that's nothing but by the knocks against it of the coffins of the poor souls that have died in the lodgings !'

"He laughed, though not without apparent secret anguish, in telling me this. I felt extremely shocked, but, willing to confine my words at least to the literal story, I only exclaimed against the unfeeling absurdity of such a confession.

"'Such a confession,' cried he, 'to a person then coming to try his lodging for her health, contains, indeed, more absurdity than we can well lay our account for.'

"I had seen Miss T. the day before.

"'So,' said he, 'did I.'

"I then said: 'Do you ever, sir, hear from her mother?'

"'No,' cried he, 'nor write to her. I drive her quite from my mind. If I meet with one of her letters, I burn it instantly. I have burnt all I can find. I never speak of her, and I desire never to hear of her more. I drive her, as I said, wholly from my mind.'

"Yet, wholly to change this discourse, I gave him a history of the Bristol milk-woman,'* and told him the tales I had heard of her writing so wonderfully, though she had read nothing but Young and Milton; 'though those,' I continued, 'could never possibly, I should think, be the first authors with anybody. Would children understand them? and grown people who have not read are children in literature.'

"'Doubtless,' said he; 'but there is nothing so little comprehended among mankind as what is genius. They give to it all, when it can be but a part. Genius is nothing more than knowing the use of tools; but there must be tools for it to use: a man who has spent all his

* Ann Yearsley.

life in this room will give a very poor account of what is contained in the next.'

" ' Certainly, sir; yet there is such a thing as invention; Shakespeare could never have seen a Caliban.'

" ' No; but he had seen a man, and knew, therefore, how to vary him to a monster. A man who would draw a monstrous cow, must first know what a cow commonly is; or how can he tell that to give her an ass's head or an elephant's tusk will make her monstrous? Suppose you show me a man who is a very expert carpenter; another will say he was born to be a carpenter—but what if he had never seen any wood? Let two men, one with genius, the other with none, look at an overturned waggon :—he who has no genius, will think of the waggon only as he sees it, overturned, and walk on; he who has genius, will paint it to himself before it was overturned, —standing still, and moving on, and heavy loaded, and empty; but both must see the waggon, to think of it at all.'

" How just and true all this, my dear Susy! He then grew animated, and talked on, upon this milk-woman, upon a once as famous shoemaker, and upon our immortal Shakespeare, with as much fire, spirit, wit, and truth of criticism and judgment, as ever yet I have heard him. How delightfully bright are his faculties, though the poor and infirm machine that contains them seems alarmingly giving way.

" Yet, all brilliant as he was, I saw him growing worse, and offered to go, which, for the first time I ever remember, he did not oppose; but, most kindly pressing both my hands :

" ' Be not,' he said, in a voice of even tenderness, ' be not longer in coming again for my letting you go now.'

" I assured him I would be the sooner, and was running

off, but he called me back, in a solemn voice, and, in a manner the most energetic, said :

" ' Remember me in your prayers !'

" I longed to ask him to remember me, but did not dare. I gave him my promise, and, very heavily indeed, I left him. Great, good, and excellent that he is, how short a time will he be our boast ! Ah, my dear Susy, I see he is going ! This winter will never conduct him to a more genial season here ! Elsewhere, who shall hope a fairer ? I wish I had bid him pray for me; but it seemed to me presumptuous, though this repetition of so kind a condescension might, I think, have encouraged me.'

' He wished to look on her once more; and on the day before his death she long remained in tears on the stairs leading to his bedroom, in the hope that she might be called in to receive his blessing. He was then sinking fast, and though he sent her an affectionate message, was unable to see her.'*

* Macaulay.

CHAPTER V.

WE have mentioned Mrs. Delany in our list of the more remarkable friends made by Miss Burney during the winter succeeding the publication of 'Cecilia.' Burke followed a fashion then prevalent when he pronounced this venerable lady the fairest model of female excellence in the previous age. Mrs. Delany owed her distinction in a great measure to the favour which she enjoyed with the royal family. Born in 1700, she was early instructed in the ways of a Court, having been brought up by an aunt who had been maid-of-honour to Queen Mary, and had received for her charge the promise of a similar employment in the household of Queen Anne. Having missed this promotion, the girl next fell into the hands of her uncle, George Granville, Lord Lansdowne, who, though celebrated by Pope as 'the friend of every Muse,' was not gentleman enough to treat his brother's child with decent consideration. He forced Mary Granville, at seventeen, into a marriage with Alexander Pendarves, a Cornish squire near sixty, of drunken habits and morose manners, who sought the match chiefly to disappoint his expectant heir. After a few years, this worthy died of a fit, to the great relief of all belonging to him, but, unfortunately for his wife, without having made the provision for her which, to do him justice, he appears to have intended. Some time later the widow paid a visit to Ireland, where she became acquainted with Dean Swift, and his intimate associate, Dr. Patrick Delany, who was famed as a scholar and preacher. After her return, Swift exchanged occasional letters with her so long as he retained his reason. In 1743, Dr. Delany, then himself a widower, came over to England to offer himself to her in marriage. She accepted him, in spite of her family, whose high stomach rose against a *mésalliance* with an Irish parson. Their influence, however, was subsequently used to procure for Delany the deanery of Down. On his death, which occurred in 1768, Mrs. Delany settled in London, and, at the time when Miss Burney was introduced to her, had a house in St. James's Place. Her most intimate friend was the old Duchess of Portland, with whom she regularly spent the summer at her Grace's dower house of Bulstrode. There she was presented to George III. and his Queen, both of whom conceived a strong regard for her. The King called her his dearest Mrs. Delany, and in 1782 commissioned Opie to paint her portrait, which was placed at Hampton Court.*

---

* 'It is pronounced like Rembrandt, but, as I told her, it does not look older than she is, but older than she does.'—Walpole to Mason, February 14, 1782.

While Frances Burney was having her first interview with Mrs. Delany, the Dowager Duchess of Portland condescended to appear upon the scene. This exalted personage, we are given to understand, had a natural aversion to female novel-writers, but, at her friend's request, consented to receive homage from the author of 'Cecilia.' Her curiosity, in fact, got the better of her pride. Before her arrival, the conversation turned on the flower-work for which Mrs. Delany was famous among her acquaintances. This was a kind of paper mosaic, invented by the old lady, and practised by her until her eyesight failed. Some specimens of it were thought worthy of being offered, as a tribute of humble duty, to Queen Charlotte. The admiration freely bestowed on this trumpery, and the doubtful reception accorded to literary merit in a woman, illustrate the tone which prevailed in the highest society a hundred years ago. To cut out bits of coloured paper, and paste them together on the leaf of an album so as to resemble flowers, was considered a wonderful achievement even for a paragon of her sex. To have written the best work of imagination that had proceeded from a female pen was held to confer only an equivocal title to eminence. The Duchess, however, exerted herself to be civil. 'She was a simple woman,' says Walpole; but she did her best. She joined Mrs. Delany in recalling the characters that had pleased them most in 'Cecilia;' she dwelt on the spirit of the writing, the fire in the composition, and, 'with a solemn sort of voice,' declared herself gratified by the morality of the book, 'so striking, so pure, so genuine, so instructive.' Fanny, always impressed by grandeur, eager after praise, thankful for notice, was charmed with these compliments. She found her Grace's manner not merely free from arrogance, but 'free also from its mortifying deputy, affability.' Yet the worship of rank, which belonged to that age, was, in little Miss Burney, always subordinate to better feelings. In her eyes the dignified visitor appeared by no means so interesting as her hostess.* Nor was it any air of courtliness that attracted her in Mrs. Delany, but a simple domestic association. Though not a person of genius, or, it should seem, of any extraordinary cultivation, this veteran of English and Irish society had preserved an unsullied, gentle, kindly spirit which showed itself in her face and carriage. Fanny could not remember to have seen so much sweetness of countenance in anyone except her own grandmother, Mrs. Sleepe. She at once began to trace, or to imagine, a resemblance between 'that saint-like woman' and her new friend, and gave herself up to the tenderness which the current of her thoughts excited.

Besides this similarity, she bethought her of another recollection which she could with propriety impart to the ladies before her. She had often heard Mr. Crisp speak of his former intercourse with the Duchess and Mrs. Delany. The latter, she learned on inquiry, had been chiefly intimate with Crisp's sisters; but the Duchess had known Crisp himself well, and was curious to learn what had become of so agreeable and accomplished a man. Her questions gave the shy, silent Fanny a theme on which she could enlarge with animation. 'I spared not,' she writes, 'for boasting of my dear daddy's kindness to me.' The accounts she had received from the

The editor of Mrs. Delany's 'Correspondence,' having a grudge against Madame d'Arblay, labours to prove that the Duchess of Portland cannot have been present at this interview. The supposed proof consists in showing from some old letters that the Duchess did not read 'Evelina' for nearly twelve months after the date spoken of. But this is nothing to the purpose. 'Evelina' does not appear to have been mentioned when its author was introduced to Miss Delany. The conversation recorded to have passed related wholly to 'Cecilia.'

Crisp family, she told Mrs. Delany, had first made her desire the acquaintance that day commenced. She ran on to relate the story of Crisp's disappearance, painted his way of life in his retreat, and entertained the company with a description of Chesington Hall, its isolated and lonely position, its ruinous condition, its nearly inaccessible roads, its quaint old pictures, and straight long garden paths.* Her flow of spirits banished all reserve, and that evening laid the foundations of a friendship that partly consoled her for the death of Crisp and the desertion of Mrs. Thrale.

The attachment between Mrs. Delany and the favourite of Chesington and Streatham grew up rapidly. The entries in Fanny's Diary show that she very soon became a constant visitor in St. James's Place. She is flattered at being so much in favour there as to find its mistress always eager to fix a time for their next and next meeting. Yet, while profuse in praise of her venerable friend, she dwells more on the qualities of the old lady's heart than on any accomplishments of mind or manner; she loves even more than she admires her; possibly some touches of high-breeding were lost on the music-master's daughter; at any rate, the first impression abides with her, and in the noted pattern of antique polish and taste† she sees always the image of the departed Mrs. Sleepe.

Except in the presence of her young grand-niece Mary Port,‡ Mrs. Delany's house had little charm of liveliness. The chief persons that frequented it belonged to the

---

* Memoirs, vol. ii., p. 313.

† The courtier-bishop Hurd described Mrs. Delany as a lady 'of great politeness and ingenuity, and of an unaffected piety.'

‡ Georgina Mary Ann Port (called 'Mary' by her great-aunt) was born on September 15, 1771. Her father having outrun his means, she was taken by Mrs. Delany, who brought her up to the age of sixteen. Not long after the death of her protectress, she married Mr. Benjamin Waddington, of Llanover. She died on January 19, 1850.

same generation as the Duchess of Portland, who spent most of her evenings there. A sombre figure in that peculiar assembly was Lady Wallingford, the impoverished widow of a gaming peer, and a daughter of the speculator Law. This lady, who never opened her lips, invariably appeared in full mourning dress, wearing a black silk robe, a hoop, long ruffles, a winged cap, and other appendages of an attire that even then was obsolete. Another visitor was the Countess of Bute, wife of George III.'s early favourite, and daughter of Lady Mary Wortley Montagu. The elderly wit Horace Walpole often joined a circle in which his old-fashioned pleasantry was still received with the old applause. Fanny, who had met him elsewhere, thought that he never showed to such advantage as when surrounded by those stately dowagers. And while Horace, and most of the other callers, had, more or less, the air of having outlived their age, the lady to whom they paid their respects had passed the better portion of her life in a still more remote period. She encouraged Miss Burney to turn over Swift's letters to her; and her most interesting anecdotes related to the days of the Dean, and Pope, and Young.

Perhaps it was, in part, some memory of the time when she herself had shared the talk of men of letters, that made her take to the young writer who had done more to raise the literary credit of women than Mrs. Montagu, or Hannah More, or the whole tribe of bluestockings united. The admired of Johnson, Burke and Reynolds was both a more entertaining guest, and a greater ornament to her drawing-room, than the respectable Mrs. Chapone, the learned Mrs. Carter, or even 'the high-bred, elegant' Mrs. Boscawen. And, whatever may have been said at a later date by distant connections of Mrs. Delany, soured by a peevish family pride which *she* disdained, her own published letters prove that she not merely appreciated Fanny's talents, but understood and valued her character. At one time she declares that 'Evelina' and 'Cecilia,' excellent as she finds them, are their author's meanest praise, and goes on to extol 'her admirable understanding, tender affection and sweetness of manners;' after three years' experience she writes of her companion : 'Her extreme diffidence of herself, notwithstanding her great genius, and the applause she has met with, adds lustre to all her excellences, and all improve on acquaintance.' It is scarcely too much to say that the correspondence in which these lines occur would never have been printed but for Miss Burney. The love and esteem expressed in her Diary have almost alone saved Mrs. Delany's name from utter oblivion ; it would be strange indeed had such regard gone unrequited by its object.

Frances Burney had certainly a remarkable capacity for friendship. Not long after her introduction in St. James's Place, she formed another acquaintance, which ripened steadily, and became, on Mrs. Delany's death, the chief intimacy of her life outside her own family. It seems to have been in the summer of 1783 that Dr. Burney and his now celebrated daughter first met with Mr. and Mrs. Locke, of Norbury Park. From some cause or other, we do not get so vivid a picture of these worthy persons as we do of most of Fanny's other friends. This is perhaps partly explained by the fact that Mr. Locke was a man of reserved and retiring temperament. But though silent in general society, he had a benevolent heart and a cultivated taste ; was a great lover of the picturesque, and a collector of works of art. Dr. Burney paid his first visit to Norbury in company with Sir Joshua Reynolds ; and many years afterwards Sir

Thomas Lawrence told Madame d'Arblay that in all his experience he had never seen a second Mr. Locke. The eldest son of the house, William Locke, was an amateur artist of some skill. Miss Burney's particular friend was, naturally, Mrs. Locke. The sketch transmitted to us of this lady is even more faint than that of her husband, whom, we are told, she strongly resembled. She was lovely, of course, and amiable: Fanny sometimes calls her bewitching; but we search in vain for anything more distinctive. After the summer of 1784, Miss Burney, except during her employment at Court, was often at Norbury. It pleased her to think that when there she was only six miles from Chesington, And while the place was still new to her, her sister Susan, who had been abroad for her health, returned, and settled with her husband, Captain Phillips, in the village of Mickleham, hard by the gates of Norbury Park. Thenceforth the Park banished all regrets for Streatham. The Thrales themselves were never more hospitable or kinder than the excellent Lockes proved to be. If we cannot get to know the latter as we know the former, it is a satisfaction, at least, to learn that Mr. Smelt, who had been sub-governor to the Prince of Wales, spoke of them to Fanny as 'that divine family.'

Mr. Smelt, previously a slight acquaintance of the Burneys, had lately shown a disposition to cultivate their society. Such attention on the part of a confidential royal servant, though easily accounted for by the fame of 'Cecilia,' was among the omens which befell about this time of what the fates had in store for the author. Another premonitory incident occurred at the beginning of 1785, when Dr. Burney was admitted to a private audience of the King and Queen, in order that he might present to them copies of his narrative of the Handel

Commemoration, which had taken place in the preceding year. The good-natured monarch, according to his wont on such occasions, entered into a familiar and discursive conversation with the Doctor. The last topic discussed was the story of the publication of Evelina. 'And is it true,' asked the King eagerly, 'that you never saw Evelina before it was printed?' 'Nor even till long after it was published,' was the reply. The King then drew from the gratified father a detailed account of Evelina's first introduction to the world, which, as the Doctor reported, afforded the greatest amusement to the Queen, as well as to his inquiring Majesty.

The old Duchess of Portland died in July, 1785. Her will made no provision for her older friend, whom no doubt she had expected to survive; and this accident indirectly determined the great mistake of Miss Burney's life. The loss of her summer quarters at Bulstrode, which for the half of every year had been her constant home, was a serious inconvenience for Mrs. Delany, whose income barely sufficed for the maintenance of her London establishment during the winter. Informed of this, the King caused a house belonging to the Crown at Windsor, near the Castle, to be fitted up for the use of his aged favourite, and settled a pension of three hundred pounds a year upon her for the rest of her days, that she might be enabled to enjoy a country life without giving up her accustomed residence in St. James's Place. The royal bounty was so complete that Mrs. Delany's maid was commanded to see that her mistress brought nothing with her but her clothes: everything else was to be provided; and when supplies were exhausted, the abigail was to make a requisition for more. The King himself superintended the workmen: when his new neighbour arrived, he was on the spot to welcome her; and she found that her benefactor had not only caused the house to be furnished with plate, china, glass, and linen, but the cellars to be stocked with wine, and the cupboards stored with sweetmeats and pickles.* Such was the plainness, and such the generosity, of George III.

Miss Burney was on a visit to her friend while these arrangements were in progress; when the latter left London for Windsor, she herself went to her father at Chesington Hall, in which old haunt Dr. Burney was then employed on his still unfinished History. In the following December, Fanny rejoined Mrs. Delany at Windsor, and during her stay there was introduced to the King and Queen. It seems that etiquette forbade her being formally presented to them, except at a drawing-room; but they were desirous of making her acquaintance, and it was at length arranged that when next their Majesties called on her hostess, as they were in the habit of doing, she should remain in the room. On the first occasion that occurred, her courage failed her at the critical moment, and she fled. A few days later, Mrs. Delany returned from her afternoon nap to find her nephew, Mr. Bernard Dewes, his little daughter, and Miss Port, engaged in the drawing-room with Miss Burney, who was teaching the child some Christmas games, in which her father and cousin joined. The Diary proceeds:

* Miss Burney's account is confirmed in every important particular by Walpole, who states that he had his information from Mrs. Delany's own mouth: Walpole to Lady Ossory, September 17, 1785. Lady Llanover, who edited the ' Delany Correspondence,' is wroth that the thankful recipient of all this minute bounty should be accused of having been helped in her house-keeping by the Duchess of Portland. In the 'Memoirs of Dr. Burney' (vol. iii., p. 50), it is stated that the Duchess, who visited at Mrs. Delany's nearly every evening, contrived to assist the *ménage*, without offending her hostess by the offer of money. If Madame d'Arblay erred in this statement—and Lady Llanover by no means satisfies us that she did err—surely the mistake was a most venial one. But Lady Llanover's outraged dignity fumes through hundreds of pages in feeble sneers at Fanny's low origin, and still more feeble attempts to convict her of inaccuracy. *Noblesse oblige.*

"We were all in the middle of the room, and in some confusion;—but she had but just come up to us to inquire what was going forwards, and I was disentangling myself from Miss Dewes, to be ready to fly off if anyone knocked at the street-door, when the door of the drawing-room was again opened, and a large man, in deep mourning, appeared at it, entering and shutting it himself without speaking.

"A ghost could not more have scared me, when I discovered by its glitter on the black, a star! The general disorder had prevented his being seen, except by myself, who was always on the watch, till Miss Port, turning round, exclaimed, 'The King!—Aunt, the King!'

"Oh, mercy! thought I, that I were but out of the room! which way shall I escape? and how pass him unnoticed? There is but the single door at which he entered, in the room! Everyone scampered out of the way: Miss Port, to stand next the door; Mr. Bernard Dewes to a corner opposite it; his little girl clung to me; and Mrs. Delany advanced to meet his Majesty, who, after quietly looking on till she saw him, approached, and, inquired how she did.

"He then spoke to Mr. Bernard, whom he had already met two or three times here.

"I had now retreated to the wall, and purposed gliding softly, though speedily, out of the room; but before I had taken a single step, the King, in a loud whisper to Mrs. Delany, said, 'Is that Miss Burney?'—and on her answering, 'Yes, sir,' he bowed, and with a countenance of the most perfect good humour, came close up to me."

Having put a question to her, and received an inaudible reply, he went back to Mrs. Delany, and spoke of the Princess Elizabeth, who, incredible as it sounds, was then recovering from an illness after having been blooded twelve times in a fortnight :

"A good deal of talk then followed about his own health, and the extreme temperance by which he preserved it. The fault of his constitution, he said, was a tendency to excessive fat, which he kept, however, in order by the most vigorous exercise, and the strictest attention to a simple diet.

"When Mrs. Delany was beginning to praise his forbearance, he stopped her.

"'No, no,' he cried, ''tis no virtue; I only prefer eating plain and little, to growing diseased and infirm.'

"During this discourse, I stood quietly in the place where he had first spoken to me. His quitting me so soon, and conversing freely and easily with Mrs. Delany, proved so delightful a relief to me, that I no longer wished myself away; and the moment my first panic from the surprise was over, I diverted myself with a thousand ridiculous notions of my own situation.

"The Christmas games we had been showing Miss Dewes, it seemed as if we were still performing, as none of us thought it proper to move, though our manner of standing reminded one of Puss in the corner. Close to the door was posted Miss Port; opposite her, close to the wainscot, stood Mr. Dewes; at just an equal distance from him, close to a window, stood myself; Mrs. Delany, though seated, was at the opposite side to Miss Port; and his Majesty kept pretty much in the middle of the room. The little girl, who kept close to me, did not break the order, and I could hardly help expecting to be beckoned, with a puss! puss! puss! to change places with one of my neighbours.

"This idea, afterwards, gave way to another more

pompous. It seemed to me we were acting a play. There is something so little like common and real life, in everybody's standing, while talking, in a room full of chairs, and standing, too, so aloof from each other, that I almost thought myself upon a stage, assisting in the representation of a tragedy—in which the King played his own part of the king; Mrs. Delany that of a venerable confidante; Mr. Dewes, his respectful attendant; Miss Port, a suppliant virgin, waiting encouragement to bring forward some petition; Miss Dewes, a young orphan, intended to move the royal compassion; and myself, a very solemn, sober, and decent mute.

" These fancies, however, only regaled me while I continued a quiet spectator, and without expectation of being called into play. But the King, I have reason to think, meant only to give me time to recover from my first embarrassment; and I feel myself infinitely obliged to his good breeding and consideration, which perfectly answered, for before he returned to me I was entirely recruited. . . .

" The King went up to the table, and looked at a book of prints, from Claude Lorraine, which had been brought down for Miss Dewes; but Mrs. Delany, by mistake, told him they were for me. He turned over a leaf or two, and then said :

" ' Pray, does Miss Burney draw too ?'

" The *too* was pronounced very civilly.

" ' I believe not, sir,' answered Mrs. Delany; 'at least, she does not tell.'

" ' Oh !' cried he, laughing, 'that's nothing! She is not apt to tell; she never does tell, you know! Her father told me that himself. He told me the whole history of her Evelina. And I shall never forget his face when he spoke of his feelings at first taking up the book !—he looked quite frightened, just as if he was doing it that moment! I never can forget his face while I live!'

" Then coming up close to me, he said:

" ' But what?—what?—how was it?'

" ' Sir,' cried I, not well understanding him.

" ' How came you—how happened it?—what?—what?'

" ' I—I only wrote, sir, for my own amusement—only in some odd, idle hours.'

" ' But your publishing—your printing—how was that?'

" ' That was only; sir—only because——'

" I hesitated most abominably, not knowing how to tell him a long story, and growing terribly confused at these questions—besides, to say the truth, his own " what? what?" so reminded me of those vile Probationary Odes,* that, in the midst of all my flutter, I was really hardly able to keep my countenance.

" The *What!* was then repeated with so earnest a look, that, forced to say something, I stammeringly answered:

" ' I thought—sir—it would look very well in print!'

" I do really flatter myself this is the silliest speech I ever made! I am quite provoked with myself for it; but a fear of laughing made me eager to utter anything, and by no means conscious, till I had spoken, of what I was saying.

" He laughed very heartily himself—well he might—and walked away to enjoy it, crying out:

" ' Very fair indeed! that's being very fair and honest!'

" Then, returning to me again, he said:

" ' But your father—how came you not to show him what you wrote?'

* The Probationary Odes for the Laureateship appeared in 1785, after the appointment of Thomas Warton to that office, on the vacancy occasioned by the death of William Whitehead.

" ' I was too much ashamed of it, sir, seriously.'

" Literal truth that, I am sure.

" ' And how did he find it out ?'

" ' I don't know myself, sir.   He never would tell me.' . . . .

" ' What entertainment you must have had from hearing people's conjectures before you were known! Do you remember any of them ?' . . . .

" ' I heard that Mr. Baretti laid a wager it was written by a man ; for no woman, he said, could have kept her own counsel.'

" This diverted him extremely.

" ' But how was it,' he continued, ' you thought most likely for your father to discover you ?'

" ' Sometimes, sir, I have supposed I must have dropped some of the manuscript: sometimes, that one of my sisters betrayed me.'

" ' Oh! your sister ?—what, not your brother ?'

" ' No, sir ; he could not, for——'

" I was going on, but he laughed so much I could not be heard, exclaiming :

" ' Vastly well! I see you are of Mr. Baretti's mind, and think your brother could keep your secret, and not your sister . . . . But you have not kept your pen unemployed all this time ?'·

" ' Indeed I have, sir.'

" ' But why ?'

" ' I—I believe I have exhausted myself, sir.'

" He laughed aloud at this, and went and told it to Mrs. Delany, civilly treating a plain fact as a mere *bon mot.*"

The King asked several other questions about Evelina, and the prospect of anything further appearing from the

R. West Ports.

A. Larsson Phi:

Valentine Green

Queen Charlotte and the Princess Royal.

author's pen. A change of subject led to the mention of hunting, when, looking round on the party, he said : ' Did you know that Mrs. Delany once hunted herself, and in a long gown and a great hoop ?' As he spoke, a violent thunder was heard at the door. Fanny again felt herself sinking into the carpet. Miss Port slid out of the room backwards, and lights shone in the hall. Enter the Queen. Her Majesty drops a profound reverence to the King, holds out both hands to her dear Mrs. Delany, and then turns her face on the short-sighted stranger, who, uncertain whether she has received a salute or not, is bewildered what to do. The King comes to her relief, repeats to his consort all that Miss Burney has already told him, and proceeds with a further catechism. The Queen, more curious about the future than the past, has questions of her own to put. ' Shall we have no more ?— nothing more ?' she asks. Fanny can only shake her head in reply, and when gracious phrases of regret and encouragement are uttered, is unable to find a word of acknowledgment. Presently the conversation, becoming general, ranges over a variety of topics, from the exemplary behaviour of the Princess Sophia, aged nearly nine, in guarding her music-master's great nose from ridicule, to Bishop Porteous's sermons, which the King thought that admired preacher would do wrong to publish, because every discourse printed would diminish his stock for the pulpit.

Three days later the King made an evening visit. The Diary describes the mode of his reception on these occasions. ' The etiquette always observed on his entrance is, first of all, to fly off to distant quarters ; and next, Miss Port goes out, walking backwards, for more candles, which she brings in, two at a time, and places upon the tables and pianoforte. Next she goes out for tea, which she then carries to his Majesty, upon a large salver, containing sugar, cream, and bread and butter and cake, while she hangs a napkin over her arm for his fingers. This, it seems, is a ceremony performed, in other places, always by the mistress of the house; but here neither of their Majesties will permit Mrs. Delany to attempt it.' While drinking his tea, the King ran on, in his usual discursive vein, about authors, actors, books, and plays. Concerning the tendency of Voltaire's works, and the personal character of Rousseau, he expressed the current opinions of English society; calling the former a monster, and telling anecdotes to illustrate 'the savage pride and insolent ingratitude' of the latter. He vexed Miss Burney by pronouncing Mrs. Siddons the most excellent player of his time, not even excepting the divine Garrick. From players he went to plays, and having deplored the immorality of the old English comedies, and the poverty of the new ones, he came at length to Shakspeare.

"'Was there ever,' cried he, 'such stuff as great part of Shakspeare? only one must not say so! But what think you? What? Is there not sad stuff? What? What?'

"'Yes, indeed, I think so, sir, though mixed with such excellences, that——'

"'Oh!' cried he, laughing good-humouredly; 'I know it is not to be said! but it's true. Only it's Shakspeare, and nobody dares abuse him.'

"Then he enumerated many of the characters and parts of plays that he objected to; and, when he had run them over, finished with again laughing, and exclaiming: 'But one should be stoned for saying so!'"

The following afternoon, the Queen came, and was also in a mood for literary criticism. She talked of the

'Sorrows of Werter,' and Klopstock's 'Messiah,' and mentioned, with praise, another book, saying :

' I picked it up on a stall. Oh, it is amazing what good books there are on stalls !'

' It is amazing to me,' said Mrs. Delany, 'to hear that.'

' Why, I don't pick them up myself; but I have a servant very clever; and if they are not to be had at the bookseller's, they are not for me any more than for another.'

In May, 1786, the Mastership of the King's Band, which had formerly been promised to Dr. Burney, once more became vacant. The Doctor was again a candidate for the appointment. We gather from his having accepted so small a post as that of Organist to Chelsea Hospital, and from some other indications, that his circumstances had not improved as he grew older. He was now sixty years of age: he must have found the work of tuition at once less easy to be met with, and more laborious to discharge, than it had been in his younger days; we cannot be mistaken in supposing that he was eager to obtain, not merely promotion, but also some permanent and lighter occupation. In his anxiety he had recourse to Mr. Smelt, who counselled him to go to Windsor, not to address the King, but to be seen by him. ' Take your daughter in your hand,' said the experienced courtier, ' and walk upon the Terrace. Your appearing there at this time the King will understand, and he is more likely to be touched by such a hint than by any direct application.' Burney lost no time in acting on the advice thus given. When he and Fanny reached the Terrace in the evening, they found the Royal Family already there. The King and Queen, the Queen's mother, and the Prince of Mecklenburg, her Majesty's brother, all walked together. Behind them followed six lovely young princesses,* with their ladies and some of the young princes, making, in the eyes of loyal subjects, 'a very gay and pleasing procession of one of the finest families in the world.' "Every way they moved," continues the narrator, "the crowd retired to stand up against the wall as they passed, and then closed in to follow. When they approached, and we were retreating, Lady Louisa Clayton placed me next herself, making her daughters stand below—without which I had certainly not been seen; for the moment their Majesties advanced, I involuntarily looked down, and drew my hat over my face. I could not endure to stare at them; and, full of our real errand, I felt ashamed even of being seen by them. Consequently, I should have stood in the herd, and unregarded; but Lady Louisa's kindness and good breeding put me in a place too conspicuous to pass unnoticed. The moment the Queen had spoken to her, which she stopped to do as soon as she came up to her, she inquired, in a whisper, who was with her. The Queen then instantly stepped near me, and asked me how I did; and then the King came forward, and, as soon as he had repeated the same question, said:

" 'Are you come to stay?'

" 'No, sir; not now.'

" 'I was sure,' cried the Queen, 'she was not come to stay, by seeing her father!'

" I was glad by this to know my father had been observed.

" 'And when,' asked the King, 'do you return again to Windsor?'

* Charlotte, b. 1766, d. 1828, m. King of Wurtemberg; Augusta, b. 1768, d. 1840 (unm.); Elizabeth, b. 1770, d. 1840, m. Landgrave of Hesse Homburg; Mary, b. 1776, d. 1840, m. her cousin, the Duke of Gloucester; Sophia, b. 1777, d. 1848 (unm.); Amelia, b. 1783. d. 1810 (unm.).

The Dukes of Cumberland, Sussex and Cambridge.
and the Princesses Augusta, Elizabeth and Mary.

" 'Very soon, I hope, sir.'

" 'And—and—and,' cried he, half laughing and hesitating significantly, 'pray, how goes on the Muse?'

"At first I only laughed too; but he repeated the inquiry, and then I answered:

" 'Not at all, sir.'

" 'No? But why?—why not?'

" 'I—I—I am afraid, sir,' stammered I.

" 'And why?' repeated he;—'of what?'

"I spoke something—I hardly know what myself—so indistinctly that he could not hear me, though he had put his head quite under my hat from the beginning of the little conference; and after another such question or two, and no greater satisfaction in the answer, he smiled very good-humouredly, and walked on, his Queen by his side.

"We stayed some time longer on the Terrace, and my poor father occasionally joined me; but he looked so conscious and depressed that it pained me to see him. He was not spoken to, though he had a bow every time the King passed him, and a curtsey from the Queen. But it hurt him, and he thought it a very bad prognostic; and all there was at all to build upon was the graciousness shown to me." Much dejected, the Doctor posted back to town with his daughter; and, on reaching home, heard that the place he sought had been disposed of by the Lord Chamberlain, in whose gift it was.

Miss Burney was persuaded that the King was displeased with the action of his official, but we venture to doubt the correctness of her belief. Beyond question, Mr. Smelt had had good reason for implying that the daughter, rather than the father, was the object of favour at Windsor. Dr. Burney was by no means a sound enough Handelian to satisfy George III. And, to say the truth, the account of the Handel Centenary Festival was but a poor performance. On the other hand, Fanny's literary success, and her manner of carrying it, had pleased and interested the royal pair. It is probable, if not absolutely certain, that the design of finding her some employment at Court had already been entertained, and that this was considered to render her father's suit for himself inopportune.

The first thought was to settle her with one of the princesses, in preference to the numerous candidates of high birth and station, but small fortune, who were waiting and supplicating for places about the persons of the King's daughters. But in the month following Dr. Burney's disappointment, a vacancy occurred in the Queen's own Household. The office of Keeper of the Robes was jointly held by two Germans, Mrs. Schwellenberg and Mrs. Haggerdorn, who had accompanied Charlotte of Mecklenburg-Strelitz, when she came to England. The health of Mrs. Haggerdorn broke down about this time, and in June, 1786, it was arranged that she should retire, and return to her own country. Who should succeed her was a matter of eager speculation and fierce competition in Court circles; but without consulting anyone, the Queen commissioned Mr. Smelt to make an offer to Frances Burney. This trusted agent was instructed to express her Majesty's wish to attach the young lady permanently to herself and her family: he was to propose to her to undertake certain duties, which were in fact those of Mrs. Haggerdorn; and he was to intimate that in case of her accepting the situation designed for her, she would have apartments in the palace, would belong to the table of Mrs. Schwellenberg, with whom the Queen's own visitors—bishops, lords, or commons—always dined; would be allowed a separate footman, and the use of a carriage in common with her senior colleague; and would receive a salary of two hundred pounds a year.

Fanny listened, and was struck with consternation. "The attendance," she wrote to her dear Miss Cambridge, "was to be incessant, the confinement to the Court continual; I was scarce ever to be spared for a single visit from the palaces, nor to receive anybody but with permission; and what a life for me, who have friends so dear to me, and to whom friendship is the balm, the comfort, the very support of existence!' It was not the sacrifice of literary prospects that alarmed her. She did not even think of 'those distinguished men and women, the flower of all political parties, with whom she had been in the habit of mixing on terms of equal intercourse,'* and from whose society she would be exiled. Her mind dwelt only on the pain of being separated from her family and intimate friends: from Susan and the Lockes; from the old familiar faces at Chesington; from her sister Charlotte, now married and settled in Norfolk; from her correspondent at Twickenham. 'I have no heart,' she says, 'to write to Mickleham or Norbury. I know how they will grieve: they have expected me to spend the whole summer with them.' Good Mr. Smelt, who, in the words of Macaulay, seems to have thought that going to Court was like going to heaven, was equally surprised and mortified at the mournful reception accorded to his flattering proposals. Mrs. Delany, in whose town house they were delivered, was not less astounded. The recipient, however, had but one thought, that, which ever way her own feelings inclined, the matter must be referred to her father, as the only person entitled to decide it. Dr. Burney, as might have been anticipated, was enraptured by the honour done to his family, and the vista which, in

* Macaulay.

his sanguine view, was opened before his daughter. Meanwhile, Mr. Smelt had gone down to Windsor, and brought back word that the Queen desired a personal interview with Miss Burney. Fanny had her audience, and it ended, as she foresaw must be the case, in her submission. When her Majesty said, with the most condescending softness, ' I am sure, Miss Burney, we shall suit one another very well,' there was nothing to be done, but to make a humble reverence, and accept. The Queen told Mrs. Delany: ' I was led to think of Miss Burney, first by her books, then by seeing her ; then by always hearing how she was loved by her friends; but chiefly by your friendship for her.'

Of course, the proposition and the acceptance were alike mistaken. The service required was unworthy of the servant, nor was she competent for the service. On the one hand, the talents of a brilliant writer were thrown away in a situation where writing was neither expected nor desired. On the other, a novice of puny figure, imperfect sight, extreme nervousness, and small aptitude for ordinary feminine duties, was most unlikely to become distinguished in the profession of a lady-in-attendance. Under the most favourable circumstances, the gains and advantages attached to her constrained life at Court were not to be compared with those which might be looked for from the diligent use of her pen in the freedom of home. Yet allowing all this, we cannot disguise from ourselves that much heedless rhetoric has been expended by several critics on the folly of Miss Burney's choice, and the infatuation of her parent. These critics, we conceive, have been led astray, partly by those more extreme trials of her servitude which no prudence could have foreseen, but principally by an erroneous estimate of her position at the time when she closed with the Queen's offer.

The picture which has been imagined of Frances
Burney sending forth, at short intervals, a series of
'Cecilias,' and receiving for each a cheque of two thousand
guineas, is attractive, but purely visionary. It would, we
venture to say, have tickled her fine sense of humour
amazingly. We are not to think of her as of a favourite
novelist of to-day, whom the booksellers and the editors
of magazines conspire to keep constantly employed. Her
longing to see herself in print seems to have been satiated
by the appearance of 'Evelina.' Her second work was a
much less spontaneous production. Indeed, it is not
clear that 'Cecilia' would have been written but for the
urgency of Crisp, seconded by other friends. Her two
fathers were agreed that she ought to exert herself while her
powers and her fame were fresh; but how much stimulus
was applied after Crisp's death, we are not informed.
Hers was not a very energetic nature, and she had some
misgiving that her invention was exhausted. At any rate,
she had now let four years go by without attempting
anything new. Her third book was not published for the
space of a lustrum after her release from Court, and then
only under strong pressure of the *res angusta domi.* There
had been some talk of laying out the amount paid for
'Cecilia' in the purchase of an annuity. But we do not
find that this saving plan was executed. What has been
contemptuously called 'board, lodging, and two hundred
a year,' was no bad provision for a single lady of thirty-
four, who was producing nothing, and had no income of
her own. Boswell, it is true, declared that he would farm
her out himself for double or treble the money; but then
Boswell did not know a great deal of female authors.
Burney was much better aware what to expect from his
daughter's enterprise and resolution; and we are by no
means sure that, in accepting for her the offered place, he

proved himself a less practical man than the ' irresponsible reviewers ' who have derided him as a moon-struck worshipper of royalty. Burke, who certainly did not undervalue Miss Burney, and who knew something of her family circumstances, was delighted at the news, and thought that the Queen had never shown more good sense than in appointing Miss Burney to her service; though he afterwards owned to having miscalculated, when the service turned out to mean confinement to such a companion as Mrs. Schwellenberg.

But neither the irksomeness of the duty, nor the character of Mrs. Schwellenberg, was known to the outer world. Both required experience to make them understood. How by degrees they disclosed themselves to Miss Burney, we shall learn presently. For the feud which sprang up between the two ladies, it must, in fairness, be owned that the elder was not wholly answerable. Miss Burney—we ought now properly to call her Mrs. Burney—had been appointed second Keeper of the Robes. She seems to have supposed that this put her on a level with Mrs. Schwellenberg, giving the latter the advantage of formal precedence only. But whatever had been the relation of Mrs. Haggerdorn to her colleague, it appears clear that Fanny, a much younger, and quite inexperienced person, was intended to be subordinate. Thus, when she expresses a fear that, by want of spirit to assert it, she had lost a right to invite guests to table, we cannot but remember that, in the terms proposed to her, the table had been described as Mrs. Schwellenberg's. The chief Keeper, as we shall see, was coarse and offensive in speech, domineering and tyrannical in action, but her junior sometimes resented a tone of superiority and command which their royal mistress evidently thought natural and reasonable.

Whatever injury Miss Burney may have sustained by entering the palace, her readers at least have no cause to complain. 'I am glad for *her* interest,' wrote Walpole, 'though sorry for my own, that Evelina and Cecilia are to be transformed into a Madame de Motteville, as I shall certainly not live to read her Memoirs, though I might another novel.' But what was to Horace a source of regret, may be to us matter for congratulation. Fanny's Diaries are now much more studied than her novels. Few of us would wish to exchange the journal of her life at Court for another fiction from her pen. The Harrels, the Delvilles, the Briggses, about whom Burke and Reynolds and Mrs. Delany talked as if they were real personages, are for most of us names that call up no association. Queen Charlotte and stout King George are better known to us than any other royal pair mentioned in English history. And for this we are in great measure indebted to the little lady who joined their household in July, 1786. The likeness of the Queen, which we remember as well as we do the features of our mothers, is entirely of her drawing; while she contributes not a few of the sketches which are combined in our impression of the monarch who loved music, and backgammon, and homely chat, and Ogden's sermons, as much as he detested popery, and whiggery, and freethinking, and Wilkes. Nor are characters of another kind wanting in this journal. Mrs. Schwellenberg's arrogance, her inso-lence, her peevishness, her ferocious selfishness, her broken English, are more familiar to the present genera-tion than the humours, the affectations, the piebald dialect of Madame Duval, or than the traits of any of the other figures in Evelina. The Senior Robe-keeper was no doubt as indifferent to posthumous reputation as she was to the contemporary opinion of all who could not displace her. That she ran any risk from the satire of her timorous assistant was a thought which never occurred to her illiterate mind. She hardly knew what satire meant. She flattered herself that Harry Bunbury could not caricature her because she had no hump. For writers of imagination she had an unbounded contempt. 'I won't have nothing what you call novels,' she once cried in Fanny's presence, 'what you call romances, what you call histories—I might not read such what you call stuff— not I!' Had she been one degree less callous, or one degree less ignorant, she might have been slower to provoke the hostility of Johnson's 'little character-monger.' Well! we have her portrait, most carefully executed. And we have also, by the same cunning hand, vivid delineations of many other persons, more or less notable, and of several interesting scenes that fell under the artist's view during her connection with the Queen. We do not go to Miss Burney's record of those five years for secrets of state, or politics, or even Court scandal—with which last, indeed, she seems to have busied herself as little as with the first two—but for a picture of the domestic life and manners of the Sovereign and his consort. It is no small proof of the journalist's tact and discretion that she was able to produce so candid a narrative of what she experienced and witnessed without giving offence to the family concerned. The Duke of Sussex is reported to have said, that he and the other surviving children of George III. had been alarmed when the Diaries of Madame d'Arblay were announced for publication, but pleased with the book when it appeared; 'though I think,' added his Royal Highness, 'that she is rather hard on poor old Schwellenberg.' The Duke, of course, had seen the Schwellenberg only in her part of an abject toad-eater. Yet there may be something in his observation. Fanny had a light touch, but, like other women, was unforgiving towards an enemy of her own sex.

Our readers must not suppose that Miss Burney, on her appointment, went to live in Windsor Castle. Some years before that time, the Castle had been forsaken by the royal family as uninhabitable. A sort of makeshift palace, known as the Upper Lodge, or the Queen's Lodge,* was erected hard by, opposite the South Terrace ; a long narrow building, with battlements fronting northward towards the old towers, and southward towards a walled garden, at the further end of which was placed the Lower Lodge, a smaller building of similar character, appropriated to the use of the Princesses. Fanny, as an attendant on the person of the Queen, was quartered in the Upper Lodge. " My Windsor apartment," she wrote, " is extremely comfortable. I have a large drawing-room, as they call it, which is on the ground-floor, as are all the Queen's rooms, and which faces the Castle and the venerable Round Tower, and opens at the further side, from the windows, to the Little Park. It is airy, pleasant, clean, and healthy. My bedroom is small, but neat and comfortable ; its entrance is only from the drawing-room, and it looks to the garden. These two rooms are delightfully independent of all the rest of the house, and contain everything I can desire for my convenience and comfort." The sitting-room had a view of the walk leading to the Terrace, access to which was obtained by a flight of steps and an iron gate. Mrs. Delany's door was at a distance of less than fifty yards from the Queen's Lodge. The paltry and uncomfortable barracks erected under George III. no longer discredit the Crown of England. The restora-

---

* It was sometimes called the ' Queen's Lodge,' because it stood on the site of the older Queen Anne's Lodge.

tion of Windsor Castle was commenced in 1800, and occupied a good many years. ' In 1823 the Queen's House was pulled down, and the present royal stables, built in 1839, occupy part of the site. It is, indeed, very difficult to identify any of the landmarks now ; everything has been so completely changed. The steps and the iron gate, the railings and the Princesses' garden, have all disappeared as completely as the Upper and Lower Lodges.'*

In the following passage we have a summary of the new Robe-keeper's usual round of daily duties :

" I rise at six o'clock, dress in a morning gown and cap, and wait my first summons, which is at all times from seven to near eight, but commonly in the exact half-hour between them. The Queen never sends for me till her hair is dressed. This, in a morning, is always done by her wardrobe-woman, Mrs. Thielky, a German, but who speaks English perfectly well. Mrs. Schwellenberg, since the first week, has never come down in a morning at all. The Queen's dress is finished by Mrs. Thielky and myself. No maid ever enters the room while the Queen is in it. Mrs. Thielky hands the things to me, and I put them on. 'Tis fortunate for me I have not the handing them ! I should never know which to take first, embarrassed as I am, and should run a prodigious risk of giving the gown before the hoop, and the fan before the neckerchief. By eight o'clock, or a little after, for she is extremely expeditious, she is dressed. She then goes out to join the King, and be joined by the Princesses, and they all proceed to the King's chapel in the Castle, to prayers, attended by the governesses of the Princesses, and the King's equerry. Various others at times attend ; but

* Loftie's ' Windsor Castle.'

only these indispensably. I then return to my own room to breakfast. I make this meal the most pleasant part of the day; I have a book for my companion, and I allow myself an hour for it. . . . At nine o'clock I send off my breakfast-things, and relinquish my book, to make a serious and steady examination of everything I have upon my hands in the way of business—in which, preparations for dress are always included, not for the present day alone, but for the Court-days, which require a particular dress; for the next arriving birthday of any of the Royal Family, every one of which requires new apparel; for Kew, where the dress is plainest; and for going on here, where the dress is very pleasant to me, requiring no show nor finery, but merely to be neat, not inelegant, and moderately fashionable. That over, I have my time at my own disposal till a quarter before twelve, except on Wednesdays and Saturdays, when I have it only to a quarter before eleven. . . . These times mentioned call me to the irksome and quick-returning labours of the toilette. The hour advanced on the Wednesdays and Saturdays is for curling and craping the hair, which it now requires twice a week. A quarter before one is the usual time for the Queen to begin dressing for the day. Mrs. Schwellenberg then constantly attends; so do I; Mrs. Thielky, of course, at all times. We help her off with her gown, and on with her powdering things, and then the hairdresser is admitted. She generally reads the newspapers during that operation. When she observes that I have run to her but half dressed, she constantly gives me leave to return and finish as soon as she is seated. If she is grave, and reads steadily on, she dismisses me, whether I am dressed or not; but at all times she never forgets to send me away while she is powdering, with a consideration not to spoil my clothes, that one

would not expect belonged to her high station. Neither
does she ever detain me without making a point of reading
here and there some little paragraph aloud. . . . Few
minutes elapse ere I am again summoned. I find her
then always removed to her state dressing-room, if any
room in this private mansion can have the epithet of
state. There, in a very short time, her dress is finished.
She then says she won't detain me, and I hear and see no
more of her till bedtime. . . .

"At five, we have dinner. Mrs. Schwellenberg and I
meet in the eating-room. We are commonly tête-à-tête.
. . . . When we have dined, we go upstairs to her apartment, which is directly over mine. Here we have coffee
till the *terracing* is over : this is at about eight o'clock. Our
tête-à-tête then finishes, and we come down again to the
eating-room. There the equerry, whoever he is, comes to
tea constantly, and with him any gentleman that the
King or Queen may have invited for the evening; and
when tea is over, he conducts them, and goes himself, to
the concert-room. This is commonly about nine o'clock.
From that time, if Mrs. Schwellenberg is alone, I never
quit her for a minute, till I come to my little supper at
near eleven. Between eleven and twelve my last summons
usually takes place, earlier and later occasionally. Twenty
minutes is the customary time then spent with the Queen :
half an hour, I believe, is seldom exceeded. I then come
back, and after doing whatever I can to forward my dress
for the next morning, I go to bed—and to sleep, too,
believe me : the early rising, and a long day's attention to
new affairs and occupations, cause a fatigue so bodily,
that nothing mental stands against it, and to sleep I fall
the moment I have put out my candle and laid down my
head."

The best-known writer of that day was wounded at

first by having to 'answer the bell,' like any chamber-maid; and she had cast on her another burden, which even her loyalty could not consider dignified. She had to mix the Queen's snuff. To perform this task belonged to her place, and it was an inflexible rule with her Majesty that discipline must be preserved. We cannot help thinking that there was a touch of regret in the King's voice when he said :

'Miss Burney, I hear you cook snuff very well.'

'Miss Burney,' exclaimed the Princess Elizabeth, 'I hope you hate snuff; for I hate it of all things in the world.'

Thus we see that disaffection lurked even in members of the Royal House.

We pause here for a moment to notice that a precaution adopted by Mrs. Phillips, in her replies to her sister's *Court Journal*, of giving fictitious names to some of the persons mentioned, was imitated, when the Diary was printed, by substituting the names invented by Susan for the real ones which occurred in the original. Thus, in the published volumes from which our extracts are taken, Mr. Turbulent stands for M. de Guiffardière,* a clergy-man who held the office of French reader to the Queen and the Princesses; Colonel Welbred is Colonel Greville; and Colonel Fairly is the Honourable Stephen Digby, who lost his first wife, a daughter of Lord Ilchester, in 1787, and married Miss Gunning, called in the Diary Miss Fuzilier, in 1790.

Next to the King and Queen, the most important figures in Fanny's new life are their fair daughters, the Princesses who inhabited the Lower Lodge. 'The history

---

* Commonly known as the Rev. Charles Giffardier. He had a prebendal stall at Salisbury, and was vicar of Newington, and rector of Berkhampstead. —Croker in the *Quarterly Review*.

of the daughters,' says Thackeray, 'as little Miss Burney
has painted them, is delightful.   They were handsome—
she calls them beautiful; they were most kind, loving,
and ladylike; they were gracious to every person; high
and low, who served them.   They had many little accomplishments of their own.   This one drew: that one played
the piano: they all worked most prodigiously, and fitted
up whole suites of rooms—pretty smiling Penelopes—with
their busy little needles . . . . The prettiest of all, I
think, is the father's darling, the Princess Amelia, pathetic
for her beauty, her sweetness, her early death, and for
the extreme passionate tenderness with which the King
loved her.'   Three weeks after Miss Burney entered on
her post, occurred the birthday of this favourite child.
On such festivals, when the weather was fine, the Royal
Family never failed to walk on the Terrace, which was
crowded with persons of distinction, who, by this mode
of showing respect, escaped the necessity of attending
the next Drawing-room.   On the present occasion, Mrs.
Delany was carried in her sedan—the gift of the King—
to the foot of the stairs, and appeared on the promenade
with the new Keeper of the Robes by her side.   " It was
really a mighty pretty procession," writes Fanny.   " The
little Princess, just turned of three years old, in a robe-
coat covered with fine muslin, a dressed close cap, white
gloves, and a fan, walked on alone and first, highly
delighted in the parade, and turning from side to side to
see everybody as she passed: for all the terracers stand
up against the walls, to make a clear passage for the
Royal Family, the moment they come in sight.   Then
followed the King and Queen, no less delighted themselves with the joy of their little darling.   The Princess
Royal, leaning on Lady Elizabeth Waldegrave, followed
at a little distance; next the Princess Augusta, holding

The Princesses. Mary, Sophia and Amelia.

by the Duchess of Ancaster; and next the Princess
Elizabeth, holding by Lady Charlotte Bertie. Office
here takes place of rank, which occasioned Lady Elizabeth
Waldegrave, as lady of her bedchamber, to walk with the
Princess Royal. Then followed the Princess Mary with
Miss Goldsworthy,* and the Princess Sophia with Made-
moiselle Montmoulin and Miss Planta;† then General
Budé and the Duke of Montague;‡ and, lastly, Major
Price, who, as equerry, always brings up the rear, walks
at a distance from the group, and keeps off all crowd
from the Royal Family."

'One sees it,' adds Thackeray: 'the band playing its
old music; the sun shining on the happy loyal crowd, and
lighting the ancient battlements, the rich elms, and purple
landscape, and bright green sward: the royal standard
drooping from the great tower yonder; as old George
passes, followed by his race, preceded by the charming
infant, who caresses the crowd with her innocent
smiles.'

The Diary proceeds: 'On sight of Mrs. Delany, the
King instantly stopped to speak to her. The Queen, of
course, and the little Princess, and all the rest, stood
still, in their ranks. They talked a good while with the
sweet old lady; during which time the King once or
twice addressed himself to me. I caught the Queen's
eye, and saw in it a little surprise, but by no means any
displeasure, to see me of the party.

"The little Princess went up to Mrs. Delany, of whom
she is very fond, and behaved like a little angel to her:
she then, with a look of inquiry and recollection, slowly,
of her own accord, came behind Mrs. Delany to look at

---

* Sub-governess of the Princesses.
† English teacher to the two eldest Princesses.
‡ Master of the Horse.

me. 'I am afraid,' said I, in a whisper, and stooping down, 'your Royal Highness does not remember me?'

"What think you was her answer? An arch little smile, and a nearer approach, with her lips pouted out to kiss me. I could not resist so innocent an invitation; but the moment I had accepted it, I was half afraid it might seem, in so public a place, an improper liberty: however, there was no help for it. She then took my fan, and having looked at it on both sides, gravely returned it me, saying, 'O! a brown fan!'"

CHAPTER VI.

A FEW days after the scene described at the end of our
last chapter, the Court set out on a visit to Lord and
Lady Harcourt at Nuneham. The arrangement was that
the royal party should pass the first day with their host
and hostess; spend the second and third in excursions to
Oxford and Blenheim respectively, sleeping each night at
Nuneham; and return the fourth day to Windsor. Miss
Burney was informed that she was to be one of her
Majesty's suite. In making this communication to her,
Mrs. Schwellenberg took occasion to say: 'I tell you
once, I shall do for you what I can; you are to have a
gown!' Seeing Fanny draw back in surprise at this
abrupt speech, the important old lady added: 'The
Queen will give you a gown; the Queen says you are not
rich.' Offended at the grossness with which the intended
gracious present was offered, our inexperienced Court
servant declared a wish to decline it. Her superior
instantly flew into a passion. 'Miss Bernar,' cried she,
quite angrily, 'I tell you once, when the Queen will give

you a gown,* you must be humble, thankful, when you are
Duchess of Ancaster!' Before the journey to Nuneham
took place, Fanny, rather unwisely, expressed her regret
that she had some time previously neglected an opportunity
of being introduced to the lady whose house she was about
to visit; she had met Lord Harcourt, she said, and
thought it might have smoothed her way to know something of his Countess also. She was promptly told that
she was utterly insignificant—that, going with the Queen,
she was sure of civil treatment; but that whether or not
she had a servant, or any change of dress, was of no consequence. There is no need,' said the senior Robe-
Keeper, 'that you should be seen. I shall do everything
that I can to assist you to appear for nobody.'

In fact, the whole expedition might have seemed to be
planned for the purpose of convincing her that any importance she had once enjoyed was now absolutely gone.
Their Majesties went to Nuneham to breakfast. Miss
Burney followed in the afternoon, with Miss Planta,
English teacher of the Princesses, Mrs. Thielky, the
Queen's wardrobe-woman, and one or two more of the
royal attendants. On their arrival, they found the house
to be 'one of those straggling, half-new, half-old, half-
comfortable, and half-forlorn mansions, that are begun in
one generation and finished in another.' We have a
graphic and amusing description of accidents encountered
and discomforts endured, before the hapless and helpless
diarist was settled for the night: the being handed from
her carriage by a common postilion; the deserted hall,
where not even a porter was to be seen; the entire
absence of a welcome, the whole family being in the

---

* Macaulay says that this promise of a gown was never performed; but he
is mistaken. Miss Burney did get the gown after some delay. It was 'a lilac
tabby,' whatever that may be, or may have been. (Diary, ii. 189.)

Park, with the King and Queen and Princesses, and the mistress of the house having deputed no one to act for her; the want of assistance in searching for her apartment; the wanderings through unknown mazy passages; the 'superfine men in yellow-laced liveries' occasionally met sauntering along, who disdained to waste a word in answer to inquiries; the sitting down at length in despair in a room destined for one of the Princesses; the alarm at being surprised there by its owner and her sisters; the subsequent promises, only made to be broken, of guidance to the wished-for haven; and finally, when that haven had at last been reached, the humiliation of being summoned to supper by a gentleman-footman haughtily calling out from the foot of the stairs, '*The equerries want the ladies!*' It is impossible to read the account of these 'difficulties and disgraces' without seeing that the shy, sensitive, flattered novel-writer had indeed mistaken her vocation when she accepted service in a royal household.

The next day was Sunday, and was appointed to be observed, after due attendance at Church, by a visit to the University of Oxford. Late on Saturday night, Miss Burney received the Queen's commands to belong to the suite on the morrow, and rejoiced exceedingly that she had brought with her a new Chambéry gauze, instead of only the dress she wore, according to her Cerbera's advice. We abridge Fanny's narrative of her laborious Sabbath:

"AUGUST 13TH.—At six o'clock my hairdresser, to my great satisfaction, arrived. Full two hours was he at work, yet was I not finished, when Swarthy, the Queen's hairdresser, came rapping at my door, to tell me her Majesty's hair was done, and she was waiting for me. I

hurried as fast as I could, and ran down without any cap.
She smiled at sight of my hasty attire, and said I should
not be distressed about a hairdresser the next day, but
employ Swarthy's assistant, as soon as he had done with
the Princesses: 'You should have had him,' she added,
'to-day, if I had known you wanted him.'

"When her Majesty was dressed, all but the hat, she
sent for the three Princesses; and the King came also.
I felt very foolish with my uncovered head; but it was
somewhat the less awkward, from its being very much a
custom, in the Royal Family, to go without caps; though
none that appear before them use such a freedom.

"As soon as the hat was on—'Now, Miss Burney,'
said the Queen, 'I won't keep you; you had better go
and dress too.'"

Breakfast and morning service followed, and then came
the Oxford expedition:

"How many carriages there were, and how they were
arranged, I observed not sufficiently to recollect; but the
party consisted of their Majesties, the Princesses Royal,
Augusta, and Elizabeth, the Duchess of Ancaster, Lord
and Lady Harcourt, Lady Charlotte Bertie, and the two
Miss Vernons. These last ladies are daughters of the
late Lord Vernon, and sisters of Lady Harcourt. General
Harcourt, Colonel Fairly, and Major Price, and Mr.
Hagget, with Miss Planta and myself, completed the
group. Miss Planta and I, of course, as the only un-
dignified persons, brought up the rear. . . . The city of
Oxford afforded us a very noble view on the road, and its
spires, towers, and domes soon made me forget all the
little objects of minor spleen that had been crossing me
as I journeyed towards them; and, indeed, by the time I

arrived in the midst of them, their grandeur, nobility, antiquity, and elevation impressed my mind so forcibly, that I felt, for the first time since my new situation had taken place, a rushing in of ideas that had no connection with it whatever. The roads were lined with decently-dressed people, and the high street was so crowded we were obliged to drive gently and carefully, to avoid trampling the people to death. Yet their behaviour was perfectly respectful and proper. Nothing could possibly be better conducted than the whole of this expedition.'

The royal party were received by the Vice-Chancellor, and all the heads of colleges and professors then in residence, who conducted them in state to the Theatre, which was crowded with spectators. The King took his seat, with his head covered, on the Chancellor's chair, the Queen and Princesses sitting below him to the left. An address, which was read by the Vice-Chancellor, contained, among other expressions of loyalty, the congratulations of the University to the King on his recent escape from the knife of Margaret Nicholson; at the same time touching on the distress which the attempt had occasioned the Queen, and paying a tribute to her amiable and virtuous character.

"'The Queen could scarcely bear it, though she had already, I doubt not, heard it at Nuneham, as these addresses must be first read in private, to have the answers prepared. Nevertheless, this public tribute of loyalty to the King, and of respect to herself, went gratefully to her heart, and filled her eyes with tears—which she would not, however, encourage, but, smiling through them, dispersed them with her fan, with which she was repeatedly obliged to stop their course down her cheeks.

The Princesses, less guarded, the moment their father's danger was mentioned, wept with but little control . . . .

" When the address was ended, the King took a paper from Lord Harcourt, and read his answer . . . . When he had done, he took off his hat, and bowed to the Chancellor and Professors, and delivered the answer to Lord Harcourt, who, walking backwards, descended the stairs, and presented it to the Vice-Chancellor . . . .

" After this, the Vice-Chancellor and Professors begged for the honour of kissing the King's hand. Lord Harcourt was again the backward messenger; and here followed a great mark of goodness in the King: he saw that nothing less than a thoroughbred old courtier, such as Lord Harcourt, could walk backwards down these steps, before himself, and in sight of so full a hall of spectators; and he therefore dispensed with being approached to his seat, and walked down himself into the area, where the Vice-Chancellor kissed his hand, and was imitated by every Professor and Doctor in the room.

" Notwithstanding this considerate good-nature in his Majesty, the sight, at times, was very ridiculous. Some of the worthy collegiates, unused to such ceremonies, and unaccustomed to such a presence, the moment they had kissed the King's hand, turned their backs to him, and walked away as in any common room; others, attempting to do better, did still worse, by tottering and stumbling, and falling foul of those behind them; some, ashamed to kneel, took the King's hand straight up to their mouths; others, equally off their guard, plumped down on both knees, and could hardly get up again; and many, in their confusion, fairly arose by pulling his Majesty's hand to raise them . . . .

" It was vacation time; there were therefore none of the students present . . . .

"At Christ Church, where we arrived at about three o'clock, in a large hall there was a cold collation prepared for their Majesties and the Princesses. It was at the upper end of the hall. I could not see of what it consisted, though it would have been very agreeable, after so much standing and sauntering, to have given my opinion of it in an experimental way. Their Majesties and the Princesses sat down to this table; as well satisfied, I believe, as any of their subjects so to do. The Duchess of Ancaster and Lady Harcourt stood behind the chairs of the Queen and the Princess Royal. There were no other ladies of sufficient rank to officiate for Princesses Augusta and Elizabeth. Lord Harcourt stood behind the King's chair; and the Vice-Chancellor, and the Head of Christ Church, with salvers in their hands, stood near the table, and ready to hand to the three noble waiters whatever was wanted: while the other Reverend Doctors and Learned Professors stood aloof, equally ready to present to the Chancellor and the Master whatever they were to forward.

"We, meanwhile, untitled attendants, stood at the other end of the room, forming a semicircle, and all strictly facing the Royal collationers . . . . A whisper was soon buzzed through the semicircle of the deplorable state of our appetite; and presently it reached the ears of some of the worthy Doctors. Immediately a new whisper was circulated, which made its progress with great vivacity, to offer us whatever we would wish, and to beg us to name what we chose. Tea, coffee, and chocolate, were whispered back. The method of producing, and the means of swallowing them, were much more difficult to settle than the choice of what was acceptable. Major Price and Colonel Fairly, however, seeing a very large table close to the wainscot behind us, desired our refreshments might be privately conveyed there, behind the semicircle, and that, while all the group backed very near it, one at a time might feed, screened by all the rest from observation. I suppose I need not inform you, my dear Susan, that to eat in presence of any of the Royal Family, is as much *hors d'usage* as to be seated. This plan had speedy success, and the very good Doctors soon, by sly degrees and with watchful caution, covered the whole table with tea, coffee, chocolate, cakes, and bread and butter . . . .

" The Duchess of Ancaster and Lady Harcourt, as soon as the first serving attendance was over, were dismissed from the royal chairs, and most happy to join our group, and partake of our repast. The Duchess, extremely fatigued with standing, drew a small body of troops before her, that she might take a few minutes' rest on a form by one of the doors; and Lady Charlotte Bertie did the same, to relieve an ankle which she had unfortunately sprained. ' Poor Miss Burney!' cried the good-natured Duchess, ' I wish she could sit down, for she is unused to this work. She does not know yet what it is to stand for five hours following, as we do . . . .'

" In one of the colleges I stayed so long in an old chapel, lingering over antique monuments, that all the party were vanished before I missed them, except Doctors and Professors; for we had a train of those everywhere; and I was then a little surprised by the approach of one of them, saying, 'You seem inclined to abide with us, Miss Burney?' — and then another, in an accent of facetious gallantry, cried, ' No, no; don't let us shut up Miss Burney among old tombs!—No, no!' "

At Magdalene College, Miss Burney and two or three other members of the suite, having slipped away to a small parlour, sat down to rest, and enjoy some apricots which Mr. Fairly had brought in his pockets. Suddenly the door opened; the Queen entered; the truants started up, and tried to look as if sitting was a posture unknown to them; while desperate exertions were made to hide the forbidden fruit. 'I discovered,' says Fanny, 'that our appetites were to be supposed annihilated, at the same time that our strength was to be invincible.' However, her fatigues ended at last, and she was permitted to spend the Monday in peace among the pictures and gardens of Nuneham, not being commanded to join in the excursion to Blenheim.

After this expedition, the year wore on slowly and tediously. There were more royal birthdays to be kept, with the usual terracings and concerts. In alternate weeks, the Court removed from Windsor to Kew for two or three days, and again returned to Windsor. There were journeys from Kew to St. James's, and back, on the days appointed for Drawing-rooms. But the ordinary routine of Windsor and Kew was monotony itself. 'The household always rose, rode, dined at stated intervals. Day after day was the same. At the same hour at night the King kissed his daughters' jolly cheeks; the Princesses kissed their mother's hand; and Madame Thielky brought the royal nightcap. At the same hour the equerries and women-in-waiting had their little dinner, and cackled over their tea. The King had his backgammon or his evening concert; the equerries yawned themselves to death in the anteroom.'* And it must be remembered that poor Miss Burney had only a partial share even in this unvaried round of existence. Her views of the Court proper were confined to glimpses through half-opened doors, and down the vistas of long corridors.

* Thackeray.

She was not even permitted to stand at the entrance of the room where 'nothing but Handel was played;' and when Mrs. Siddons once came to the Lodge to read a play, the Keepers of the Robes were only allowed access to 'a convenient adjoining room.' She was licensed to receive hardly anyone from the outer world, except her father and sisters, Mrs. Delany, and the Lockes; beyond these, she had to use the utmost caution in admitting visitors; while her associates within the palace were restricted to the King's equerries, Mr. Turbulent, Mrs. Schwellenberg, Miss Planta, and a few other persons in positions resembling her own. She saw no other company but the strangers who from time to time were sent to dine at Mrs. Schwellenberg's table.

His Majesty's equerries were certainly not selected for their brilliant attainments, or their powers of conversation, or even for their polished manners. One of these gentlemen, a Colonel Goldsworthy, whom Miss Burney had not before seen, arrived for his turn of duty at the end of September. 'He seems to me,' says the Diary, 'a man of but little cultivation or literature, but delighting in a species of dry humour, in which he shines most successfully, by giving himself up for its favourite butt.' He soon began to warn Fanny of the discomforts of winter service in the ill-built and ill-contrived Queen's Lodge. 'Wait till November and December, and then you'll get a pretty taste of them . . . . Let's see, how many blasts must you have every time you go to the Queen? First, one upon opening your door; then another, as you get down the three steps from it, which are exposed to the wind from the garden-door downstairs; then a third, as you turn the corner to enter the passage; then you come plump upon another from the hall door; then comes another, fit to knock you down, as you turn to the upper passage; then, just as you turn towards the Queen's room comes another; and last, a whiff from the King's stairs, enough to blow you half a mile off. One thing,' he added, 'pray let me caution you about—don't go to early prayers in November; if you do, that will completely kill you! . . . . When the Princesses, used to it as they are, get regularly knocked up before this business is over, off they drop one by one:—first the Queen deserts us; then Princess Elizabeth is done for; then Princess Royal begins coughing; then Princess Augusta gets the snuffles; and all the poor attendants, my poor sister* at their head, drop off, one after another, like so many snuffs of candles: till at last, dwindle, dwindle, dwindle—not a soul goes to the Chapel but the King, the parson, and myself; and there we three freeze it out together!'

That the King was considerate to his attendants, the following story by the same elegant wit will testify. It was told after a hard day's hunting: " ' After all our labours,' said he, 'home we come, with not a dry thread about us, sore to the very bone, and forced to smile all the time, and then:

" ' Here, Goldsworthy!' cries his Majesty; so up I comes to him, bowing profoundly, and my hair dripping down to my shoes. 'Goldsworthy, I say,' he cries, 'will you have a little barley-water?'

" ' And, pray, did you drink it?'

" ' I drink it?—drink barley-water? No, no; not come to that neither. But there it was, sure enough!—in a jug fit for a sick-room; just such a thing as you put upon a hob in a chimney, for some poor miserable soul that keeps his bed! And: 'Here, Goldsworthy,' says his Majesty, 'here's the barley-water!'

* Miss Goldsworthy, sub-governess of the Princesses.

" ' And did the King drink it himself ?'

" ' Yes, God bless his Majesty ! but I was too humble a subject to do the same as the King !' "

In January, 1787, the Court removed to London for the winter. During their residence in the capital, the Royal Family occupied Buckingham House, then called the Queen's House. But the season in town was interrupted by short weekly visits to Windsor. The only Sundays of the year which George III. spent in London were the six Sundays of Lent. Miss Burney went to the play once or twice, and also attended ' the Tottenham Street oratorios.' She had more than one illness in the early part of this year; but her custodians courteously entreated their prisoner, and gave her liberty to go to her friends to refresh herself. Under this permission, she had opportunities of meeting Mrs. Cholmondeley, Sir·Joshua, Mrs. Montagu, Mrs. Vesey, Horace Walpole,* and sundry other old acquaintances. But at the beginning of June the relaxations of this pleasant time, as well as the fatiguing journeys backwards and forwards to Windsor, came to an end, and the household were again settled in the Upper Lodge. The rest of the year passed in much the same way as the summer and autumn of 1786 had done, but with fewer noticeable incidents.

In August occurred the commanded visit of Mrs. Siddons, to which we have before referred :

" In the afternoon . . . . her Majesty came into the room, and, after a little German discourse with Mrs.

* ' The last time I saw her (Mrs. Vesey) before I left London,' writes Walpole, ' Miss Burney passed the evening there, looking quite recovered and well ; and so cheerful and agreeable that the Court seems only to have improved the ease of her manner, instead of stamping more reserve on it, as I feared. But what slight graces it can give will not compensate to us and the world for the loss of her company and her writings.'—Walpole to Hannah More, June 15, 1787.

Schwellenberg, told me Mrs. Siddons had been ordered to the Lodge, to read a play, and desired I would receive her in my room.

"I felt a little queer in the office; I had only seen her twice or thrice, in large assemblies, at Miss Monckton's, and at Sir Joshua Reynolds's, and never had been introduced to her, nor spoken with her. However, in this dead and tame life I now lead, such an interview was by no means undesirable.

"I had just got to the bottom of the stairs, when she entered the passage gallery. I took her into the tea-room, and endeavoured to make amends for former distance and taciturnity, by an open and cheerful reception. I had heard from sundry people (in old days) that she wished to make the acquaintance; but . . . . now that we came so near, I was much disappointed in my expectations . . . . I found her the Heroine of a Tragedy—sublime, elevated, and solemn. In face and person, truly noble and commanding; in manners, quiet and stiff; in voice, deep and dragging; and in conversation, formal, sententious, calm, and dry. I expected her to have been all that is interesting; the delicacy and sweetness with which she seizes every opportunity to strike and to captivate upon the stage had persuaded me that her mind was formed with that peculiar susceptibility which, in different modes, must give equal powers to attract and to delight in common life. But I was very much mistaken. As a stranger, I must have admired her noble appearance and beautiful countenance, and have regretted that nothing in her conversation kept pace with their promise; and, as a celebrated actress, I had still only to do the same. Whether fame and success have spoiled her, or whether she only possesses the skill of representing and embellishing materials with which she is furnished by others, I know not; but still I remain disappointed.

"She was scarcely seated, and a little general discourse begun, before she told me—all at once—that 'there was no part she had ever so much wished to act as that of Cecilia.' I made some little acknowledgment, and hurried to ask when she had seen Sir Joshua Reynolds, Miss Palmer, and others with whom I knew her acquainted. The play she was to read was 'The Provoked Husband.' She appeared neither alarmed nor elated by her summons, but calmly to look upon it as a thing of course, from her celebrity."

The company that assembled in Mrs. Schwellenberg's apartments occupied their leisure hours with small-talk, mild flirtations, and trifling amusements, varied by occasional misunderstandings. The first Keeper of the Robes domineered over them all, and her rule was a savage tyranny, tempered by ill-health. Her infirmities sometimes detained her in London for weeks together. During her absence, her junior presided at the dinner-table, and made tea for the equerries. Great was the joy whenever the old lady went up to town to consult her physician. Then Mr. Turbulent,* more gay and flighty than beseemed a married clergyman,† would practise on the patent prudery of Fanny's character by broaching strange theories of morality, and breaking out in wild rhapsodies of half-amatory admiration. Then the colonels-in-waiting, relieved from the watchful eyes of Cerbera, exerted themselves for the entertainment of the fair tea-maker. They were not always successful. Miss Burney cared but little for

---

* What induced Macaulay to describe this gentleman as 'half-witted,' we are at a loss to conjecture. He possessed, as Miss Burney bears witness, remarkable cleverness, extraordinary attainments and great powers of conversation.

† He had a wife to whom he was strongly attached.

Mrs Siddons.

Colonel Goldsworthy's rough humour, and still less for the vocal performances of a certain Colonel Manners, who, in love with his own voice, and with what he called the songs that he heard at church, insisted on regaling his friends with snatches from Tate and Brady, married to the immortal notes of the National Anthem. Fanny once or twice caused some unpleasantness by endeavouring to escape from the duty of receiving the equerries in the evening. As soon as the Schwellenberg returned, she was again thrown into the background. Destitute of every attraction, yet constantly demanding notice, the principal could not bear to see the least attention bestowed on anyone else. 'Apparently,' says the Diary, 'she never wishes to hear my voice but when we are *tête-à-tête*, and then never is in good-humour when it is at rest.' When in company, she would sometimes talk about a pair of tame frogs which she kept, and fall into an ecstasy while describing ' their ladder, their table, and their amiable ways of snapping live flies.' 'And I can make them croak when I will,' she would say, 'when I only go so to my snuff-box—knock, knock, knock—they croak all what I please.' Rather to our surprise, we hear of this lady being once engaged in reading : the author was Josephus, 'which is the only book in favour at present, and serves for all occasions, and is quoted to solve all difficulties.' But the sole effectual mode of amusing her, after the gentlemen had retired, was to join her in a game at cards. Fanny disliked cards, and knew little of trumps or honours ; but to avert threatened attacks of spasms, she was at length fain to waive her objections, and learn piquet. When in the least crossed, Mrs. Schwellenberg put no restraint on her temper, language, or demeanour. If her servants kept her waiting for her coach, she would talk of having them trans-

ported; if Miss Burney spoke of taking tea with Mrs.
Delany, she would leave her unhelped at the dinner-table.

Such was *la Présidente.*   More than once, Miss Burney
felt her ill-usage so intolerable that she was only held
back from resigning her appointment by reluctance to
mortify her father.   The most violent dispute between
them occurred towards the end of November, 1787, when,
during a journey to town for a Drawing-Room, Mrs.
Schwellenberg had insisted upon keeping the window of
the carriage on her companion's side open, though a sharp
wind was blowing, which before their arrival in London
set up an inflammation in poor Fanny's eyes.   The scene
on the journey back is thus described :

"The next day, when we assembled to return to
Windsor, Mr. de Luc was in real consternation at sight
of my eyes; and I saw an indignant glance at my coadjutrix, that could scarce content itself without being
understood. . . .

" Some business of Mrs. Schwellenberg's occasioned a
delay of the journey, and we all retreated back; and
when I returned to my room, Miller, the old head housemaid, came to me, with a little neat tin saucepan in her
hand, saying, ' Pray, ma'am, use this for your eyes: 'tis
milk and butter, *such as I used to make for Madame Haggerdorn* when she travelled in the winter with Mrs. Schwellenberg.'

" I really shuddered when she added, that all that poor
woman's misfortunes with her eyes, which, from inflammation after inflammation, grew nearly blind, were attributed by herself to these journeys, in which she was
forced to have the glass down at her side in all weathers,
and frequently the glasses behind her also !

" Upon my word this account of my predecessor was

the least exhilarating intelligence I could receive! Goter told me, afterwards, that all the servants in the house had remarked *I was going just the same way!*

" Miss Planta presently ran into my room, to say she had hopes we should travel without this amiable being; and she had left me but a moment when Mrs. Stainforth succeeded her, exclaiming, ' Oh, for Heaven's sake, don't leave her behind; for Heaven's sake, Miss Burney, take her with you !'

" 'Twas impossible not to laugh at these opposite interests; both, from agony of fear, breaking through all restraint.

" Soon after, however, we all assembled again, and got into the coach. Mr. de Luc, who was my *vis-à-vis*, instantly pulled up the glass.

" ' Put down that glass !' was the immediate order.

" He affected not to hear her, and began conversing.

" She enraged quite tremendously, calling aloud to be obeyed without delay. He looked compassionately at me, and shrugged his shoulders, and said, ' But, ma'am——"

" ' Do it, Mr. de Luc, when I tell you! I will have it! When you been too cold, you might bear it !'

" ' It is not for me, ma'am, but poor Miss Burney.'

" ' O, poor Miss Burney might bear it the same! put it down, Mr. de Luc! without, I will get out! put it down, when I tell you! It is my coach! I will have it selfs! I might go alone in it, or with one, or with what you call nobody, when I please !'

" Frightened for good Mr. de Luc, and the more for being much obliged to him, I now interfered, and begged him to let down the glass. Very reluctantly he complied, and I leant back in the coach, and held up my muff to my eyes.

"What a journey ensued! To see that face when lighted up with fury is a sight for horror! I was glad to exclude it by my muff.

"Miss Planta alone attempted to speak. I did not think it incumbent on me to 'make the agreeable,' thus used; I was therefore wholly dumb: for not a word, not an apology, not one expression of being sorry for what I suffered, was uttered. The most horrible ill-humour, violence, and rudeness, were all that were shown. Mr. de Luc was too much provoked to take his usual method of passing all off by constant talk: and as I had never seen him venture to appear provoked before, I felt a great obligation to his kindness.

"When we were about half-way, we stopped to water the horses. He then again pulled up the glass, as if from absence. A voice of fury exclaimed, 'Let it down! without, I won't go!'

"'I am sure,' cried he, 'all Mrs. de Luc's plants will be killed by this frost!'

"For the frost was very severe indeed.

"Then he proposed my changing places with Miss Planta, who sat opposite Mrs. Schwellenberg, and consequently on the sheltered side.

"'Yes!' cried Mrs. Schwellenberg, 'Miss Burney might sit there, and so she ought!'

"I told her briefly I was always sick in riding backwards.

"'Oh, ver well! when you don't like it, don't do it. You might bear it when you like it! What did the poor Haggerdorn bear it! when the blood was all running down from her eyes!'

"This was too much! 'I must take, then,' I cried, 'the more warning!'"

Even this quarrel blew over. Mrs. Schwellenberg* continued to look black, and hurl thunderbolts, as long as the peccant eyes remained inflamed, but as these gradually grew well, her brows cleared and her incivility wore off, till the sufferer became far more in favour than she had ever presumed to think herself till that time. She was 'my good Miss Berney' at every other word; no one else was listened to if she would speak, and no one else was accepted for a partner at piquet if she would play. Fanny found no cause to which she could attribute this change, and believed the whole mere matter of caprice.

In the autumn of 1787, the newspapers began to make frequent mention of Miss Burney's name. Paragraphs appeared regretting her long silence, and the employment to which it was supposed to be attributable.† Fanny had many regrets connected with her situation: she lamented her dependence on her odious colleague; she lamented the inferiority of most of her associates; she lamented her separation from her old friends; but we have no reason to think that she repined at the want of liberty to print and publish. At least we cannot discover any passage in her Diary indicating such a feeling. Presently the paragraphs proceeded to mingle rumours with regrets. The 'World' was informed that Miss Burney 'had resigned her place about the Queen, and had been promoted to attend the Princesses, an office far more suited to her character and abilities.' Then followed

---

* Croker was told by the Right Hon. Joseph Planta, on the authority of Miss Planta, that Mrs. Schwellenberg was so despotic that she was better served, and more attended to than the Queen herself. 'Her servant always waited at the step of her door that she might not have to ring a bell; and a very constant expression of hers was, that if such and such a thing was good enough for her Majesty, it was not good enough for *her.*'—Jesse's 'George III.,' vol. ii., App., p. 539.

† 'I flatter myself *you* will never be royally gagged and promoted to fold muslins, as has been lately wittily said on Miss Burney, in the List of five hundred living authors.'—Walpole to Hannah More, July 12, 1788.

a contradiction. 'The rumour of resignation was premature, and only arose from thoughts of the benefit the
education of the Princesses might reap from Miss Burney's
virtues and accomplishments.' Such speculations made
it needful for their subject to explain herself to the Queen.
Fanny hastened to repudiate all participation in the idea
that it could be promotion to her to be transferred from
the service of her Majesty to that of the Princesses; she
disclaimed, with equal warmth, having the slightest wish
for such a transference. There can be no doubt that she
was perfectly sincere. The Queen, she felt, had some
regard for her, and she had a decided attachment to the
Queen. 'Oh,' she sighed, 'were there no Mrs. Schwellenberg!'

One cannot help wondering if the question whether
some more worthy position at Court might not be found
for Miss Burney occurred to the Queen, or to herself, at
this interview. If such a thought did present itself, it
does not seem to have been mentioned by either. Fanny
had early conceived the notion that the Queen intended
to employ her as an English reader. She was not
altogether wrong. She had been occasionally called on
to read, but the result did not prove very satisfactory.
At the first trial her voice was quite unmanageable; when
she had concluded, the Queen talked of the *Spectator* she
had read, but forebore saying anything of any sort about
the reader. Of a subsequent attempt we have this record:
'Again I read a little to the Queen—two *Tatlers*; both
happened to be very stupid; neither of them Addison's,
and therefore reader and reading were much on a par:
for I cannot arrive at ease in this exhibition to her
Majesty; and where there is fear or constraint, how de-
ficient, if not faulty, is every performance!' For the office
of preceptress to the Princesses she was even less fitted

than for that of reader to their mother. Probably Mrs.
Goldsworthy and Miss Planta were much better qualified
to instruct their young charges than Miss Burney would
have been. This may be confessed without the slightest
reflection on her extraordinary talents. She could afford
to have it known that her education had been neglected.
It was nothing that she had withdrawn rather ungra-
ciously from Johnson's Latin lessons. It was little that
she did not understand a word of the German which the
Royal Family commonly spoke among themselves. Hardly
any Englishwomen in those days read Latin, or were
acquainted with the language of Goethe and Wieland.
But Miss Burney had not even a strong taste for reading.
At the height of her fame, her knowledge of ordinary
English authors was surprisingly limited. Queen Charlotte,
who read a good deal in French and English, as well as in
German, was disappointed by the scanty furniture of her
attendant's book-shelves. And whenever her Majesty or
anyone else at Court mentioned any standard or current
work in her presence, it almost invariably happened that
she had not read it. One evening, Cowper's 'Task' was
referred to, and she was asked if she knew the poem;
'Only by character,' was her answer. She had not even
that amount of acquaintance with Churchill's Satires, the
very existence of which seems to have been unknown to
her. Akenside's works she knew of only by some quotations which she had heard from Mr. Locke. It may, perhaps, be urged that Cowper was then quite a new writer,
and that the fame of Mark Akenside and Charles
Churchill, though bright when she was a child, had
become dim before she grew up. Well, then, take Goldsmith. No poems were more popular than Oliver's when
Fanny began to see the world in Martin's Street; yet we
have her confession that she never read the 'Traveller,'

or ' The Deserted Village,' till a friend made her a present
of them in 1790.*   This being so, we cannot wonder that
she had never heard of Falconer's ' Shipwreck ' when
Colonel Digby produced a copy of that work.   She appears
to have been barely aware of Cumberland's ' Observer,' a
production in which she herself and most of her friends
were referred to, until the Queen read some passages to
her, and afterwards lent her the volumes.   She had not
seen Hawkins's ' Life of Johnson ' when the King first
mentioned it to her, and ' talked it over with great
candour and openness.'   Nor did she take much interest
in literary questions.   The Scotch ballad of ' The
Gaberlunzie Man,' then lately printed in Germany, she
threw aside almost contemptuously, though it had been
lent her by the Queen.   About Shakspeare her views
were those of a most loyal subject.   She reads Hamlet
to Mrs. Delany, and this is her comment : ' How noble
a play it is, considered in parts ! how wild and how
improbable, taken as a whole !   But there are speeches,
from time to time, of such exquisite beauty of language,
sentiment, and pathos, that I could wade through the
most thorny of roads to arrive at them.'   The Queen, as
Thackeray has observed, could give shrewd opinions
about books, and we suspect she presently learned to value
her second Robe-Keeper for her brightness of intelligence,
her powers of description, and her lively humour, rather
than for the solidity or the variety of her attainments.

* ' Diary,' vol. iii., p. 245.

CHAPTER VII.

The Trial of Warren Hastings—Westminster Hall—Description of it on the
Opening Day of the Trial—Edmund Burke—The other Managers—Proces-
sion of the Peers—Entrance of the Defendant—The Arraignment—Speech
of Lord Chancellor Thurlow—Reply of Warren Hastings—Opening of the
Trial—Mr. Windham—His Admiration of Dr. Johnson—His Reflections
on the Spectacle—Bearing of the Lord Chancellor—Windham on Hastings
—William Pitt—Major Scott—Conversation with Windham—Partisanship
—Close of the First Day's Proceedings—Conference on it with the Queen—
Another Day at the Trial—Burke's Great Speech—Resemblance between
Hastings and Windham—Fox's Eloquence—Death of Mrs. Delany.

ON the 13th of February, 1788, began the trial of Warren
Hastings.   Miss Burney was furnished by the Queen with
two tickets for the opening ceremony.   She went accordingly, accompanied by her brother Charles, and also by a
Miss Gomme, of whom she was commanded to undertake
the charge.   We abridge her description of this great
spectacle.   It should be premised that the zeal with
which she espoused the side of the defence was due not
solely to the favour shown to Mr. and Mrs. Hastings by
the Court, but in an equal degree, at least, to her own
personal friendship for the accused statesman and his
wife, with whom she had become acquainted before she
joined the royal service :

" We got to Westminster Hall between nine and ten
o'clock . . . .
" The Grand Chamberlain's Box is in the centre of the
upper end of the Hall : there we sat, Miss Gomme and

myself, immediately behind the chair placed for Sir Peter Burrell. To the left, on the same level, were the green benches for the House of Commons, which occupied a third of the upper end of the Hall, and the whole of the left side: to the right of us, on the same level, was the Grand Chamberlain's Gallery . . . .

"The bottom of the Hall contained the Royal Family's Box and the Lord High Steward's . . . .

"A gallery also was run along the left side of the Hall, above the green benches, which is called the Duke of Newcastle's Box, the centre of which was railed off into a separate apartment for the reception of the Queen and four eldest Princesses, who were then *incog.*, not choosing to appear in state, and in their own Box.

"In the middle of the floor was placed a large table, and at the head of it the seat for the Chancellor, and round it seats for the Judges, the Masters in Chancery, the Clerks, and all who belonged to the Law ; the upper end, and the right side of the room, was allotted to the Peers in their robes; the left side to the Bishops and Archbishops.

"Immediately below the Great Chambelain's Box was the place allotted for the Prisoner. On his right side was a box for his own Counsel, on his left the Box for the Managers, or Committee, for the Prosecution; and these three most important of all the divisions in the Hall were all directly adjoining to where I was seated . . . .

"The business did not begin till near twelve o'clock. The opening to the whole then took place, by the entrance of the *Managers of the Prosecution ;* all the company were already long in their boxes or galleries.

"I shuddered, and drew involuntarily back, when, as the doors were flung open, I saw Mr. Burke, as Head of the Committee, make his solemn entry. He held a scroll in his hand, and walked alone, his brow knit with corroding care and deep labouring thought—a brow how different to that which had proved so alluring to my warmest admiration when first I met him! so highly as he had been my favourite, so captivating as I had found his manners and conversation in our first acquaintance, and so much as I owed to his zeal and kindness to me and my affairs in its progress! How did I grieve to behold him now the cruel Prosecutor (such to me he appeared) of an injured and innocent man!

"Mr. Fox followed next, Mr. Sheridan, Mr. Windham, Messrs. Anstruther, Grey, Adam, Michael Angelo Taylor, Pelham, Colonel North, Mr. Frederick Montagu, Sir Gilbert Elliot, General Burgoyne, Dudley Long, etc. . . .

"When the Committee Box was filled, the House of Commons at large took their seats on their green benches . . . .

"Then began the procession, the Clerks entering first, then the Lawyers according to their rank, and the Peers, Bishops, and Officers, all in their coronation robes; concluding with the Princes of the Blood,—Prince William, son to the Duke of Gloucester, coming first, then the Dukes of Cumberland, Gloucester, and York, then the Prince of Wales; and the whole ending by the Chancellor, with his train borne.

"They then all took their seats.

"A Serjeant-at-Arms arose, and commanded silence. . . .

"Then some other officer, in a loud voice, called out, as well as I can recollect, words to this purpose :—'Warren Hastings, Esquire, come forth! Answer to the charges brought against you; save your bail, or forfeit your recognizance!'

"Indeed I trembled at these words, and hardly could keep my place when I found Mr. Hastings was being brought to the bar. He came forth from some place immediately under the Great Chamberlain's Box, and was preceded by Sir Francis Molyneux, Usher of the Black Rod; and at each side of him walked his Bails, Messrs. Sullivan and Sumner.

"The moment he came in sight, which was not for full ten minutes after his awful summons, he made a low bow to the Chancellor and Court facing him. I saw not his face, as he was directly under me. He moved on slowly, and, I think, supported between his two Bails, to the opening of his own Box; there, lower still, he bowed again; and then, advancing to the bar, he leant his hands upon it, and dropped on his knees; but a voice in the same moment proclaiming he had leave to rise, he stood up almost instantaneously, and a third time profoundly bowed to the Court.

"What an awful moment this for such a man!—a man fallen from such a height of power to a situation so humiliating—from the almost unlimited command of so large a part of the Eastern World to be cast at the feet of his enemies, of the great tribunal of his country, and of the nation at large, assembled thus in a body to try and to judge him! Could even his prosecutors at that moment look on—and not shudder at least, if they did not blush?

"The crier, I think it was, made, in a loud and hollow voice, a public proclamation, 'That Warren Hastings, Esquire, late Governor-General of Bengal, was now on his trial for high crimes and misdemeanours, with which he was charged by the Commons of Great Britain; and that all persons whatsoever who had aught to allege against him were now to stand forth.'

"A general silence followed, and the Chancellor, Lord Thurlow, now made his speech . . . .

"Again Mr. Hastings made the lowest reverence to the

Sir J. Reynolds.   A. Dawson Ph. sc.   Thos Watson.

Warren Hastings.

Court, and, leaning over the bar, answered, with much agitation, through evident efforts to suppress it, 'My Lords—impressed—deeply impressed—I come before your Lordships, equally confident in my own integrity, and in the justice of the Court before which I am to clear it.' . . . .

"A general silence again ensued, and then one of the lawyers opened the cause. He began by reading from an immense roll of parchment the general charges against Mr. Hastings, but he read in so monotonous a chant that nothing else could I hear or understand than now and then the name of Warren Hastings.

"During this reading, to which I vainly lent all my attention, Mr. Hastings, finding it, I presume, equally impossible to hear a word, began to cast his eyes around the House, and having taken a survey of all in front and at the sides, he turned about and looked up; pale looked his face—pale, ill, and altered. I was much affected by the sight of that dreadful harass which was written on his countenance. Had I looked at him without restraint, it could not have been without tears. I felt shocked, too, shocked and ashamed, to be seen by him in that place. I had wished to be present from an earnest interest in the business, joined to firm confidence in his powers of defence; but *his* eyes were not those I wished to meet in Westminster Hall . . . .

"Another lawyer now arose, and read so exactly in the same manner, that it was utterly impossible to discover even whether it was a charge or an answer.

"Such reading as this, you may well suppose, set everybody pretty much at their ease; and but for the interest I took in looking from time to time at Mr. Hastings, and watching his countenance, I might as well have been away. He seemed composed after the first half-hour, and calm; but he looked with a species of indignant contempt towards his accusers, that could not, I think, have been worn had his defence been doubtful. Many there are who fear for him; for me, I own myself wholly confident in his acquittal . . . .

"At length I was called by a 'How d'ye do, Miss Burney?' from the Committee Box! And then I saw young Mr. Burke, who had jumped up on the nearest form to speak to me. Pleasant enough! I checked my vexation as well as I was able, since the least shyness on my part to those with whom formerly I had been social must instantly have been attributed to Court influence; and therefore, since I could not avoid the notice, I did what I could to talk with him as heretofore. He is, besides, so amiable a young man, that I could not be sorry to see him again, though I regretted it should be just in that place, and at this time . . . .

"The moment I was able to withdraw from young Mr. Burke, Charles, who sat behind me, leant down and told me a gentleman had just desired to be presented to me.

"'Who?' quoth I.

"'Mr. Windham,' he answered.

"I really thought he was laughing, and answered accordingly; but he assured me he was in earnest, and that Mr. Windham had begged him to make the proposition. What could I do? There was no refusing: yet a planned meeting with another of the Committee, and one deep in the prosecution, and from whom one of the hardest charges has come—could anything be less pleasant as I was then situated?

"The Great Chamberlain's Box is the only part of the hall that has any communication with either the Committee Box or the House of Commons, and it is also the very nearest to the prisoner. Mr. Windham I had seen twice before—both times at Miss Monckton's; and anywhere else I should have been much gratified by his desire of a third meeting, as he is one of the most agreeable, spirited, well-bred, and brilliant conversers I have ever spoken with. He is a neighbour, too, now, of Charlotte's. He is member for Norwich, and a man of family and fortune, with a very pleasing, though not handsome face, a very elegant figure, and an air of fashion and vivacity . . . .

" I was sorry to see him make one of a set that appeared so inveterate against a man I believe so injuriously treated; and my concern was founded upon the good thoughts I had conceived of him, not merely from his social talents, which are yet very uncommon, but from a reason dearer to my remembrance. He loved Dr. Johnson—and Dr. Johnson returned his affection. Their political principles and connexions were opposite, but Mr. Windham respected his venerable friend too highly to discuss any points that could offend him ; and showed for him so true a regard, that, during all his late illnesses, for the latter part of his life, his carriage and himself were alike at his service, to air, visit, or go out, whenever he was disposed to accept them.

" Nor was this all ; one tender proof he gave of warm and generous regard, that I can never forget, and that rose instantly to my mind when I heard his name, and gave him a welcome in my eyes when they met his face. It is this : Dr. Johnson, in his last visit to Lichfield, was taken ill, and waited to recover strength for travelling back to town in his usual vehicle, a stage-coach. As soon as this reached the ears of Mr. Windham, he set off for Lichfield in his own carriage, to offer to bring him back to town in it, and at his own time . . . .

" Charles soon told me he was at my elbow . . . .

13—2

"After the first compliments he looked around him, and exclaimed, 'What an assembly is this! How striking a *spectacle!* I had not seen half its splendour down there. You have it here to great advantage; you lose some of the Lords, but you gain all the Ladies. You have a very good place here.'

"'Yes; and I may safely say I make a very impartial use of it : for since here I have sat, I have never discovered to which side I have been listening!'

"He laughed, but told me they were then running through the charges.

"'And is it essential,' cried I, 'that they should so run them through that nobody can understand them? Is that a form of law?'

"He agreed to the absurdity; and then, looking still at the *spectacle,* which indeed is the most splendid I ever saw, arrested his eyes upon the Chancellor. 'He looks very well from hence,' cried he; 'and how well he acquits himself on these solemn occasions! With what dignity, what loftiness, what high propriety, he comports himself!' . . . .

"Suddenly, his eye dropped down upon poor Mr. Hastings : the expression of his face instantly lost the gaiety and ease with which it had addressed me; he stopped short in his remarks; he fixed his eyes steadfastly on this new, and but too interesting object, and after viewing him some time in a sort of earnest silence, he suddenly exclaimed, as if speaking to himself, and from an impulse irresistible—'What a sight is that! to see that man, that small portion of human clay, that poor feeble machine of earth, enclosed now in that little space, brought to that Bar, a prisoner in a spot six foot square—and to reflect on his late power! Nations at his command! Princes ͻstrate at his feet!—What a change! how must he feel —'

" He stopped, and I said not a word. I was glad to see him thus impressed; I hoped it might soften his enmity. I found, by his manner, that he had never, from the Committee Box, looked at him . . . .

" Recovering, now, from the strong emotion with which the sight of Mr. Hastings had filled him, he looked again around the Court, and pointed out several of the principal characters present, with arch and striking remarks upon each of them, all uttered with high spirit, but none with ill-nature.

" ' Pitt,' cried he, ' is not here!—a noble stroke that for the annals of his administration! A trial is brought on by the whole House of Commons in a body, and he is absent at the very opening! However,' added he, with a very meaning laugh, ' I'm glad of it, for 'tis to his eternal disgrace!'

" Mercy! thought I, what a friend to kindness is party!

" ' Do you see Scott?' cried he.

" ' No, I never saw him; pray show him me.'

" ' There he is, in green; just now by the Speaker, now moved by the Committee; in two minutes more he will be somewhere else, skipping backwards and forwards; what a grasshopper it is!'

" ' I cannot look at him,' cried I, ' without recollecting a very extraordinary letter from him, that I read last summer in the newspaper, where he answers some attack that he says has been made upon him, because the term is used of " a very insignificant fellow;" and he printed two or three letters in the Public Advertiser, in following days, to prove, with great care and pains, that he knew it was all meant as an abuse of himself, from those words!'

" ' And what,' cried he, laughing, ' do you say to that notion now you see him?'

" ' That no one,' cried I, examining him with my glass, ' can possibly dispute his claim !'

" What pity that Mr. Hastings should have trusted his cause to so frivolous an agent ! I believe, and indeed it is the general belief, both of foes and friends, that to his officious and injudicious zeal the present prosecution is wholly owing."

A long conversation—or rather several conversations, for the talk was interrupted more than once—ensued, in the course of which Miss Burney, much to the astonishment of Windham, who knew her friendship for Burke, declared herself a partisan of Hastings, while at the same time she admitted that she knew nothing of the merits of the case—had not even read the charges against the late Governor-General. " I had afterwards," she writes, " to relate a great part of this to the Queen herself. She saw me engaged in such close discourse, and with such apparent interest on both sides, with Mr. Windham, that I knew she must else form conjectures innumerable. So candid, so liberal is the mind of the Queen, that she not only heard me with the most favourable attention towards Mr. Windham, but was herself touched even to tears by the relation. We stayed but a short time after this last conference ; for nothing more was attempted than reading over the charges and answers, in the same useless manner."

Miss Burney went again to Westminster Hall on the second day of Burke's opening speech :

" All I had heard of his eloquence, and all I had conceived of his great abilities, was more than answered by his performance. Nervous, clear, and striking was almost all that he uttered : the main business, indeed, of his coming forth was frequently neglected, and not seldom

wholly lost; but his excursions were so fanciful, so entertaining, and so ingenious, that no miscellaneous hearer,
like myself, could blame them. It is true he was unequal,
but his inequality produced an effect which, in so long a
speech, was perhaps preferable to greater consistency,
since, though it lost attention in its falling off, it recovered
it with additional energy by some ascent unexpected and
wonderful. When he narrated, he was easy, flowing, and
natural; when he declaimed, energetic, warm, and brilliant.
The sentiments he interspersed were as nobly conceived
as they were highly coloured; his satire had a poignancy
of wit that made it as entertaining as it was penetrating;
his allusions and quotations, as far as they were English
and within my reach, were apt and ingenious; and the
wild and sudden flights of his fancy, bursting forth from
his creative imagination in language fluent, forcible, and
varied, had a charm for my ear and my attention wholly
new and perfectly irresistible."

She was again visited in her box by Windham, who, on
Hastings happening to look up, remarked that he did not
like his countenance. "I could have told him," says
Fanny, "that he is reckoned extremely like himself; but
after such an observation I would not venture, and only
said: 'Indeed, he is extremely altered: it was not so he
looked when I conceived for him that prepossession I
have owned to you.'" The Queen's reporter, for such
she was, attended a third time on the day after the
Lords had enraged the Managers by deciding that
they must complete their case upon all the charges
before the accused was called on for any defence. She
heard Mr. Fox speak for five hours with a violence
that did not make her forget what she was told of his
being in a fury. His eloquence was not nearly so much

to her taste as Burke's. Fox's countenance struck her as hard and callous; his violence, she thought, had that sort of monotony that seemed to result from its being factitious, and she felt less pardon for that than for any extravagance in Mr. Burke, whose excesses seemed at least to be un-affected and sincere. Mr. Fox appeared to her to have no such excuse; 'he looked all good-humour and negligent ease the instant before he began a speech of uninterrupted passion and vehemence, and he wore the same careless and disengaged air the very instant he had finished.' After other attendances at the trial, Miss Burney's mind was withdrawn from the subject in which she took so much interest by the last illness and death of Mrs. Delany. The old lady, who died on the 15th of April, 1788, left some small remembrances to the friend whose companionship had soothed her latter days.

CHAPTER VIII.

FOR many years George III. had enjoyed unbroken good
health. 'The King,' wrote a well-informed gossipper*
in January, 1788, 'walks twelve miles on his way from
Windsor to London, which is more than the Prince of
Wales can do.' Early in June, however, his Majesty was
disturbed by passing symptoms, which proved to be fore-
runners of an illness famous in English history. The
complaint, in its first stage, was called a bilious attack;
and when the patient appeared to have thrown it off, he
was advised by his physician to drink the waters at
Cheltenham for a month, in order to complete his recovery. On June 8, the King sent his old friend Dr.
Hurd, Bishop of Worcester, a letter, in which he announced his intended journey into Gloucestershire; and,
at the same time, proposed to enlarge his excursion by
paying a visit to Hartlebury, and afterwards attending the
Festival of the Three Choirs, which that year was to be

---

* Mr. Storer, the friend of George Selwyn.

held at Worcester. His Majesty went on to say that, as feeding the hungry was a Christian duty, he should expect his correspondent, while welcoming the sovereign to his cathedral city, to provide some cold meat for his refreshment.

The hearty old English gentleman, in fact, was minded to enjoy his holiday in the homely way that pleased him best. On July 12, the Court travelled from Windsor to Cheltenham, where Bays Hill Lodge, a seat of the Earl of Fauconberg, situated just outside the town, had been engaged for the royal party. The Lodge was so small that their Majesties, with the three eldest Princesses who accompanied them, could only be housed there at a considerable sacrifice of state and ceremony. No bed could be provided within its walls for any male person but the King. The female attendants on the Queen and her daughters were limited to one lady-in-waiting, Miss Burney, Miss Planta, and the wardrobe women.

' Is *this* little room for your Majesty?' exclaimed Fanny, in astonishment.

' Stay till you see your own,' retorted the Queen, laughing, ' before you call this little.'

Colonel Gwynn, the King's equerry, and Colonel Digby, the Queen's vice-chamberlain, slept in a house at some distance. The Queen consented to dine with these officers, though until then the German etiquette in which she was trained had prevented her from sitting at table with men of much higher rank.

During his stay at Cheltenham, the King drank the waters at six o'clock every morning, and afterwards took exercise in the 'Walks.' This parade was conducted in the same manner as the terracing at Windsor. The King led the way, with the Queen leaning on his arm; the Princesses followed them; and the equerry brought up the rear. The unaccustomed spectacle drew crowds from the town and the country round, causing at first a good deal of inconvenience, which the King bore with his usual good-nature. In the course of July, he made excursions with his family to several places of interest in the neighbourhood: to Oakley Grove, the seat of Lord Bathurst, patron of Pope and Prior, and friend of Bolingbroke and Atterbury; to the Abbey Church of Tewkesbury; to Gloucester Cathedral; to Croome Court, the abode of Lord Coventry and his beautiful Countess.

Miss Burney and Miss Planta were not of the suite on these expeditions, and altogether enjoyed much more liberty than fell to their lot at Windsor or Kew. Sometimes they amused themselves by making little excursions on their own account. On the day of the royal visit to Oakley Grove, they went over to Gloucester, where Miss Planta had an acquaintance in the person of the philanthropic printer, Robert Raikes, still remembered as the originator of Sunday-schools. Mr. Raikes felt himself a man of importance; he had been invited to Windsor, and had had the honour of a long conversation with the Queen. Apparently the notice taken of him had left traces on his manner. 'He is somewhat too flourishing,' Fanny whispered to her Diary, 'somewhat too forward, somewhat too voluble; but he is worthy, benevolent, good-natured, and good-hearted, and therefore the overflowings of successful spirits and delighted vanity must meet with some allowance.' Bating this little self-complacency, the good man proved himself a capital host and guide, entertaining the royal attendants in a handsome and painstaking manner, which obtained their warm acknowledgments.

But Miss Burney beguiled her leisure principally in improving her acquaintance with Colonel Digby, who paid her marked attention during their attendance at the Gloucestershire watering-place. This courteous, insinuating colonel suited her taste far better than the more soldier-like equerries whom she met at Court. She had conceived a decided inclination for him from the moment of his first introduction to her. 'He is a man,' she then wrote, 'of the most scrupulous good-breeding; diffident, gentle, and sentimental in his conversation, and assiduously attentive in his manners.' He had now the additional recommendation that belongs to a widower grieving over joys departed, yet not despairing of consolation. In this state of mind, he neglected no opportunity of making himself agreeable to a lady whose disposition was so congenial to his own. Even a fit of the gout, which detained him from his official duties, could not prevent him from limping over to the Lodge to sit with Miss Burney. They talked of many things, but chiefly of books, of the affections, of happiness, and of religion. The famous authoress astonished her admirer not a little by the discovery she was fain to make of the many books she had never yet read. Her candour encouraged him to produce his own stores of literature, which were much more extensive than hers. This pensive gentleman, we need scarcely say, was addicted to reciting poetry and passages of pious sentiment. One line especially, which was often in his mouth, about 'the chastity of silent woe,' Fanny found peculiarly beautiful, though it might have reminded her of the Irish Commissary whom she had met at Brighton. Very soon quotations were succeeded by readings. The pair studied together Akenside's poems, Falconer's 'Shipwreck,' Carr's Sermons, and a work* entitled 'Original Love-Letters,' with which we own ourselves unacquainted. Presently,

* By William Combe [1741-1823], author of 'Doctor Syntax.'

however, as the air of Cheltenham did not appear to suit the Colonel's gout, he began to think of taking leave of absence.

A visit from the Duke of York was expected while the Court was at Cheltenham. So eager was the King for the society of this his favourite son, that he caused a portable wooden house to be moved from the further end of the town, and joined on to Bays Hill Lodge, for the reception of the Prince and his attendants. The work consumed much time and money, but the fond father was bent on lodging his Frederick close to himself. All this care and affection met with the too familiar return. The Duke arrived on August 1, according to his appointment; and Miss Burney describes the King's joy as only less extreme than the transport he had shown when, a year before, she had seen the darling appear at Windsor after long absence in Germany. But the Prince, so much looked for, would remain no more than a single night. Military business, he declared, required him to be in London by the next day but one, which was Sunday; however, he would travel all Saturday night that he might be able to spend a second evening with his parents. ' I wonder,' cried Colonel Digby, with the sententious propriety which charmed our Fanny, ' how these Princes, who are thus forced to steal even their travelling from their sleep, find time to say their prayers !'

On August 5 the Court visited Worcester for the purpose of attending the Musical Festival. When the royal *cortége* stopped at the Bishop's palace, " the King had an huzza that seemed to vibrate through the whole town, the Princess Royal's carriage had a second, and the equerries a third. The mob then," proceeds the Diary, " as ours drew on in succession, seemed to deliberate whether or not we also should have a cheer; but one of them soon decided the matter by calling out, ' These are the maids of honour !' and immediately gave us an huzza that made us quite ashamed." The opening performance of the Festival next morning did not much gratify the historian. ' It was very long and intolerably tedious, consisting of Handel's gravest pieces and fullest choruses, and concluding with a sermon, concerning the institution of the charity, preached by Dr. Langhorne.'* A second morning performance to which she went did not strike her more favourably. One of the evening concerts she liked better. Of another she observes that it ' was very Handelian, though not exclusively so.'

At the close of the Festival the royal party and their suite returned to Cheltenham. On the same evening Colonel Digby took his departure, 'leaving me,' says Fanny, ' firmly impressed with a belief that I shall find in him a true, an honourable, and even an affectionate friend for life.' Next day an express came from him with a letter for Miss Burney, begging her to inform the Queen that the Mastership of St. Katharine's Hospital, which was in her Majesty's gift, had just become void by the death of the occupant. In a few more days it was announced that the vacant appointment had been conferred on Mr. Digby.

By August 16, the Court was again established at Windsor, and a rumour began to circulate of the Colonel's gallantry at Cheltenham, mingled with a second rumour of his being then confined by gout at a house where lived Miss Gunning, for whom he had been supposed to have an admiration. Both reports were disregarded by Mrs. Schwellenberg's assistant, who could think of nothing but the change from the pleasant society which she had lately enjoyed to the arrogance, the contentiousness, the pre-

* The writer and translator, 1735-1799.

suming ignorance, that assailed her in the hated dining-room at the Queen's Lodge. 'What scales,' she wrote, 'could have held and weighed the heart of F. B. as she drove past the door of her revered lost comforter, to enter the apartment inhabited by such qualities!'

One strange visitor, however, she had at starting, who provided her with some little amusement:

"AUGUST 18TH.—Well, now I have a new personage to introduce to you, and no small one; ask else the stars, moon and planets! While I was surrounded with band-boxes, and unpacking, Dr. Shepherd* was announced. Eager to make his compliments on the safe return, he forced a passage through the back avenues and stairs, for he told me he did not like being seen coming to me at the front door, as it might create some jealousies amongst the other Canons! A very commendable circumspection! but whether for my sake or his own he did not particularize.

" M. de Lalande, he said, the famous astronomer, was just arrived in England, and now at Windsor, and he had expressed a desire to be introduced to me. . . . .

" His business was to settle bringing M. de Lalande to see me in the evening. I told him I was much honoured, and so forth, but that I received no evening company, as I was officially engaged. He had made the appointment, he said, and could not break it, without affronting him; besides, he gave me to understand it would be an honour to me for ever to be visited by so great an astronomer. . . .

" In the midst of tea, with a room full of people, I was called out to Dr. Shepherd! . . . . I hurried into the next room, where I found him with his friend, M. de Lalande. What a reception awaited me! how unexpected a one from a famed and great astronomer! M. de Lalande

* One of the Canons of Windsor.

advanced to meet me—I will not be quite positive it was on tiptoe, but certainly with a mixture of jerk and strut that could not be quite flat-footed. He kissed his hand with the air of a *petit maître,* and then broke forth into such an harangue of Eloges, so solemn with regard to its own weight and importance, and so *fade* with respect to the little personage addressed, that I could not help thinking it lucky for the planets, stars, and sun, they were not bound to hear his comments, though obliged to undergo his calculations.

"On my part sundry profound reverences with now and then an '*Oh, monsieur!*' or '*c'est trop d'honneur,*' acquitted me so well, that the first harangue being finished, on the score of general and grand reputation, *Eloge* the second began, on the excellence with which '*cette célèbre demoiselle*' spoke French!

"This may surprise you, my dear friends; but you must consider M. de Lalande is a great *discoverer.*

"Well, but had you seen Dr. Shepherd! he looked lost in sleek delight and wonder, that a person to whom he had introduced M. de Lalande should be an object for such fine speeches.

"This gentleman's figure, meanwhile, corresponds no better with his discourse than his scientific profession, for he is an ugly little wrinkled old man, with a fine showy waistcoat, rich lace ruffles, and the grimaces of a dentist. I believe he chose to display that a Frenchman of science could be also a man of gallantry.

"I was seated between them, but the good doctor made no greater interruption to the florid professor than I did myself: he only grinned applause, with placid, but ineffable satisfaction.

"Nothing therefore intervening, *Eloge* the third followed, after a pause no longer than might be necessary for due admiration of *Eloge* the second. This had for *sujet* the fair female sex; how the ladies were now all improved; how they could write, and read, and spell; how a man nowadays might talk with them and be understood, and how delightful it was to see such pretty creatures turned rational!

"And all this, of course, interspersed with particular observations and most pointed applications; nor was there in the whole string of compliments which made up the three *bouquets,* one single one amongst them that might have disgraced any *petit maître* to utter, or any *petite maîtresse* to hear.

"The third being ended, a rather longer pause ensued. I believe he was dry, but I offered him no tea. I would not voluntarily be accessory to detaining such great personages from higher avocations. I wished him next to go and study the stars; from the moon he seemed so lately arrived there was little occasion for another journey.

"I flatter myself he was of the same opinion, for the fourth *Eloge* was all upon his unhappiness in tearing himself away from so much merit, and ended in as many bows as had accompanied his entrance.

"I suppose, in going, he said, with a shrug, to the Canon, '*M. le Docteur, c'est bien gênant, mais il faut dire des jolies choses aux dames!*'

"He was going the next day to see Dr. Maskelyne's* Observatory. Well! I have had him first in mine!"

The King, at his return to Windsor, appeared to be restored to his usual health. In less than two months, however, he was again out of order. We give the most noteworthy passage in Miss Burney's account of his subsequent illness as it fell under her observation. She

---

* Dr. Maskelyne (1732-1811) was Astronomer Royal at the time.

was doing double duty at this time, in the absence of Mrs. Schwellenberg, who had gone to Weymouth for her health. The Court was at Kew when the first apprehensions arose :

"OCTOBER 17TH.—Our return to Windsor is postponed till to-morrow. The King is not well; he has not been quite well some time, yet nothing I hope alarming, though there is an uncertainty as to his complaint not very satisfactory.

" 19TH.—The Windsor journey is again postponed, and the King is but very indifferent. Heaven preserve him! there is something unspeakably alarming in his smallest indisposition. I am very much with the Queen, who, I see, is very uneasy, but she talks not of it.

" 20TH.—The King was taken very ill in the night, and we have all been cruelly frightened; but it went off, and, thank Heaven! he is now better.

" 25TH.—The King was so much better, that our Windsor journey at length took place, with permission of Sir George Baker,* the only physician his Majesty will admit.

" I had a sort of conference with his Majesty, or rather I was the object to whom he spoke, with a manner so uncommon, that a high fever alone could account for it; a rapidity, a hoarseness of voice, a volubility, an earnestness—a vehemence, rather—it startled me inexpressibly, yet with a graciousness exceeding all I ever met with before—it was almost kindness! Heaven—Heaven preserve him! The Queen grows more and more uneasy. She alarms me sometimes for herself; at other times she has a sedateness that wonders me still more.

" SUNDAY, OCT. 26TH.—The King was prevailed upon

---

* Physician in Ordinary to the King : born 1722 ; died 1809.

not to go to chapel this morning. I met him in the passage from the Queen's room; he stopped me, and conversed upon his health near half an hour, still with that extreme quickness of speech and manner that belongs to fever; and he hardly sleeps, he tells me, one minute all night; indeed, if he recovers not his rest, a most delirious fever seems to threaten him. He is all agitation, all emotion, yet all benevolence and goodness, even to a degree that makes it touching to hear him speak. He assures everybody of his health; he seems only fearful to give uneasiness to others, yet certainly he is better than last night. Nobody speaks of his illness, nor what they think of it.

"NOVEMBER 1ST.—Our King does not advance in amendment; he grows so weak that he walks like a gouty man, yet has such spirits that he has talked away his voice, and is so hoarse it is painful to hear him. The Queen is evidently in great uneasiness. God send him better! . . .

" During the reading this morning, twice, at pathetic passages, my poor Queen shed tears. ' How nervous I am!' she cried; ' I am quite a fool! Don't you think so ?'

" No, ma'am !' was all I dared answer.

" The King was hunting. Her anxiety for his return was greater than ever. The moment he arrived he sent a page to desire to have coffee and take his bark in the Queen's dressing-room. She said she would pour it out herself, and sent to inquire how he drank it.

" The King is very sensible of the great change there is in himself, and of her disturbance at it. It seems, but Heaven avert it! a threat of a total breaking up of the constitution. This, too, seems his own idea. I was present at his first seeing Lady Effingham on his return to Windsor this last time. 'My dear Effy,' he cried, 'you see me, all at once, an old man.'

"I was so much affected by this exclamation, that I wished to run out of the room. Yet I could not but recover when Lady Effingham, in her well-meaning but literal way, composedly answered, 'We must all grow old, sir; I am sure I do.'

"He then produced a walking-stick which he had just ordered. 'He could not,' he said, 'get on without it; his strength seemed diminishing hourly.'

"He took the bark, he said; 'but the *Queen,*' he cried, 'is my physician, and no man need have a better; she is my *Friend,* and no man *can* have a better.'

"How the Queen commanded herself I cannot conceive. . . . Nor can I ever forget him in what passed this night. When I came to the Queen's dressing-room he was still with her. He constantly conducts her to it before he retires to his own. He was begging her not to speak to him when he got to his room, that he might fall asleep, as he felt great want of that refreshment. He repeated this desire, I believe, at least a hundred times, though, far enough from needing it, the poor Queen never uttered one syllable; He then applied to me, saying he was really very well, except in that one particular, that he could not sleep. . . .

"3RD.—We are all here in a most uneasy state. The King is better and worse so frequently, and changes so, daily, backwards and forwards, that everything is to be apprehended, if his nerves are not some way quieted. I dreadfully fear he is on the eve of some severe fever. The Queen is almost overpowered with some secret terror. I am affected beyond all expression in her presence, to see what struggles she makes to support serenity. To-day she gave up the conflict when I was alone with her, and burst into a violent fit of tears. It was very, very terrible to see! . . .

"5TH.—I found my poor Royal Mistress, in the morning, sad and sadder still; something horrible seemed impending. . . .

"I was still wholly unsuspicious of the greatness of the cause she had for dread. Illness, a breaking up of the constitution, the payment of sudden infirmity and premature old age for the waste of unguarded health and strength —these seemed to me the threats awaiting her; and great and grievous enough, yet how short of the fact! . . .

"At noon the King went out in his chaise, with the Princess Royal, for an airing. I looked from my window to see him; he was all smiling benignity, but gave so many orders to the postilions, and got in and out of the carriage twice, with such agitation, that again my fear of a great fever hanging over him grew more and more powerful. Alas! how little did I imagine I should see him no more for so long—so black a period!

"When I went to my poor Queen, still worse and worse I found her spirits. . . .

"The Princess Royal soon returned. She came in cheerfully, and gave, in German, a history of the airing, and one that seemed comforting.

"Soon after, suddenly arrived the Prince of Wales. He came into the room. He had just quitted Brighthelmstone. Something passing within seemed to render this meeting awfully distant on both sides. She asked if he should not return to Brighthelmstone? He answered yes, the next day. He desired to speak with her; they retired together. . .

"Only Miss Planta dined with me. We were both nearly silent: I was shocked at I scarcely knew what, and she seemed to know too much for speech. She stayed with me till six o'clock, but nothing passed, beyond general solicitude that the King might get better.

" Meanwhile, a stillness the most uncommon reigned over the whole house. Nobody stirred ; not a voice was heard ; not a motion. I could do nothing but watch, without knowing for what : there seemed a strangeness in the house most extraordinary.

" At seven o'clock Columb came to tell me that the music was all forbid, and the musicians ordered away !

" This was the last step to be expected, so fond as his Majesty is of his concert, and I thought it might have rather soothed him : I could not understand the prohibition ; all seemed stranger and stranger."

One after another, the usual evening visitors made their appearance. First the equerries, and then Colonel Digby, who had reached the palace that afternoon, came in to tea. "Various small speeches now dropped, by which I found the house was all in disturbance, and the King in some strange way worse, and the Queen taken ill !" Presently the whole truth was divulged. " The King, at dinner, had broken forth into positive delirium, which long had been menacing all who saw him most closely ; and the Queen was so overpowered as to fall into violent hysterics. All the Princesses were in misery, and the Prince of Wales had burst into tears. No one knew what was to follow—no one could conjecture the event."

At ten o'clock, Miss Burney went to her own room to be in readiness for her usual summons to the Queen :

" Two long hours I waited—alone, in silence, in ignorance, in dread ! I thought they would never be over ; at twelve o'clock I seemed to have spent two whole days in waiting. I then opened my door, to listen, in the passage, if anything seemed stirring. Not a sound could I hear. My apartment seemed wholly separated from life and motion. Whoever was in the house kept at the other end, and not even a servant crossed the stairs or passage by my rooms.

"I would fain have crept on myself, anywhere in the world, for some inquiry, or to see but a face, and hear a voice, but I did not dare risk losing a sudden summons.

"I re-entered my room, and there passed another endless hour, in conjectures too horrible to relate.

"A little after one, I heard a step—my door opened—and a page said I must come to the Queen.

"I could hardly get along—hardly force myself into the room; dizzy I felt, almost to falling. But the first shock passed, I became more collected. Useful, indeed, proved the previous lesson of the evening: it had stilled, if not mortified my mind, which had else, in a scene such as this, been all tumult and emotion.

"My poor Royal Mistress! never can I forget her countenance—pale, ghastly pale she looked; she was seated to be undressed, and attended by Lady Elizabeth Waldegrave and Miss Goldsworthy; her whole frame was disordered, yet she was still and quiet.

"These two ladies assisted me to undress her, or rather I assisted them, for they were firmer, from being longer present; my shaking hands and blinded eyes could scarce be of any use.

"I gave her some camphor julep, which had been ordered her by Sir George Baker. 'How cold I am!' she cried, and put her hand on mine; marble it felt! and went to my heart's core!

"The King, at the instance of Sir George Baker, had consented to sleep in the next apartment, as the Queen was ill. For himself, he would listen to nothing. Accordingly, a bed was put up for him, by his own order, in the Queen's second dressing-room, immediately adjoining to the bedroom. He would not be further removed. Miss Goldsworthy was to sit up with her, by the King's direction.

"I would fain have remained in the little dressing-room, on the other side the bedroom, but she would not permit it . . . . I went to bed, determined to preserve my strength to the utmost of my ability, for the service of my unhappy mistress. I could not, however, sleep. I do not suppose an eye was closed in the house all night.

"6TH.—I rose at six, dressed in haste by candle-light, and unable to wait for my summons in a suspense so awful, I stole along the passage in the dark, a thick fog intercepting all faint light, to see if I could meet with Sandys,* or anyone, to tell me how the night had passed.

" When I came to the little dressing-room, I stopped, irresolute what to do. I heard men's voices; I was seized with the most cruel alarm at such a sound in her Majesty's dressing-room. I waited some time, and then the door opened, and I saw Colonel Goldsworthy and Mr. Batterscomb. I was relieved from my first apprehension, yet shocked enough to see them there at this early hour. They had both sat up there all night, as well as Sandys. Every page, both of the King and Queen, had also sat up, dispersed in the passages and ante-rooms; and oh, what horror in every face I met!

" I waited here, amongst them, till Sandys was ordered by the Queen to carry her a pair of gloves. I could not resist the opportunity to venture myself before her. I glided into the room, but stopped at the door: she was in bed, sitting up; Miss Goldsworthy was on a stool by her side!

* Wardrobe-woman to the Queen.

"I feared approaching without permission, yet could not prevail with myself to retreat. She was looking down, and did not see me. Miss Goldsworthy, turning round, said, ''Tis Miss Burney, ma'am.'

"She leaned her head forward, and in a most soft manner, said, ' Miss Burney, how are you ?'

"Deeply affected, I hastened up to her; but, in trying to speak, burst into an irresistible torrent of tears.

"My dearest friends, I do it at this moment again, and can hardly write for them ; yet I wish you to know all this piercing history right.

"She looked like death—colourless and wan; but nature is infectious; the tears gushed from her own eyes, and a perfect agony of weeping ensued, which, once begun, she could not stop; she did not, indeed, try; for when it subsided, and she wiped her eyes, she said, ' I thank you, Miss Burney—you have made me cry; it is a great relief to me—I had not been able to cry before, all this night long.'

"Oh, what a scene followed ! what a scene was related ! The King, in the middle of the night, had insisted upon seeing if his Queen was not removed from the house ; and he had come into her room, with a candle in his hand, opened the bed-curtains, and satisfied himself she was there, and Miss Goldsworthy by her side. This observance of his directions had much soothed him ; but he stayed a full half-hour, and the depth of terror during that time no words can paint. The fear of such another entrance was now so strongly upon the nerves of the poor Queen that she could hardly support herself.

"The King—the royal sufferer—was still in the next room, attended by Sir George Baker and Dr. Heberden,*

* William Heberden. Born in 1710; Fellow of St. John's College, Cambridge ; practised medicine at Cambridge ; removed to London in 1748 ; wrote ' Medical Commentaries ;' passed the later years of his life at Windsor, where he died in 1801.

and his pages, with Colonel Goldsworthy occasionally, and as he called for him. He kept talking unceasingly; his voice was so lost in hoarseness and weakness, it was rendered almost inarticulate; but its tone was still all benevolence—all kindness—all touching graciousness.

"It was thought advisable the Queen should not rise, lest the King should be offended that she did not go to him; at present he was content, because he conceived her to be nursing for her illness.

"But what a situation for her! She would not let me leave her now; she . . . frequently bid me listen, to hear what the King was saying or doing. I did, and carried the best accounts I could manage, without deviating from truth, except by some omissions. Nothing could be so afflicting as this task; even now, it brings fresh to my ear his poor exhausted voice. 'I am nervous,' he cried; 'I am not ill, but I am nervous: if you would know what is the matter with me, I am nervous. But I love you both very well; if you would tell me truth: I love Dr. Heberden best, for he has not told me a lie: Sir George has told me a lie—a white lie, he says, but I hate a white lie! If you will tell me a lie, let it be a black lie!'

"This was what he kept saying almost constantly, mixed in with other matter, but always returning, and in a voice that truly will never cease vibrating in my recollection."

In the course of the morning, a third physician—Dr. Warren*—arrived. His opinion was eagerly awaited by the Queen; but he did not come to her, though repeatedly summoned. At length, Lady Elizabeth brought news that he and the other two physicians were gone over to the Castle to the Prince of Wales.

* Richard Warren. Born about 1732; Fellow of the Royal and Antiquarian Societies; Physician in Ordinary to George III. and the Prince of Wales; died in 1797.

" I think a deeper blow I had never witnessed. Already to become but second, even for the King! The tears were now wiped : indignation arose, with pain, the severest pain, of every species.

" In about a quarter of an hour Colonel Goldsworthy sent in to beg an audience. It was granted, a long cloak only being thrown over the Queen.

" He now brought the opinion of all the physicians in consultation, ' That her Majesty would remove to a more distant apartment, since the King would undoubtedly be worse from the agitation of seeing her, and there could be no possibility to prevent it while she remained so near.'

" She instantly agreed, but with what bitter anguish! Lady Elizabeth, Miss Goldsworthy, and myself attended her ; she went to an apartment in the same row, but to which there was no entrance except by its own door. It consisted of only two rooms, a bedchamber, and a dressing-room. They are appropriated to the lady-in-waiting when she is here.

" At the entrance into this new habitation the poor wretched Queen once more gave way to a perfect agony of grief and affliction; while the words, ' What will become of me! What will become of me!' uttered with the most piercing lamentation, struck deep and hard into all our hearts. Never can I forget their desponding sound ; they implied such complicated apprehension."

Of the scene in the King's rooms that night, Miss Burney had only a momentary glimpse. Being sent on some commission for the Queen, " When I gently opened," she writes, " the door of the apartment to which I was directed, I found it quite filled with gentlemen and attendants, arranged round it on chairs and sofas, in dead

silence. It was a dreadful start with which I retreated;
for anything more alarming and shocking could not be
conceived—the poor King within another door, unconscious anyone was near him, and thus watched, by dread
necessity, at such an hour of the night!" How the hours
passed she heard the next day.

"7TH.—While I was yet with my poor royal sufferer
this morning the Prince of Wales came hastily into the
room. He apologized for his intrusion, and then gave a
very energetic history of the preceding night. It had
been indeed most affectingly dreadful! The King had
risen in the middle of the night, and would take no denial
to walking into the next room. There he saw the large
congress I have mentioned : amazed and in consternation, he demanded what they did there? Much followed
that I have heard since, particularly the warmest eloge
on his dear son Frederick, his favourite, his friend.
' Yes,' he cried, ' Frederick is my friend !'—and this son
was then present amongst the rest, but not seen !

"Sir George Baker was there, and was privately exhorted by the gentlemen to lead the King back to his
room ; but he had not courage : he attempted only to
speak, and the King penned him in a corner, told him he
was a mere old woman—that he wondered he had ever
followed his advice, for he knew nothing of his complaint,
which was only nervous !

"The Prince of Wales, by signs and whispers, would
have urged others to have drawn him away, but no one
dared approach him, and he remained there a considerable time, ' Nor do I know when he would have been
got back,' continued the Prince, ' if at last Mr. Digby*
had not undertaken him. I am extremely obliged to Mr.

* We have substituted the real name here for the ' Mr. Fairly ' of the printed
Diary.

Digby indeed. He came boldly up to him, and took him by the arm, and begged him to go to bed, and then drew him along, and said he must go. Then he said he would not, and cried, ' Who are you ?' ' I am Mr. Digby, sir,' he answered, ' and your Majesty has been very good to me often, and now I am going to be very good to you, for you must come to bed, sir : it is necessary to your life. And then he was so surprised that he let himself be drawn along just like a child; and so they got him to bed. I believe else he would have stayed all night !' "

On the following morning, an incident occurred which showed the revolution that had taken place in the palace. Mr. Smelt had travelled post from York on hearing of the King's illness, but had not yet been able to see either him or the Queen. Accidentally meeting with the Prince of Wales, he was received by his old pupil with much apparent kindness of manner, and invited to remain at Windsor till he could be admitted to the Queen's presence. Not small, then, was his surprise when, on returning shortly afterwards to the Upper Lodge, the porter handed him his great-coat, saying that he had express orders from the Prince to refuse him re-admission.[*] ' From this time,' continues Miss Burney, ' as the poor King grew worse, general hope seemed universally to abate; and the Prince of Wales now took the government of the house into his own hands. Nothing was done but by his orders, and he was applied to in every difficulty. The Queen interfered not in anything; she lived entirely in her two new rooms, and spent the

---

[*] It is fair to mention that the Prince afterwards apologized to his old sub-governor on meeting him at Kew.—Diary, iii. 117. Even Walpole, chary as he usually is of praise, has done justice to the " singular virtues and character," the " ignorance of the world as well as its depravity," of this estimable person. " Happy for the Prince," adds Walpole, " had he had no other governor ; at least no other director of his morals and opinions of government."—See Walpole's ' Reign of George III.,' vol. iv., pp. 312, 313.

whole day in patient sorrow and retirement with her daughters.'

The next news which reached the suite was that the Prince had issued commands to the porter to admit only four persons into the house on any pretence whatever; and these were ordered to repair immediately to the equerry-room below stairs, while no one whatsoever was to be allowed to go to any other apartment. 'From this time,' adds the Diary, 'commenced a total banishment from all intercourse out of the house, and an unremitting confinement within its walls.' The situation was rendered even more intolerable by the sudden return of Mrs. Schwellenberg from Weymouth. On the 10th, Miss Burney writes: 'This was a most dismal day. The dear and most suffering King was extremely ill, the Queen very wretched, poor Mrs. Schwellenberg all spasm and horror, Miss Planta all restlessness, the house all mystery, and my only informant and comforter [Colonel Digby] distanced.'

Then began a series of tantalizing fluctuations. From November 12 to the 15th, the King showed some signs of amendment; but on Sunday, the 16th, all was dark again in the Upper Lodge. 'The King was worse. His night had been very bad; all the fair promise of amendment was shaken; he had now some symptoms even dangerous to his life. Oh, good heaven! what a day did this prove! I saw not a human face, save at dinner; and then what faces! gloom and despair in all, and silence to every species of intelligence.' The special prayer for the King's recovery was used this day for the first time in St. George's Chapel. Evidences of the general distress were apparent on all sides. 'Every prayer in the service in which he was mentioned brought torrents of tears from all the suppliants that joined in them.' Fanny ran away after the service to avoid inquiries.

Of the afternoon she writes: 'It was melancholy to see the crowds of former welcome visitors who were now denied access. The Prince reiterated his former orders; and I perceived from my window those who had ventured to the door returning back in tears.' She received letters of inquiry, but was not at liberty to write a word. The night of the 19th was no better than that of the 16th. 'Mr. Charles Hawkins came,' proceeds the Diary. 'He had sat up. Oh, how terrible a narrative did he drily give of the night!—short, abrupt, peremptorily bad, and indubitably hopeless. I did not dare alter, but I greatly softened this relation, in giving it to my poor Queen.' On this day Dr. Warren told Mr. Pitt that there was now every reason to believe that the King's disorder was no other than actual lunacy.

All the equerries, except one who was ill, were now on duty. The King, in his rambling talk, reproached them with want of attention. They lost their whole time at table, he said, by sitting so long over their bottle; 'and Mr. Digby,' he added on one occasion, 'is as bad as any of them; not that he stays so long at table, or is so fond of wine, but yet he's just as late as the rest; for he's so fond of the company of learned ladies, that he gets to the tea-table with Miss Burney, and there he stays and spends his whole time.' Colonel Digby, in repeating this speech to the lady interested, was good enough to explain to her that what the King had in his head was—Miss Gunning. The Colonel went on to mention Miss Gunning's learning and accomplishments with great praise, yet 'with that sort of general commendation that disclaims all peculiar interest;' touched, in a tone of displeasure, on the report that had been spread concerning him and her; lightly added something about its utter falsehood; and concluded by saying that this, in the then

confused state of the King's mind, was what his Majesty
meant by 'learned ladies.' More puzzled than enlightened
by this explanation, Fanny, with some hesitation, assented
to the insinuating Chamberlain's suggestion that she should
think no more of what the King had said, but allow the
Colonel ' to come and drink tea with her very often.'

From the 20th to the 28th there was no improvement
in the condition of the sick monarch. Nearly all who
saw him, whether physicians or members of the suite,
began to abandon hope of his recovery ; only Sir Lucas
Pepys, an old friend of the Burneys, who was now added
to the medical attendants, inclined to a more encouraging
view. The proceedings of the 28th are entered in the
Diary, as follows :

" Sir Lucas made me a visit, and informed me of all the
medical proceedings ; and told me, in confidence, we were
to go to Kew to-morrow, though the Queen herself had
not yet concurred in the measure ; but the physicians
joined to desire it, and they were supported by the
Princes. The difficulty how to get the King away from
his favourite abode was all that rested. If they even
attempted force, they had not a doubt but his smallest
resistance would call up the whole country to his fancied
rescue ! Yet how, at such a time, prevail by persuasion ?

" He moved me even to tears, by telling me that none of
their own lives would be safe if the King did not recover,
so prodigiously high ran the tide of affection and loyalty.
All the physicians received threatening letters daily, to
answer for the safety of their monarch with their lives !
Sir George Baker had already been stopped in his
carriage by the mob, to give an account of the King; and
when he said it was a bad one, they had furiously exclaimed, ' The more shame for you !'

"After he left me, a Privy Council was held at the Castle, with the Prince of Wales; the Chancellor, Mr. Pitt, and all the officers of state were summoned, to sign a permission for the King's removal. The poor Queen gave an audience to the Chancellor—it was necessary to sanctify their proceedings. The Princess Royal and Lady Courtown attended her. It was a tragedy the most dismal!

" The Queen's knowledge of the King's aversion to Kew made her consent to this measure with the extremest reluctance; yet it was not to be opposed: it was stated as much the best for him, on account of the garden: as here there is none but what is public to spectators from the terrace, or tops of houses. I believe they were perfectly right, though the removal was so tremendous.

" The physicians were summoned to the Privy Council, to give their opinions, upon oath, that this step was necessary.

" Inexpressible was the alarm of everyone, lest the King, if he recovered, should bear a lasting resentment against the authors and promoters of this journey. To give it, therefore, every possible sanction, it was decreed that he should be seen both by the Chancellor and Mr. Pitt.

" The Chancellor went into his presence with a tremor such as, before, he had been only accustomed to inspire; and when he came out, he was so extremely affected by the state in which he saw his Royal master and patron that the tears ran down his cheeks, and his feet had difficulty to support him.

" Mr. Pitt was more composed, but expressed his grief with so much respect and attachment, that it added new weight to the universal admiration with which he is here beheld.

"All these circumstances, with various others of equal sadness which I must not relate, came to my knowledge through Sir Lucas, Mr. de Luc, and my noon attendance upon her Majesty, who was compelled to dress for her audience of the Chancellor.

"SATURDAY, NOVEMBER 29TH.—Shall I ever forget the varied emotions of this dreadful day!

"I rose with the heaviest of hearts, and found my poor Royal Mistress in the deepest dejection: she told me now of our intended expedition to Kew. Lady Elizabeth hastened away to dress, and I was alone with her for some time.

"Her mind, she said, quite misgave her about Kew: the King's dislike was terrible to think of, and she could not foresee in what it might end. She would have resisted the measure herself, but that she had determined not to have upon her own mind any opposition to the opinion of the physicians.

"The account of the night was still more and more discouraging: it was related to me by one of the pages, Mr. Brawan; and though a little I softened or omitted particulars, I yet most sorrowfully conveyed it to the Queen.

"Terrible was the morning!—uninterruptedly terrible! all spent in hasty packing up, preparing for we knew not what, nor for how long, nor with what circumstances, nor scarcely with what view! We seemed preparing for captivity, without having committed any offence; and for banishment, without the least conjecture when we might be recalled from it.

"The poor Queen was to get off in private: the plan settled between the Princes and the physicians was that her Majesty and the Princesses should go away quietly, and then that the King should be told that they were gone, which was the sole method they could devise to prevail with him to follow. He was then to be allured by a promise of seeing them at Kew; and, as they knew he would doubt their assertion, he was to go through the rooms and examine the house himself.

"I believe it was about ten o'clock when her Majesty departed: drowned in tears, she glided along the passage, and got softly into her carriage, with two weeping Princesses, and Lady Courtown, who was to be her Lady-in-waiting during this dreadful residence.

"Then followed the third Princess, with Lady Charlotte Finch. They went off without any state or parade, and a more melancholy scene cannot be imagined. There was not a dry eye in the house. The footmen, the housemaids, the porter, the sentinels—all cried even bitterly as they looked on. . . .

"It was settled the King was to be attended by three of his gentlemen in the carriage, and to be followed by the physicians, and preceded by his pages. But all were to depart on his arrival at Kew, except his own Equerry-in-waiting. . . .

"Miss Planta and I were to go as soon as the packages could be ready, with some of the Queen's things. Mrs. Schwellenberg was to remain behind, for one day, in order to make arrangements about the jewels. . . .

"In what confusion was the house! Princes, Equerries, physicians, pages—all conferring, whispering, plotting, and caballing, how to induce the King to set off!

"At length we found an opportunity to glide through the passage to the coach; Miss Planta and myself, with her maid and Goter. . . . .

"We were almost wholly silent all the way.

"When we arrived at Kew, we found the suspense with which the King was awaited truly terrible. Her Majesty had determined to return to Windsor at night, if he came not. We were all to forbear unpacking in the meanwhile. . . .

"Dinner went on, and still no King. We now began to grow very anxious, when Miss Planta exclaimed that she thought she heard a carriage. We all listened. 'I hope!' I cried. . . The sound came nearer, and presently a carriage drove into the front court. I could see nothing, it was so dark; but I presently heard the much-respected voice of the dear unhappy King, speaking rapidly to the porter, as he alighted from the coach. . . .

"The poor King had been prevailed upon to quit Windsor with the utmost difficulty: he was accompanied by General Harcourt, his aide-de-camp, and Colonels Goldsworthy and Welbred—no one else! He had passed all the rest with apparent composure, to come to his carriage, for they lined the passage, eager to see him once more! and almost all Windsor was collected round the rails, etc., to witness the mournful spectacle of his departure, which left them in the deepest despondence, with scarce a ray of hope ever to see him again.

"The bribery, however, which brought, was denied him! —he was by no means to see the Queen! . . .

"I could not sleep all night—I thought I heard the poor King. He was under the same range of apartments, though far distant, but his indignant disappointment haunted me. The Queen, too, was very angry at having promises made in her name which could not be kept. What a day altogether was this!

"SUNDAY, NOVEMBER 30TH.—Here, in all its dread colours, dark as its darkest prognostics, began the Kew campaign. I went to my poor Queen at seven o'clock: the Princess Augusta arose and went away to dress, and I received her Majesty's commands to go down for inquiries. She had herself passed a wretched night, and already lamented leaving Windsor.

"I waited very long in the cold dark passages below, before I could find anyone of whom to ask intelligence. The parlours were without fires, and washing. I gave directions afterwards to have a fire in one of them by seven o'clock every morning.

"At length I procured the speech of one of the pages, and heard that the night had been the most violently bad of any yet passed!—and no wonder!

"I hardly knew how to creep upstairs, frozen both within and without, to tell such news; but it was not received as if unexpected, and I omitted whatever was not essential to be known.

"Afterwards arrived Mrs. Schwellenberg, so oppressed between her spasms and the house's horrors, that the oppression she inflicted ought perhaps to be pardoned. It was, however, difficult enough to bear! Harshness, tyranny, dissension, and even insult, seemed personified. I cut short details upon this subject—they would but make you sick."

CHAPTER IX.

State of Kew Palace—Dr. Willis and his Son called in—Progress under the
New Doctors—Party Spirit—The Regency Question—Attacks on the Queen
—Fluctuations in the King's State—Violence of Burke—Extraordinary Scene
between the King and Miss Burney in Kew Gardens—Marked Improvement
of the King—The Regency Bill postponed—The King informs Miss Burney
of his Recovery—The Restoration—Demonstrations of Joy—Return to
Windsor—Old Routine resumed—Reaction.

THE beginning of December saw the diminished and
imprisoned household suffering under an increase of
apprehensions. The condition of the King became even
more alarming; the Queen began to sink as she had
not done before. From the outer world came sinister
rumours, the duration of the malady threatening a
Regency—'a word,' says Fanny, 'which I have not yet
been able to articulate.' Inside, the palace at Kew was
'in a state of cold and discomfort past all imagination.'
It had never been a winter residence, and there was
nothing prepared to fit it for becoming one. Not only
were the bedrooms of the Princesses without carpets, but
so out of repair was the building, that a plentiful supply of
sandbags had to be provided to moderate the gales that
blew through the doors and windows. The parlour in
which Miss Burney had to sit with the Schwellenberg
was carpetless, chilly, and miserable; and even this was
locked in the morning on Fanny's admission of having
used it before breakfast; Cerbera barking out that,
'when everybody went to her room, she might keep an

inn—what you call hotel.' These domestic incon-
veniences endured for some time. By degrees, however,
the worst of them were obviated. The bare boards were
wholly or partially covered; the apartments allotted to
the family were refurnished and redistributed; and Miss
Burney was no longer exposed to the cold damps of a
dark passage while awaiting the page who brought her
for the Queen the first news of how the night had been
passed by the patient.

Hitherto no progress had been made towards a
successful treatment of the King's malady. In the early
days of December, however, even the Queen felt it useless
to disguise any longer the nature of the attack, and ex-
perts in mental disease were accordingly added to the
staff of physicians. Fortunately, a right choice was made
at the first trial. The new advisers selected were Dr.
Francis Willis, a clergyman who for twenty-eight years had
devoted himself to the cure of lunacy, and his son, Dr.
John Willis, who was associated with him in practice.
The arrival of these two country practitioners—they
came from Lincolnshire—revived the hopes which the
Court physicians, by their dissensions and general
despondency, had well-nigh destroyed. Though decried
by the regular faculty as interlopers, if not charlatans, the
Doctors Willis took the hearts of all at Kew Palace by
storm. Mr. Digby pronounced them ' fine, lively, natural,
independent characters. Miss Burney, on making their
acquaintance, heartily re-echoed this praise :

" I am extremely struck with both these physicians.
Dr. Willis is a man of ten thousand; open, honest,
dauntless, light-hearted, innocent, and high-minded: I
see him impressed with the most animated reverence and
affection for his royal patient; but it is wholly for his

character—not a whit for his rank. Dr. John, his eldest
son, is extremely handsome, and inherits, in a milder
degree, all the qualities of his father; but living more in
the general world, and having his fame and fortune still
to settle, he has not yet acquired the same courage, nor is
he, by nature, quite so sanguine in his opinions. The
manners of both are extremely pleasing, and they both
proceed completely their own way, not merely unacquainted with Court etiquette, but wholly, and most
artlessly, unambitious to form any such acquaintance."

The new doctors at once modified the treatment to
which the King had been subject, and the effects of the
change were speedily apparent:

"DECEMBER 11TH.—To-day we have had the fairest
hopes; the King took his first walk in Kew garden!
There have been impediments to this trial hitherto, that
have been thought insurmountable, though, in fact, they
were most frivolous. The walk seemed to do him good,
and we are all in better spirits about him than for this
many and many a long day past."

It was not to be expected that the advance to restoration would proceed without break or check. On the 17th
we have the entry: ' My account this morning was quite
afflictive once more;' but under date of the 22nd we
read: ' With what joy did I carry this morning an exceeding good account of the King to my royal mistress!
It was trebly welcome, as much might depend upon it in
the resolutions of the House concerning the Regency,
which was of to-day's discussion;' and in some notes
summing up the remaining days of the year, we have:
' The King went on, now better, now worse, in a most
fearful manner; but Sir Lucas Pepys never lost sight of
hope, and the management of Dr. Willis and his two

sons* was most wonderfully acute and successful. Yet, so much were they perplexed and tormented by the inter-ruptions given to their plans and methods, that they were frequently almost tempted to resign the undertaking from anger and confusion.'

The new year opened amid the same alternations of progress and relapse. In society, the war of politics took a new departure from the King's derangement. Sup-porters of the Administration were confident of his speedy recovery; the Opposition were indefatigable in spreading the belief that his disorder was incurable. The animosity on both sides rose to a height which had not been equalled even at Pitt's first entrance into office. 'It is a strange subject,' wrote the Archbishop of Canterbury, 'for party to insist upon, and disgraceful to the country that it should be so; but so it is.' Uneasiness and un-certainty prevailed everywhere. Some of Miss Burney's best friends began to be dismayed at her position, and at the prospect before her. Her sister Charlotte, now Mrs. Francis, wrote from Norfolk, urging that Dr. Burney's consent should be obtained to her resignation, and offer-ing her, on behalf of Mr. Francis and herself, a permanent residence in their house. Evidently, Fanny's family regarded her as a helpless person, requiring to be looked after and taken care of. Her faith, however, in the com-forting predictions of the Willises and Sir Lucas Pepys remained unshaken, and she would not hear of quitting her post.

A fresh trouble had by this time arisen. The Queen could not escape becoming involved in the strife of parties. The Prince of Wales and the Duke of York were naturally impatient to push their afflicted father from his seat.

* Dr. Willis was now assisted by a younger son, named Thomas, who, like himself, was in holy orders, as well as by his eldest son John.

What they wanted in brains was amply supplied by the combined genius of the Whig leaders—by Fox, and Burke, and Sheridan—all embittered at having been so often checkmated by the young statesman whom they had flouted as a mere boy. What the Princes lacked in tenacity of purpose was driven into them by the incessant cry of myriad place-hunters, yelling like famished wolves. The first thought of the faction was how to clutch power as soon as might be ; their second, how to engross it as exclusively as possible. No scruple was made of declaring that all places would be vacated and refilled, even if the Regency were to last only a single day.* That there would be a complete change of Administration was a matter of course. But beyond this, changes were meditated in the army, and other departments of the State, which it was known must grievously offend the King, should they come to his knowledge. Among other promotions, every colonel in favour with the Prince or the Duke was to be raised to the rank of Major-General. Mrs. Fitzherbert, it was said, was to be created a Duchess.†

Next to Pitt and his colleagues, the chief obstacle to the speedy execution of these notable projects was Queen Charlotte. It was not to be expected that a wife would be as ready as the heir-apparent to believe in the confirmed insanity of the head of the house. It was excusable, to say the least, that one who for more than twenty - eight years had filled, without reproach, the station of Queen Consort, should object to be effaced with her lord, until the necessity for his seclusion was unmistakably demonstrated. And when discord raged in the medical council, when Dr. Warren pronounced the King

* 'Cornwallis Papers,' vol. i., p. 406.
† 'Buckingham Papers,' vol. ii., p. 104 ; 'Auckland Correspondence,' vol. ii., pp. 251, 289.

to be 'rather worse' than he had been at Windsor, while to Sir Lucas and the specialists, as well as to ordinary observers, his condition appeared most hopeful, she might surely be pardoned for leaning to the favourable view. Partisans, however, were too excited to listen to reason. The clergyman from Lincolnshire was denounced in the Opposition newspapers as a mere empiric and creature of Pitt. The most scurrilous abuse was heaped upon the Queen. Both in the press, and in the House of Commons, she was accused of being in league with Willis to misrepresent the state of the King's health, in order to prevent the Prince, her son, from being invested with the authority of Regent. Pitt, having no option but to propose a Regency, was proceeding with the utmost caution, and seeking to lay on the expectant Viceroy several restrictions, which his character seemed to call for, and which assuredly have not been disapproved by the judgment of posterity. Besides limiting the Prince's power to confer peerages and pensions, and to alienate royal property, the Premier recommended that the care and management of the King's person, as well as the appointments in the household, should be entrusted to the Queen. Perhaps no part of the Government's plan aroused more angry hostility than this. ' How would the King on his recovery,' demanded Burke in Parliament, ' be pleased at seeing the patronage of the Household taken from the Prince of Wales, his representative, and given to the Queen? He must be shocked at the idea.' Allusions to these attacks on one who so little deserved them occur in Miss Burney's Diary about this time:

"JANUARY 10TH.—The King again is not so well; and new evidences are called for in the House, relative to his state. My poor Royal Mistress now droops. I grieve—

grieve to see her !—but her own name and conduct called in question ! Who can wonder she is shocked and shaken ? Was there not enough before, firmly as she supported it ?

"11TH.—This morning Dr. John gave me but a bad account of the poor King. His amendment is not progressive; it fails, and goes back, and disappoints most grievously; yet it would be nothing were the case and its circumstances less discussed, and were expectation more reasonable.

"12TH.—A melancholy day : news bad both at home and abroad. At home, the dear, unhappy King still worse; abroad, new examinations voted of the physicians ! Good Heaven ! what an insult does this seem from Parliamentary power, to investigate and bring forth to the world every circumstance of such a malady as is ever held sacred to secrecy in the most private families ! How indignant we all feel here no words can say."

Macaulay is very severe on poor Miss Burney for the want of correct constitutional principles shown in this last entry. He cites the passage to prove that the second Robe-Keeper's 'way of life was rapidly impairing her powers of reasoning and her sense of justice;' that, as he elsewhere says, this existence was as incompatible with health 'of mind as the air of the Pomptine Marshes with health of body.' The critic is perfectly right in stating that the motion which roused indignation at Kew was made by Mr. Pitt, who was regarded as the King's champion, though he should have added that it was brought forward in response to a challenge from the Opposition. But Miss Burney felt as a woman, and wrote as a woman, not as a politician. Had she been a politician, she would still have been entitled to the indulgence which was being claimed and abused by every speaker and journalist on the side opposed to the Court. Consider the debates and the scandalous charges that she read daily in the newspapers. And if she erred, she erred in company with a large number of other heretics who should have been far better fortified in sound doctrine than herself. If the atmosphere of the palace was unwholesome, it was much less contaminating than the malaria of Carlton House. If the novelist was wrong in thinking that the House of Commons ought not to concern itself with the details of the King's illness, what is to be said of the eminent Whigs who maintained that the Legislature had nothing to do with any question relating to the disposition of the regal authority? What shall be said for Alexander Wedderburn, then Chief Justice of the Common Pleas, and afterwards Lord Chancellor, who advised the Prince of Wales to seize on the Regency without consulting either House of Parliament? Or what can be urged for Fox himself, who asserted his patron's right to take this course, in the very face of the assembled Commons? 'It is melancholy,' says Macaulay, 'to see genius sinking into such debasement.' What words, then, shall we apply to Edmund Burke, who scandalized both sides of the House by declaring that 'the Almighty had hurled the monarch from his throne, and plunged him into a condition which drew down upon him the pity of the meanest peasant in his kingdom'? Miss Burney, still feeling and writing as a woman, could not accuse her old friend Burke of being debased, though she sadly laments over him as 'that most misguided of vehement and wild orators.'* Such was the virulence engendered in a spectator of the misery at Court by associating with Leonard Smelt and Colonel Digby.

* Diary, vol. iii., p. 163.

" Kew Palace, Monday, February 2nd.—What an adventure had I this morning! one that has occasioned me the severest personal terror I ever experienced in my life.

" Sir Lucas Pepys still persisting that exercise and air were absolutely necessary to save me from illness, I have continued my walks, varying my gardens from Richmond to Kew, according to the accounts I received of the movements of the King. For this I had her Majesty's permission, on the representation of Sir Lucas.

" This morning, when I received my intelligence of the King from Dr. John Willis, I begged to know where I might walk in safety. ' In Kew Gardens,' he said, ' as the King would be in Richmond.'

" ' Should any unfortunate circumstance,' I cried, ' at any time, occasion my being seen by his Majesty, do not mention my name, but let me run off without call or notice.'

" This he promised. Everybody, indeed, is ordered to keep out of sight.

" Taking, therefore, the time I had most at command, I strolled into the gardens. I had proceeded, in my quick way, nearly half the round, when I suddenly perceived, through some trees, two or three figures. Relying on the instructions of Dr. John, I concluded them to be workmen and gardeners; yet tried to look sharp, and in so doing, as they were less shaded, I thought I saw the person of his Majesty!

" Alarmed past all possible expression, I waited not to know more, but turning back, ran off with all my might. But what was my terror to hear myself pursued!—to hear the voice of the King himself loudly and hoarsely calling after me, ' Miss Burney! Miss Burney!'

" I protest I was ready to die. I knew not in what

state he might be at the time; I only knew the orders to keep out of his way were universal; that the Queen would highly disapprove any unauthorised meeting, and that the very action of my running away might deeply, in his present irritable state, offend him. Nevertheless, on I ran, too terrified to stop, and in search of some short passage, for the garden is full of little labyrinths, by which I might escape.

"The steps still pursued me, and still the poor hoarse and altered voice rang in my ears :—more and more foot-steps resounded frightfully behind me,—the attendants all running, to catch their eager master, and the voices of the two Doctor Willises loudly exhorting him not to heat himself so unmercifully.

"Heavens, how I ran! I do not think I should have felt the hot lava from Vesuvius—at least, not the hot cinders—had I so run during its eruption. My feet were not sensible that they even touched the ground.

"Soon after, I heard other voices, shriller, though less nervous, call out, 'Stop! stop! stop!'

"I could by no means consent : I knew not what was purposed, but I recollected fully my agreement with Dr. John that very morning, that I should decamp if surprised, and not be named.

"My own fears and repugnance, also, after a flight and disobedience like this, were doubled in the thought of not escaping : I knew not to what I might be exposed, should the malady be then high, and take the turn of resentment. Still, therefore, on I flew; and such was my speed, so almost incredible to relate or recollect, that I fairly believe no one of the whole party could have overtaken me,, if these words, from one of the attendants, had not reached me, 'Doctor Willis begs you to stop!'

"'I cannot! I cannot!' I answered, still flying on,

when he called out, 'You must, ma'am; it hurts the King to run.'

" Then, indeed, I stopped—in a state of fear really amounting to agony. I turned round, I saw the two Doctors had got the King between them, and three attendants of Dr. Willis's were hovering about. They all slackened their pace, as they saw me stand still; but such was the excess of my alarm, that I was wholly insensible to the effects of a race which, at any other time, would have required an hour's recruit.

" As they approached, some · little presence of mind happily came to my command : it occurred to me that, to appease the wrath of my flight, I must now show some confidence : I therefore faced them as undauntedly as I was able, only charging the nearest of the attendants to stand by my side.

" When they were within a few yards of me, the King called out, ' Why did you run away ?'

" Shocked at a question impossible to answer, yet a little assured by the mild tone of his voice, I instantly forced myself forward to meet him, though the internal sensation, which satisfied me this was a step the most proper to appease his suspicions and displeasure, was so violently combated by the tremor of my nerves, that I fairly think I may reckon it the greatest effort of personal courage I have ever made.

" The effort answered : I looked up, and met all his wonted benignity of countenance, though something still of wildness in his eyes. Think, however, of my surprise, to feel him put both his hands round my two shoulders, and then kiss my cheek !

" I wonder I did not really sink, so exquisite was my affright when I saw him spread out his arms ! Involuntarily, I concluded he meant to crush me : but the Willises, who have never seen him till this fatal illness, not knowing how very extraordinary an action this was from him, simply smiled and looked pleased, supposing, perhaps, it was his customary salutation!

" I believe, however, it was but the joy of a heart unbridled, now, by the forms and proprieties of established custom and sober reason. To see any of his household thus by accident, seemed such a near approach to liberty and recovery, that who can wonder it should serve rather to elate than lessen what yet remains of his disorder!

" He now spoke in such terms of his pleasure in seeing me, that I soon lost the whole of my terror; astonishment to find him so nearly well, and gratification to see him so pleased, removed every uneasy feeling, and the joy that succeeded, in my conviction of his recovery, made me ready to throw myself at his feet to express it.

" What a conversation followed! When he saw me fearless, he grew more and more alive, and made me walk close by his side, away from the attendants, and even the Willises themselves, who, to indulge him, retreated. I own myself not completely composed, but alarm I could entertain no more.

" Everything that came uppermost in his mind he mentioned; he seemed to have just such remains of his flightiness as heated his imagination without deranging his reason, and robbed him of all control over his speech, though nearly in his perfect state of mind as to his opinions.

" What did he not say!—He opened his whole heart to me,—expounded all his sentiments, and acquainted me with all his intentions.

" The heads of his discourse I must give you briefly, as I am sure you will be highly curious to hear them, and as no accident can render of much consequence what a man says in such a state of physical intoxication.

16

"He assured me he was quite well—as well as he had ever been in his life; and then inquired how I did, and how I went on? and whether I was more comfortable?

"If these questions, in their implication, surprised me, imagine how that surprise must increase when he proceeded to explain them! He asked after the coadjutrix, laughing, and saying, 'Never mind her!—don't be oppressed—I am your friend! don't let her cast you down! —I know you have a hard time of it—but don't mind her!'

"Almost thunderstruck with astonishment, I merely curtseyed to his kind 'I am your friend,' and said nothing.

"Then presently he added, 'Stick to your father— stick to your own family—let them be your objects.'

"How readily I assented!

"Again he repeated all I have just written, nearly in the same words, but ended it more seriously: he suddenly stopped, and held me to stop too, and putting his hand on his breast, in the most solemn manner, he gravely and slowly said, 'I will protect you!—I promise you that— and therefore depend upon me!'

'I thanked him; and the Willises, thinking him rather too elevated, came to propose my walking on. 'No, no, no!' he cried, a hundred times in a breath; and their good humour prevailed, and they let him again walk on with his new companion.

"He then gave me a history of his pages, animating almost into a rage, as he related his subjects of displeasure with them, particularly with Mr. Ernst,* who,

---

* Many stories have been told of the deranged King having been brutally treated by this man Ernst, who is said on one occasion to have thrown the patient violently down, exclaiming to the attendants, 'There is your King for you!' But Ernst, who was a Page of the Back Stairs, received a pension on his retirement. It seems probable, therefore, that Ernst's supposed brutality was, as Miss Burney suggests, an illusion of the King's malady.

he told me, had been brought up by himself. I hope his ideas upon these men are the result of the mistakes of his malady.

"Then he asked me some questions that very greatly distressed me, relating to information given him in his illness, from various motives, but which he suspected to be false, and which I knew he had reason to suspect : yet was it most dangerous to set anything right, as I was not aware what might be the views of their having been stated wrong. I was as discreet as I knew how to be, and I hope I did no mischief; but this was the worst part of the dialogue.

"He next talked to me a great deal of my dear father, and made a thousand inquiries concerning his 'History of Music.' This brought him to his favourite theme, Handel ; and he told me innumerable anecdotes of him, and particularly that celebrated tale of Handel's saying of himself, 'While that boy lives, my music will never want a protector.' And this, he said, I might relate to my father.

"Then he ran over most of his oratorios, attempting to sing the subjects of several airs and choruses, but so dreadfully hoarse that the sound was terrible.

"Dr. Willis, quite alarmed at this exertion, feared he would do himself harm, and again proposed a separation. 'No, no, no!' he exclaimed, 'not yet; I have something I must just mention first.'

"Dr. Willis, delighted to comply, even when uneasy at compliance, again gave way.

"The good King then greatly affected me. He began upon my revered old friend, Mrs. Delany ; and he spoke of her with such warmth—such kindness! 'She was my friend!' he cried, 'and I loved her as a friend! I have made a memorandum when I lost her—I will show it you.'

" He pulled out a pocket-book, and rummaged some time, but to no purpose.

" The tears stood in his eyes—he wiped them, and Dr. Willis again became very anxious. ' Come, sir,' he cried, ' now do you come in and let the lady go on her walk,—come, now, you have talked a long while,—so we'll go in—if your Majesty pleases.'

" ' No, no !' he cried, ' I want to ask her a few questions ;—I have lived so long out of the world, I know nothing !'

" This touched me to the heart. We walked on together, and he inquired after various persons, particularly Mrs. Boscawen, because she was Mrs. Delany's friend ! Then, for the same reason, after Mr. Frederick Montagu, of whom he kindly said, ' I know he has a great regard for me, for all he joined the Opposition.' Lord Grey de Wilton, Sir Watkin Wynn, the Duke of Beaufort, and various others, followed.

" He then told me he was very much dissatisfied with several of his State officers, and meant to form an entire new establishment. He took a paper out of his pocket-book, and showed me his new list.

" This was the wildest thing that passed ; and Dr. John Willis now seriously urged our separating ; but he would not consent; he had only three more words to say, he declared, and again he conquered.

" He now spoke of my father, with still more kindness, and told me he ought to have had the post of Master of the Band, and not that little poor musician Parsons, who was not fit for it: ' But Lord Salisbury,' he cried, ' used your father very ill in that business, and so he did me ! However, I have dashed out his name, and I shall put your father's in,—as soon as I get loose again !'

" This again—how affecting was this !

"'And what,' cried he, 'has your father got, at last? nothing but that poor thing at Chelsea? O fie! fie! fie! But never mind! I will take care of him! I will do it myself!'

"Then presently he added, 'As to Lord Salisbury, he is out already, as this memorandum will show you, and so are many more. I shall be much better served; and when once I get away, I shall rule with a rod of iron!'

"This was very unlike himself, and startled the two good doctors, who could not bear to cross him, and were exulting at my seeing his great amendment, but yet grew quite uneasy at his earnestness and volubility.

"Finding we now must part, he stopped to take leave, and renewed again his charges about the coadjutrix. 'Never mind her!' he cried, 'depend upon me! I will be your friend as long as I live!—I here pledge myself to be your friend!' And then he saluted me again just as at the meeting, and suffered me to go on.

"What a scene! how variously was I affected by it! but, upon the whole, how inexpressibly thankful to see him so nearly himself—so little removed from recovery!

"I went very soon after to the Queen, to whom I was most eager to avow the meeting, and how little I could help it. Her astonishment, and her earnestness to hear every particular, were very great. I told her almost all. Some few things relating to the distressing questions I could not repeat; nor many things said of Mrs. Schwellenberg, which would much, and very needlessly, have hurt her."

About February 6, a further improvement in the King's state took place, which proved to be decisive. From this time, not only were his equerries allowed to attend him again in the evening, but the Queen was once more

admitted to his chamber. Singularly enough, the progress
of his recovery coincided exactly with the progress of the
Regency Bill. The latter was brought into the House of
Commons on the 5th, and on the following day a printed
copy was shown to Fanny. " I shuddered," she writes,
" to hear it named." On the 10th she reports : " The
amendment of the King is progressive, and without any
reasonable fear, though not without some few drawbacks.
The Willis family were surely sent by Heaven to restore
peace, and health, and prosperity to this miserable house!"
On the 12th the Regency Bill passed the Commons, and
was carried up to the House of Lords ; it was there
subsequently read a second time, went through Committee, and was ordered for a third reading. But that
stage was not to arrive. Miss Burney writes on the 13th :
" Oh, how dreadful will be the day when that unhappy
Bill takes place ! I cannot approve the plan of it ; the
King is too well to make such a step right. It will break
his spirits, if not his heart, when he hears and under-
stands such a deposition.

" SATURDAY, 14TH.—The King is infinitely better. Oh
that there were patience in the land, and this Regency
Bill postponed !"

Macaulay, quoting part of the entry for the 13th, leaves
it to be inferred that the writer disapproved of ' Pitt's
own Bill' under any circumstances ; he carefully omits
the words which show that her objection was to the plan
being proceeded with when the King's recovery was so
far advanced as to render it inapplicable. The Ministry
speedily made it plain that they were of the same mind
as Miss Burney. On the 17th, the Peers, on the motion
of the Lord Chancellor, adjourned the further consideration of the Regency Bill ; and a week later the measure
was finally abandoned.

"What a different house," says the Diary of the 19th, "is this house become!—sadness and terror, that wholly occupied it so lately, are now flown away, or rather are now driven out; and though anxiety still forcibly prevails, 'tis in so small a proportion to joy and thankfulness, that it is borne as if scarce an ill!" Before the month ended, Miss Burney had an assurance of the King's entire restoration from his own mouth. "The King I have seen again—in the Queen's dressing-room. On opening the door, there he stood! He smiled at my start; and, saying he had waited on purpose to see me, added, 'I am quite well now—I was nearly so when I saw you before; but I could overtake you better now.'"

All England had been intent on the little palace at Kew, where distress was now turned into rejoicing. To none of his subjects was the recovery of the royal patient a matter of indifference. To a limited party it was a source of bitter disappointment and chagrin. To the immense majority it brought unbounded satisfaction. It was the engrossing topic of the day. 'Nobody,' said an observer, 'talks, writes, thinks, or dreams of anything else.' On the 1st of March thanksgivings for the happy event were offered in all the churches of the capital. On the 10th the physicians took their departure from Kew. On the same day Parliament was opened by Commission under the sign manual. At sunset began a spectacle worthy of the occasion. 'London,' wrote Wraxall, 'displayed a blaze of light from one extremity to the other; the illuminations extending, without any metaphor, from Hampstead and Highgate to Clapham, and even as far as Tooting; whilst the vast distance between Greenwich and Kensington presented the same dazzling appearance. The poorest mechanics contributed their proportion, and instances were exhibited of cobblers' stalls decorated with one or two farthing candles.*

The Queen carried all the Princesses, except the youngest, up to town, to feast their eyes on streets as brilliant and crowded as Vauxhall on a gala night. It may cool our historic fervour to remember that the blaze of light which astonished our ancestors was produced by nothing more luminous than oil-lamps, and that the crowds of 1789 would pass for a sorry muster in the huge Babylon of to-day; but, after all, the scene exhibited in London, when even the cobblers' stalls were illuminated, was not without its significance on the eve of the meeting of the States General at Versailles. Cowper, usurping the functions of Thomas Warton, then poet-laureate, sang of Queen Charlotte's private expedition :

> ' Glad she came that night to prove,
> A witness undescried,
> How much the object of HER love
> Was loved by ALL beside.'

Miss Burney describes how the festive evening was spent at Kew. The Queen, at her own expense, had arranged for an illumination of the palace and courtyard as a surprise to her consort. Biagio Rebecca, by her order, had painted a grand transparency, displaying representations of " the King, Providence, Health, and Britannia, with elegant devices. When this was lighted and prepared, the Princess Amelia went to lead her papa to the front window; but first she dropped on her knees, and presented him a paper," containing some congratulatory verses which, at the Queen's desire, the narrator " had scribbled in her name for the happy occasion," and which concluded with a postscript :

> ' The little bearer begs a kiss
> From dear papa for bringing this.'

---

* Wraxall's Posthumous Memoirs, vol. iii., pp. 369, 370.

"I need not, I think, tell you," continues Fanny, "that the little bearer begged not in vain. The King was extremely pleased. He came into a room belonging to the Princesses, in which we had a party to look at the illuminations, and there he stayed above an hour: cheerful, composed, and gracious; all that could merit the great national testimony to his worth this day paid him." When at one o'clock in the morning the Queen returned to Kew, she found the King standing bare-headed at the porch, ready to hand her from the coach, and eager to assure himself of her safety. So far from being dissatisfied with anything that she had done during his illness, his affection for her was confirmed by the zeal with which she had watched over his interests.

On the 14th of March the Court left Kew for Windsor. "All Windsor," says the Diary, "came out to meet the King. It was a joy amounting to ecstasy. I could not keep my eyes dry all day long. A scene so reversed! Sadness so sweetly exchanged for thankfulness and delight!" But the period of excitement was now over. The old routine of duty recommenced, with few incidents to relieve its monotony: there was an entertainment or two for the suite in the royal borough to celebrate the restoration; then one by one the friends and acquaintances who were assembled round the household in the early days of March dispersed to their homes; no society remained at the Upper Lodge but Cerbera and the gentlemen-in-waiting—who did *not* include Colonel Digby; hardly any change marked the succession of days, save an occasional visit to Kew, and now and then a journey to town for a drawing-room. In the Public Thanksgiving, held at St. Paul's on the 23rd of April, Fanny appears to have had no part, though she received as mementoes of the occasion a medal of green and gold,

and a fan ornamented with the words: *Health restored to
one, and happiness to millions.*   Once, when in London, she
had a visit from Miss Gunning, who called to inquire after
the Queen's health, and who 'looked serious, sensible,
interesting,' though she said but little, and in that little
managed to introduce the name of Mr. Digby.   Degree
by degree, Fanny's spirits sank to the point of actual despondency, till she writes, 'A lassitude of existence creeps
sensibly upon me.'   A fit of illness did not assist to
restore her cheerfulness.   Thus ended March, and thus
passed April, May, and the greater part of June.   The
King had raised some alarm by declaring his intention of
going to Germany in the summer, but, to the satisfaction
of the suite in general, and of one of the Queen's Robe-
Keepers in particular, when the time came, the physicians
advised a stay at an English watering - place in preference.

CHAPTER X.

ON the 25th of June the Court set out on a progress from
Windsor to Weymouth. Miss Burney and Miss Planta, as
was usual on these occasions, were of the suite; the
Schwellenberg, as usual, remained behind. 'The crowds
increased as we advanced, and at Winchester the town
was *one head*.' At Romsey, on the steps of the Town
Hall, a band of musicians, some in coarse brown coats
and red neckcloths, some even in smock-frocks, made a
chorus of 'God save the King,' in which a throng of
spectators joined with shouts that rent the air. 'Carriages
of all sorts lined the roadside—chariots, chaises, landaus,
carts, waggons, whiskies, gigs, phaetons—mixed and intermixed, filled within and surrounded without by faces all
glee and delight.' On the verge of the New Forest the
King was met by a party of foresters, habited in green,
with bows and bugles, who, according to ancient custom,

presented him with a pair of milk-white greyhounds, wearing silver collars, and led by silken cords.

Arrived at Lyndhurst, he drove to the old hunting-seat of Charles II., then tenanted by the Duke of Gloucester. "It is a straggling, inconvenient old house," writes Fanny, "but delightfully situated in a village—looking, indeed, at present, like a populous town, from the amazing concourse of people that have crowded into it. . . . During the King's dinner, which was in a parlour looking into the garden, he permitted the people to come to the window; and their delight and rapture in seeing their monarch at table, with the evident hungry feeling it occasioned, made a contrast of admiration and deprivation truly comic. They crowded, however, so excessively, that this can be permitted no more. They broke down all the paling, and much of the hedges, and some of the windows, and all by eagerness and multitude, for they were perfectly civil and well-behaved. . . . We continued at Lyndhurst five days. . . . On the Sunday we all went to the parish church; and after the service, instead of a psalm, imagine our surprise to hear the whole congregation join in 'God save the King!' Misplaced as this was in a church, its intent was so kind, loyal, and affectionate, that I believe there was not a dry eye amongst either singers or hearers."

On the 30th of June the royal party quitted Lyndhurst, and arrived at Weymouth in the course of the evening. 'The journey was one scene of festivity and rejoicing.' The change of air, the bustle of travelling, the beauty of the summer landscapes, the loyalty of the population, had restored Fanny's tone, and brought back the glow she had experienced at the time of the King's convalescence. Her enthusiasm lent a touch of enchantment to everything she saw. Salisbury and Blandford welcomed their sovereign with displays and acclamations that fairly carried her away. At Dorchester the windows and roofs of the quaint old houses seemed packed with eager faces. 'Girls, with chaplets, beautiful young creatures, strewed the entrance of various villages with flowers.'

Nor were the good people of Weymouth and Melcomb Regis a whit behind in loyalty, though greatly at a loss how to vary the expression of their feelings. "Not a child could we meet that had not a bandeau round its head, cap or hat, of 'God save the King'; all the bargemen wore it in cockades; and even the bathing-women had it in large coarse girdles round their waists. It is printed in golden letters upon most of the bathing-machines, and in various scrolls and devices it adorns every shop, and almost every house, in the two towns . . . . Nor is this all. Think but of the surprise of his Majesty when, the first time of his bathing, he had no sooner popped his royal head under water than a band of music, concealed in a neighbouring machine, struck up, 'God save great George our King'! One thing, however, was a little unlucky:—When the mayor and burgesses came with the address, they requested leave to kiss hands. This was graciously accorded; but the mayor advancing in a common way, to take the Queen's hand, as he might that of any lady mayoress, Colonel Gwynn, who stood by, whispered:

" 'You must kneel, sir.'

" He found, however, that he took no notice of this hint, but kissed the Queen's hand erect. As he passed him, in his way back, the Colonel said:

" 'You should have knelt, sir !'

" 'Sir,' answered the poor Mayor, ' I cannot.'

" 'Everybody does, sir.'

" 'Sir,—I have a wooden leg !'

" But the absurdity of the matter followed—all the rest did the same; taking the same privilege, by the example, without the same or any cause !"

Miss Burney's way of life at Weymouth seems to have been much the same as if she had belonged to a private party. "I have here a very good parlour, but dull from its aspect. Nothing but the sea at Weymouth affords any life or spirit. My bedroom is in the attics. Nothing like living at a Court for exaltation. Yet even with this gratification, which extends to Miss Planta, the house will only hold the females of the party . . . . It is my intention to cast away all superfluous complaints into the main ocean, which I think quite sufficiently capacious to hold them; and really my little frame will find enough to carry and manage without them . . . . His Majesty is in delightful health, and much improved in spirits. All agree he never looked better . . . . The Queen is reading Mrs. Piozzi's 'Tour' to me, instead of my reading it to her. She loves reading aloud, and in this work finds me an able commentator. How like herself, how characteristic is every line!—Wild, entertaining, flighty, inconsistent, and clever!" As at Cheltenham, much of the stiffness of Windsor etiquette was thrown aside. The King and his family spent most of their time in walking or riding, and the Queen required but little attendance. Now and again the royal party varied the usual amusements of a wateringplace by a visit to the *Magnificent* line-of-battle ship, stationed at the entrance of the bay, by a cruise in the *Southampton* frigate, which lay further in, or by an excursion to Dorchester, Lulworth Castle, or Sherborne Castle. During these intervals, the Robe-Keeper was left to her own occupations. She passed much of her leisure with the wife of the equerry, Mrs. Gwynn, Goldsmith's 'Jessamy Bride,' who had many stories to tell of her old admirer,* and could exchange anecdotes with Fanny of

* "His coffin was re-opened at the request of the Jessamy Bride, that a lock might be cut from his hair. It was in Mrs. Gwynn's possession when she died, after nearly seventy years."—Forster's "Goldsmith."

Johnson, Baretti, the Thrales, Sir Joshua and his nieces. Strolling with this acquaintance one morning on the sands, Miss Burney " overtook a lady of very majestic port and demeanour, who solemnly returned Mrs. Gwynn's salutation, and then addressed herself to me with similar gravity. I saw a face I knew, and of very uncommon beauty, but did not immediately recollect it was Mrs. Siddons. Her husband was with her, and a sweet child. I wished to have tried if her solemnity would have worn away by length of conversation : but I was obliged to hasten home."

The great actress, as she told Fanny, had come to Weymouth solely for her health ; but she could not resist the royal command to appear at the little theatre, where Mrs. Wells and Quick were already performing. " The King," says the Diary, " has taken the centre front box for himself, and family, and attendants. The side boxes are too small. The Queen ordered places for Miss Planta and me, which are in the front row of a box next but one to the royals. Thus, in this case, our want of rank to be in their public suite gives us better seats than those *high* enough to stand behind them !

" JULY 29TH.—We went to the play, and saw Mrs. Siddons in Rosalind. She looked beautifully, but too large for that shepherd's dress ; and her gaiety sits not naturally upon her—it seems more like disguised gravity. I must own my admiration for her confined to her tragic powers ; and there it is raised so high that I feel morti- fied, in a degree, to see her so much fainter attempts and success in comedy."

A few days later we read that Mrs. Siddons, as Lady Townly, in her looks and the tragic part was exquisite ; and again : " Mrs. Siddons performed Mrs. Oakley. What pity thus to throw away her talents ! But the

Queen dislikes tragedy; and the honour to play before
the Royal Family binds her to the little credit acquired
by playing comedy.

"SUNDAY, AUGUST 9TH.—The King had a council
yesterday, which brought most of the great officers of State
to Weymouth. This evening her Majesty desired Miss
Planta and me to go to the rooms, whither they commonly go themselves on Sunday evenings; and after
looking round them, and speaking where they choose,
they retire to tea in an inner apartment with their own
party, but leave the door open, both to see and be seen.
The rooms are convenient and spacious: we found them
very full. As soon as the royal party came, a circle was
formed, and they moved round it, just as before the ball
at St. James's, the King one way, with his Chamberlain,
the new-made Marquis of Salisbury,* and the Queen
the other, with the Princesses, Lady Courtown, etc. The
rest of the attendants planted themselves round in the
circle. I had now the pleasure, for the first time, to see
Mr. Pitt; but his appearance is his least recommendation;
it is neither noble nor expressive."

Three days later occurs a significant entry:

"WEDNESDAY, AUGUST 12TH.—This is the Prince of
Wales's birthday; but it has not been kept."

On the 13th the royal party left Weymouth for Exeter,
where they arrived to a late dinner. Two days afterwards
they proceeded through a fertile and varied country to
Saltram, the seat of Earl Morley, a minor. All along the
route, the enthusiasm of loyalty which had accompanied
the King from Windsor continued undiminished. Arches
of flowers were erected at every town, with such devices
as rustic ingenuity could imagine, to express the welcome

---

* James, seventh Earl of Salisbury, was advanced in August, 1789, to the
title of Marquis.

of the inhabitants. Everywhere there were crowds, cheers, singing, peals of bells, rejoicings, garlands, and decorations. The view from Saltram commanded Plymouth Sound, Mount Edgecombe, and a wide stretch of the fine adjacent country. Visits were made from this noble house to the great naval port, to the beauties of the famous Mount, to the woods and steeps of Maristow, and the antique curiosities of Cothele on the banks of the Tamar. On the 27th the Court quitted Saltram for Weymouth, and in the middle of September finally departed from Weymouth on its return to Windsor. Two nights and the intervening day were spent at Longleat, the seat of the Marquis of Bath. "Longleat," writes Miss Burney, " was formerly the dwelling of Lord Lansdowne, uncle to Mrs. Delany; and here, at this seat, that heartless uncle, to promote some political views, sacrificed his incomparable niece, at the age of seventeen, marrying her to an unwieldy, uncultivated country esquire, near sixty years of age, and scarce ever sober—his name Pendarves. With how sad an awe, in recollecting her submissive unhappiness, did I enter these doors!—and with what indignant hatred did I look at the portrait of the unfeeling Earl, to whom her gentle repugnance, shown by almost incessant tears, was thrown away, as if she, her person, and her existence, were nothing in the scale, where the disposition of a few boroughs opposed them! Yet was this the famous Granville—the poet, the fine gentleman, the statesman, the friend and patron of Pope, of whom he wrote :

'What Muse for Granville can refuse to sing?'

Mine, I am sure, for one."

The house, at the time of this visit, though magnificent, and of an immense magnitude, was very much out of repair, and by no means cheerful or comfortable.

Gloomy grandeur, Fanny thought, was the character of the building and its fitting-up. " My bedroom," she says, " was furnished with crimson velvet, bed included, yet so high, though only the second story, that it made me giddy to look into the park, and tired to wind up the flight of stairs. It was formerly the favourite room, the housekeeper told me, of Bishop Ken, who put on his shroud in it before he died. Had I fancied I had seen his ghost, I might have screamed my voice away, unheard by any assistant to lay it; for so far was I from the rest of the mansion, that not the lungs of Mr. Bruce could have availed me." The last place at which the King stopped on his homeward journey was Tottenham Park, the seat of the Earl of Ailesbury. Here occurred an instance of the enormous expense to which the great nobles sometimes went in entertaining their sovereign. ' The good lord of the mansion put up a new bed for the King and Queen that cost him £900.'

On September 18 the Court arrived at Windsor. ' Deadly dead sank my heart ' is our traveller's record of her sensation on re-entering the detested dining-room. Nothing happened during the remainder of the year to raise her spirits. In October, the days began to remind her of the terrible miseries of the preceding autumn. She found 'a sort of recollective melancholy always ready to mix ' with her thankfulness for the King's continued good health. And about the same time disquieting news came from over the water of the march to Versailles, the return to Paris, and the shouts of the hungry and furious *poissardes* proclaiming the arrival of ' the baker, his wife, and the little apprentice.' Events of this kind could not but excite uneasiness at any Court, however popular for the time. These shadows were presently succeeded by another, equally undefined, but of a more personal character. In the middle of November, Fanny was told by Miss Planta, in confidence, that Mr. Digby had written to acquaint his royal patrons with his approaching marriage. 'I believed not a syllable of the matter,' says the Diary; 'but I would not tell her that.' Only a few days later, however, the same kind friend informed Miss Burney that 'it was all declared, and that the Princesses had wished Miss Gunning joy at the Drawing-Room.' 'Now first,' says Fanny, 'my belief followed assertion;—but it was only because it was inevitable, since the Princesses could not have proceeded so far without certainty.' The wedding took place early in January; and from this time the bridegroom appeared no more at Court, which became to one of the attendants an abode of unrelieved gloom.

Some of her friends were frank enough in their comments on her situation. There was something, no doubt, in Miss Burney's aspect which drew such remarks as these from the wife of an Irish bishop: " Well; the Queen, to be sure, is a great deal better dressed than she used to be; but for all that, I really think it is but an odd thing for you !—Dear, I think it's something so out of the way for you !—I can't think how you set about it. It must have been very droll to you at first. A great deal of honour, to be sure, to serve a Queen, and all that; but, I dare say a lady's-maid could do it better . . . . It must be a mighty hurry-scurry life ! You don't look at all fit for it, to judge by appearances, for all its great honour, and all that." Colonel Digby had previously accused her of being *absent* in her official occupation, and she had owned that she had at first found attention *unattainable.* " She had even," she added, " and not seldom, handed the Queen her fan before her gown, and her gloves before her cap !" The Vice-Chamberlain thought this very likely,

17—2

and observed that such matters did not seem trifles to her Majesty.

The Diary for the earlier months of 1790 contains little more than what the writer calls 'loose scraps of anecdotes,' of which we can find room for only one or two specimens. Here is an account of a conversation with Colonel Manners, who, besides being an equerry, was also a Member of Parliament :

"I had been informed he had once made an attempt to speak, during the Regency business, last winter; I begged to know how the matter stood, and he made a most frank display of its whole circumstances.

"'Why, they were speaking away,' he cried, 'upon the Regency, and so—and they were saying the King could not reign, and recover; and Burke was making some of his eloquence, and talking; and, says he, 'hurled from his throne'—and so I put out my finger in this manner, as if I was in a great passion, for I felt myself very red, and I was in a monstrous passion I suppose, but I was only going to say 'Hear! Hear!' but I happened to lean one hand down upon my knee, in this way, just as Mr. Pitt does when he wants to speak ; and I stooped forward, just as if I was going to rise up and begin ; but just then I caught Mr. Pitt's eye, looking at me so pitifully ; he thought I was going to speak, and he was frightened to death, for he thought—for the thing was, he got up himself, and he said over all I wanted to say ; and the thing is, he almost always does ; for just as I have something particular to say, Mr. Pitt begins, and goes through it all, so that he don't leave anything more to be said about it ; and so I suppose, as he looked at me so pitifully, he thought I should say it first, or else that I should get into some scrape, because I was so warm and looking so red.'

"Any comment would disgrace this; I will therefore only tell you his opinion, in his own words, of one of our late taxes.*

"'There's only one tax, ma'am, that ever I voted for against my conscience, for I've always been very particular about that; but that is the *bacheldor's* tax, and that I hold to be very unconstitutional, and I am very sorry I voted for it, because it's very unfair; for how can a man help being a *bacheldor*, if nobody will have him? and, besides, it's not any fault to be taxed for, because we did not make ourselves *bacheldors*, for we were made so by God, for nobody was born married, and so I think it's a very unconstitutional tax.'"

Miss Burney's desultory journals for this year contain few notices of her life at Court. We hear, indeed, in the spring, of her being summoned to a new employment, and called upon four or five times to read a play before the Queen and Princesses. But this proved a very occasional break in the routine of drudgery which she could no longer support with cheerfulness. Henceforth she seems to avoid all mention of other engagements and incidents at Windsor or Kew as matters too wearisome to think of or write about. We have, instead, accounts of days spent at the Hastings trial, where, as before, she spent much time in conversing with Windham. The charges were now being investigated in detail, and it was often difficult to make up an interesting report for her mistress. Sometimes, however, when evidence weighed the proceedings down, Burke would speak from time to time, and lift them up; or Windham himself, much to Fanny's satisfaction, would take part in the arguments.

* In 1785, Mr. Pitt introduced an increase in the tax paid on men-servants, when they were kept by bachelors

But Westminster Hall was attractive mainly by contrast to the palace ; in the Great Chamberlain's Box there was no danger of receiving a summons to the Queen, no fear of being late for an attendance in the royal dressing-room. During the recess, when there was no trial to attend, Miss Burney's thoughts were a good deal occupied by the illness and death of a faithful man-servant, and with the subsequent disposal of his savings, which caused her some trouble.

Once, at the end of May, she had an opportunity of unburdening her mind to her father. They met in Westminster Abbey at one of the many commemorations of Handel which occurred about this time ; and, neither of them caring very much for the great master's music, they spent three hours chiefly in conversation. For four years they had not been so long alone together. Dr. Burney happened to mention that some of the French exiles wished him to make them acquainted with the author of ' Cecilia,' and repeated the astonished speech of the Comtesse de Boufflers on learning that this was out of his power : ' Mais, monsieur, est-ce possible ! Made-moiselle votre fille n'a-t-elle point de vacances ?' Such an opening was just what Fanny wanted, and she availed herself of it to pour out her whole heart. With many expressions of gratitude for the Queen's goodness, she owned that her way of life was distasteful to her ; she was lost to all private comfort, dead to all domestic endearment, worn with want of rest and laborious attendance. Separated from her relations, her friends, and the society she loved, she brooded over the past with hopeless regret, and lived like one who had no natural connections. " Melancholy was the existence, where happiness was excluded, though not a complaint could be made ! where the illustrious personages who were served possessed almost all human excellence—yet where those who were their servants, though treated with the most benevolent condescension, could never, in any part of the live-long day, command liberty, or social intercourse, or repose !" " The silence of my dearest father," she adds, "now silencing myself, I turned to look at him; but how was I struck to see his honoured head bowed down almost into his bosom with dejection and discomfort ! We were both perfectly still a few moments; but when he raised his head I could hardly keep my seat to see his eyes filled with tears ! ' I have long,' he cried, ' been uneasy, though I have not spoken ; . . . . but . . . . if you wish to resign—my house, my purse, my arms, shall be open to receive you back !' "

It cannot fairly be said that, during the preceding four years, Miss Burney had been debarred from literary work. The conditions of her lot were hard, and it may have been one of them that she should publish nothing while in the Queen's service; but she certainly had enjoyed considerable leisure for composition. Witness the full and carefully-written journal which she had kept during the greater part of her tenure of office. Perhaps the frequent interruptions to which she was liable hindered her from concentrating her thoughts on the production of a regular narrative. Indefatigable as she was with her pen, we can see that she was far less strenuous when much intellectual exertion was required. When she was offered her post, her Muse was at a standstill, as she told the King; and since she entered the household, she had written nothing capable of being printed, except two or three small copies of verses not worth printing, and the rough draft of a tragedy. She had begun this tragedy during the King's illness, in order to distract her attention; and after laying it aside for sixteen months, she resumed her task in the spring of 1790, and completed the play in August. Well or ill done, she was pleased, she told her sisters, to have done something ' at last—she who had so long lived in all ways as nothing.' In the early part of this year the news-papers announced, as they had done several times before, that the distinguished novelist, who had so long been silent, had at length finished a new tale ready for the press. As often as this rumour appeared, a flutter of apprehension ran through the ante-rooms of the Upper and Lower Lodges. Fanny's genius for seizing the points of a character, and presenting them in a ludicrous light, could not fail to be recognised wherever she went. Years before, the fiery Baretti had warned her that if she dared to put him in a book, she should feel the effects of an Italian's vengeance.* Joseph Baretti, who had stilettoed his man, and who lived to libel Mrs. Piozzi, was the very person to fulfil a promise of this kind. But for his threat, his tempting eccentricities might have exposed him to considerable peril. But the carpet-knights and waiting-women of Windsor stood in no immediate danger. ' There is a new book coming out, and we shall all be in it !' exclaimed the conscience-stricken Mr. Turbulent. The colonels frowned, bit their lips, and tried not to look uncomfortable. ' Well, anybody's welcome to me and my character !' cried poor Miss Planta, whom Fanny used to patronize. ' Never mind ! she's very humane !' observed one of the Willises, well aware that, whoever else might suffer, he and his family were exempt from ridicule. Miss Burney smiled demurely at the tributes paid to her power. Full well she knew that, so far as the characters of her colleagues were worth preserving, she had them all

* Diary, vol. ii., p. 581.

safe, under lock and key, in her Diary. But not a line of the dreaded novel had been written. The passion, which possessed her in her early days, for planning a story, and contriving situations for the actors in it, had faded away as the freshness of youth departed.

The months rolled on, and her spirits did not improve, while her health steadily declined. Some of her female friends—Mrs. Gwynn, Miss Cambridge, Mrs. Ord—saw her at Windsor or Kew after the close of the London season, and were painfully impressed with the alteration which they noted in her. The reports which these ladies carried up to town were speedily known throughout her father's circle of acquaintances. The discontent that had been felt at her seclusion increased tenfold when it was suspected that there was danger of the prisoner's constitution giving way. A sort of cabal was formed to bring influence to bear upon Dr. Burney. The lead in this seems to have been taken by Sir Joshua Reynolds, who, despite his failing eyesight and his Academic troubles, was zealous as ever in the cause of his old favourite. Dr. Burney had yielded to Fanny's wish of retiring; but he was not in affluent circumstances, he had expected great things from the Court appointment, his daughter had not much worldly wisdom, and in dread of the censure that awaited him in high quarters, if he suffered her to throw away a competency without visible necessity, he was for putting off the evil day of resignation as long as possible. It was therefore important that friends whose approbation he valued should unite to make him understand that the case, in their judgment, called for prompt determination. He was much worked upon in the autumn by a letter from Horace Walpole to Frances, in which the writer, with a touch of heartiness quite unusual to him, lamented her confinement to a closet at Court, and asked whether her talents were given to be buried in obscurity? About the same time, he was warned by his daughter, Mrs. Francis, that Windham, her neighbour in Norfolk, who had observed for himself the change in Fanny's appearance, was meditating an attack on him as soon as they should meet in town. The politician had already sounded Burney to little purpose; 'it is resolution,' he told Charlotte, 'not inclination, the Doctor wants.' 'I will set the Literary Club upon him!' he cried. 'Miss Burney has some very true friends there, and I am sure they will all eagerly assist. We will present him an address.'

The general feeling infected James Boswell, though not very intimate with the Burney family. In this same autumn, Boswell was on a visit to the Dean of Windsor, who was also Bishop of Carlisle. Miss Burney met him one morning at the choir-gate of St. George's Chapel:

" We saluted with mutual glee: his comic-serious face and manner have lost nothing of their wonted singularity; nor yet have his mind and language, as you will soon confess.

" ' I am extremely glad to see you indeed,' he cried, ' but very sorry to see you here. My dear ma'am, why do you stay?—it won't do, ma'am! you must resign!— we can put up with it no longer. I told my good host the Bishop so last night; we are all grown quite out-rageous!' Whether I laughed the most, or stared the most, I am at a loss to say; but I hurried away, not to have such treasonable declarations overheard, for we were surrounded by a multitude. He accompanied me, how-ever, not losing one moment in continuing his exhorta-tions: ' If you do not quit, ma'am, very soon, some violent measures, I assure you, will be taken. We shall address Dr. Burney in a body; I am ready to make the harangue myself. We shall fall upon him all at once.'

"I stopped him to inquire about Sir Joshua; he said he saw him very often, and that his spirits were very good. I asked about Mr. Burke's book. 'Oh,' cried he, 'it will come out next week: 'tis the first book in the world, except my own, and that's coming out also very soon; only I want your help.' 'My help?' 'Yes, madam; you must give me some of your choice little notes of the Doctor's; we have seen him long enough upon stilts; I want to show him in a new light. Grave Sam, and great Sam, and solemn Sam, and learned Sam —all these he has appeared over and over. Now I want to entwine a wreath of the graces across his brow; I want to show him as gay Sam, agreeable Sam, pleasant Sam: so you must help me with some of his beautiful billets to yourself.'"

Fanny evaded this request by declaring that she had not any stores at hand; she could not, she afterwards said, consent to print private letters addressed to herself. The self-satisfied biographer followed her to the Queen's Lodge, continuing his importunity, and repeating his exhortations to her to resign at once. At the entrance, he pulled out a proof-sheet of the First Book in the world, and began to read from it a letter of Dr. Johnson to himself. 'He read it,' says the Diary, 'in strong imitation of the Doctor's manner, very well, and not caricature. But Mrs. Schwellenberg was at her window, a crowd was gathering to stand round the rails, and the King and Queen and Royal Family now approached from the Terrace. I made rather a quick apology, and with a step as quick as my now weakened limbs have left in my power, I hurried to my apartment.'

By what representations Dr. Burney was brought to view his daughter's condition in its true light we are not distinctly informed. We find, however, that, before October ended, a memorial to the Queen, written by Fanny in her father's name and her own, requesting permission for the Robe-Keeper to resign, had been approved by the Doctor, who expressed his desire that it should be presented at the first favourable opportunity. Then came a pause: the invalid was taking bark, which for a short time recruited her strength; and she cherished the hope of obtaining a ship for her brother James before she left the Court. But her hopes both for her brother and herself proved illusory. In December, her loss of health became so notorious that no part of the house could wholly avoid acknowledging it. 'Yet,' she writes, 'was the terrible piquet the catastrophe of every evening, though frequent pains in my side forced me, three and four times in a game, to creep to my own room for hartshorn and for rest.' The remaining members of the household were more considerate than the mistress of the card-table. The ladies had the fellow-feeling of fellow-sufferers; even Mr. Turbulent frankly counselled Miss Burney to retreat before it was too late. A general opinion prevailed that she was falling into a decline, and that, at best, she was reduced to a choice between her place and her life. " There seemed now," she says, " no time to be lost; when I saw my dear father he recommended to me to be speedy, and my mother was very kind in urgency for immediate measures. I could not, however, summon courage to present my memorial; my heart always failed me, from seeing the Queen's entire freedom from such an expectation; for though I was frequently so ill in her presence that I could hardly stand, I saw she concluded me, while life remained, inevitably

·hers." Fanny's nervousness, in fact, had made her less anxious to deliver her letter than her father was to have it delivered, and some further persuasion from him was required before the paper reached her Majesty's hands.

At length it was presented, and the result was exactly what the writer had anticipated. The Schwellenberg stormed, of course: to resign was to return to nothingness; to forfeit the protection of the Court was to become an outcast; to lose the beatific vision of the Sovereign and his consort was hardly less than to be excluded from heaven. The Queen thought the memorial very modest and proper, but was surprised at its contents. Indomitable herself, she could not understand how anyone else could suffer from more than passing illness. She therefore proposed that her sick attendant should have six weeks' leave of absence, which, with change of air and scene, and the society of her family, the Locks and the Cambridges, would ensure a perfect cure. This proposal was duly communicated to Dr. Burney. The good man's answer arrived by return of post. With much gratitude for the royal goodness, he declared, on medical authority, that nothing short of an absolute retirement gave any prospect of recovery. "A scene almost horrible ensued," says Miss Burney, "when I told Cerbera the offer was declined. She was too much enraged for disguise, and uttered the most furious expressions of indignant contempt at our proceedings. I am sure she would gladly have confined us both in the Bastille, had England such a misery, as a fit place to bring us to ourselves, from a daring so outrageous against imperial wishes."

The Queen herself betrayed a blank disappointment at Dr. Burney's inflexibility, but neither exhibited displeasure nor raised any further obstacle. Yet the prisoner's liberation was still at a distance. In January, 1791, she was prostrated by an attack of some acute illness which lasted through the two following months. On returning to her duty, she found that search was being made for a suitable person to succeed her. But the selection proved difficult, and her Majesty, of course, could not be pressed. It was at length arranged that Miss Burney should be set free soon after the celebration of the King's birthday in June. This matter settled, her position grew easier. Her colleague not only laid aside asperity of manner, but became even 'invariable in kindness.' And Fanny now began to do the old lady more justice than she had ever done before. She acknowledged, in short, that Cerbera's bark was worse than her bite ; that though selfish, harsh, and overbearing, she was not unfriendly ; that she was even extremely fond of her junior's society, when the latter could force herself to appear gay and chatty. On such occasions the morose German would melt, and tell the Queen : 'The Bernar bin reely agribble.' 'Mrs. Schwellenberg, too,' adds the Diary, 'with all her faults, is heart and soul devoted to her royal mistress, with the truest faith and loyalty.' As for this mistress, she treated her retiring servant with all her former confidence, clouded only by a visible, though unavowed, regret at the prospect of their separation. Thus the closing weeks of this life at Court were spent in comparative tranquillity, though there were intervals of great weakness and depression.

"On the opening of this month," says the Diary for June, "her Majesty told me that the next day Mr. Hastings was to make his defence, and warmly added, ' I would give the world you could go to it !'" There was no resisting such an appeal, and accordingly, under date of June 2nd, we read : " I went once more to Westminster Hall, which was more crowded than on any day since the trial commenced, except the first. Peers, commoners,

and counsel, peeresses, commoneresses, and the numerous
indefinites, crowded every part, with a just and fair curiosity
to hear one day's defence, after seventy-three of accusa-
tion.' Miss Burney heard the accused read his vindication,
and listened with an interest which she knew would be
shared by the King and Queen ; she heard something also
about herself, which she did not communicate to their
Majesties. She attended to the story of Hastings when
told by himself as she had never attended to it before ;
her sympathy followed him when he expressed disdain of
his persecutors, when he arraigned the late Minister, Lord
North, of double-dealing, and the then Minister, Mr. Pitt,
of cowardly desertion. She shared his indignation when
the Managers interrupted him ; she exulted when the
Lords quelled the interruption by cheering the speaker,
and when Lord Kenyon, who presided in the place of the
Chancellor, said, ' Mr. Hastings, proceed.' She contrasted
the fortitude of the defendant, who for so many days had
been silent under virulent abuse, with the intemperate
eagerness of his assailants, who could not exercise the
like self-control even for three brief hours. In short, she
felt as warm-hearted women always have felt, and as it is
suspected that even icy politicians, men of light and leading on their respective sides, occasionally do feel in the
present enlightened age. "The conclusion of the defence,"
continues this excited partisan, "I heard better, as Mr.
Hastings spoke considerably louder from this time : the
spirit of indignation animated his manner, and gave
strength to his voice. You will have seen the chief parts
of his discourse in the newspapers ; and you cannot, I
think, but grow more and more his friend as you peruse
it. He called pathetically and solemnly for instant judgment ; but the Lords, after an adjournment, decided to
hear his defence by evidence, and in order, the next

Session. How grievous such continued delay to a man past sixty, and sighing for such a length of time for redress from a prosecution as yet unparalleled in our annals!"

When it was over, Windham approached her, and 'in a tone of very deep concern, and with a look that fully concurred in it,' said, 'Do I see Miss Burney? Indeed,' he went on, 'I was going to make a speech not very gallant.' 'But it is what I should like better,' cried the lady; for it is kind, if you were going to say I look miserably ill, as that is but a necessary consequence of feeling so, and miserably ill I have felt this long time past.' She prevented more by going on to say how happy she was that he had been absent from the Managers' Box, and had not joined in the attempt made by his fellow-managers to disconcert Mr. Hastings. 'Indeed, I was kept in alarm to the very last moment; for at every figure I saw start up just now—Mr. Fox, Mr. Burke, Mr. Grey—I concluded yours would be the next.' 'You were prepared, then,' cried he with no little malice, 'for a " voice issuing from a distant pew." ' This unexpected quotation from Cecilia " put me quite out," says Fanny, " whereupon he seized his opportunity to put himself in. For, after a little laugh at his victory, he very gravely, and even almost solemnly, said, 'But there is another subject—always uppermost with me—which I have not ventured to speak of to you ; though to others you know not how I have raved and raged! But I believe, I am sure, you know what I allude to.' 'Twas impossible, thus challenged, to dissemble. 'Yes,' I answered; 'I own, I believe I understand you ; and, indeed, I should be tempted to say further—if you would forget it when heard, and make no implications—that, from what has come round to me from different quarters, I hold myself to be very much obliged to you . . . .' When we came home I was immediately summoned to her Majesty, to whom I gave a full and fair account of all I had heard of the defence; and it drew tears from her expressive eyes, as I repeated Mr. Hastings' own words, upon the hardship and injustice of the treatment he had sustained." At night, the reporter was called upon to repeat her narrative to the King, to whom she was equally faithful, " sparing nothing of what had dropped from the persecuted defendant relative to the Ministers of the Crown."

Two days afterwards came the King's birthday, and Miss Burney was well enough to enjoy a lively scene— the last that she was to witness at Court:

"At dinner Mrs. Schwellenberg presided, attired magnificently. Miss Goldsworthy, Mrs. Stainforth, Messrs. de Luc and Stanhope dined with us; and, while we were still eating fruit, the Duke of Clarence entered. He was just risen from the King's table, and waiting for his equipage to go home and prepare for the ball. To give you an idea of the energy of his Royal Highness's language, I ought to set apart a general objection to writing, or rather intimating, certain forcible words, and beg leave to show you, in genuine colours, a royal sailor. We all rose, of course, upon his entrance, and the two gentlemen placed themselves behind their chairs, while the footmen left the room; but he ordered us all to sit down, and called the men back to hand about some wine. He was in exceeding high spirits, and in the utmost good humour. He placed himself at the head of the table, next Mrs. Schwellenberg, and looked remarkably well, gay, and full of sport and mischief, yet clever withal as well as comical. 'Well, this is the first day I have ever dined with the King at St. James's on his birthday.

Pray, have you all drunk his Majesty's health?' 'No, your Roy'l Highness: your Roy'l Highness might make dem do dat,' said Mrs. Schwellenberg. 'O, by —— will I! Here, you (to the footman); bring champagne! I'll drink the King's health again, if I die for it! Yet, I have done pretty well already: so has the King, I promise you! I believe his Majesty was never taken such good care of before. We have kept his spirits up, I promise you; we have enabled him to go through his fatigues: and I should have done more still, but for the ball and Mary—I have promised to dance with Mary!' Princess Mary made her first appearance at Court to-day: she looked most interesting and unaffectedly lovely: she is a sweet creature, and perhaps, in point of beauty, the first of this truly beautiful race, of which Princess Mary may be called *pendant* to the Prince of Wales. Champagne being now brought for the Duke, he ordered it all round. When it came to me, I whispered to Westerhaults to carry it on: the Duke slapped his hands violently on the table, and called out, 'O, by ——, you shall drink it!' There was no resisting this. We all stood up, and the Duke sonorously gave the royal toast."

The indefatigable diarist, says Thackeray, continues for pages reporting H.R.H.'s conversation, and indicating, with a humour not unworthy of the clever little author of 'Evelina,' the increasing excitement of the young Sailor Prince, who drank more and more champagne, stopped old Mrs. Schwellenberg's remonstrances by kissing her hand, and telling her to shut her potato-trap, and who did not keep 'sober for Mary.' Mary had to find another partner that night, for the royal William Henry could not keep his legs. When the Princess afterwards told Miss Burney of her brother's condition at the ball, and Fanny accounted for it by relating what had passed at the attendants' dinner-table, she found that she had been anticipated by the Duke himself. 'Oh!' cried the Princess; 'he told me of it himself the next morning, and said: "You may think how far I was gone, for I kissed the Schwellenberg's hand!"' The lady saluted was duly sensible of the honour paid her. 'Dat Prince Villiam,' she observed to her junior—'oders de Duke of Clarence—bin raelly ver merry—oders vat you call tipsy.'

Mademoiselle Jacobi,* Fanny's destined successor, arrived in the first days of July, and the prison door was now thrown open. Miss Burney imagined that, as the day of her discharge approached, the Queen's manner to her became rather less cordial, and betokened an inward feeling that the invalided servant ought, at every hazard, to have remained with her employer. This, we believe, is a common opinion among mistresses in all ranks of life, when called upon to surrender a trusted dependent. The King, with that weakness which the better-half always despises, was disposed to be much more indulgent. As if to compensate for his consort's vexation, he showed himself increasingly courteous and kind at every meeting, making opportunities to talk over Boswell's book, which had

---

* Macaulay asserts that, shortly after her release, Miss Burney "visited her old dungeon, and found her successor already far on the way to the grave, and kept to strict duty, from morning till midnight, with a sprained ankle, and a nervous fever." This is a strange misstatement. Mademoiselle Jacobi had leave of absence to nurse her sprain: it was not "in the old dungeon" that Miss Burney saw her on the occasion referred to, but in a small room at Brompton, where she was sitting with her leg on bolsters, and unable to put her foot to the ground. Fanny, in January, 1792, took a turn of duty at St. James's, by the Queen's request, because "Mademoiselle Jacobi was still lame." Diary, vol. iii., pp. 385-87. However, we read afterwards that, towards the end of 1797, Mademoiselle Jacobi "retired to Germany, ill and dissatisfied with everything in England." She, as well as Miss Burney, received a pension.

recently appeared, and listening to Fanny's anecdotes of
Johnson with the utmost complacency and interest. The
Princesses did not conceal their sorrow at the impending
change. 'Indeed,' says the Diary, 'the most flattering
marks of attention meet me from all quarters. Mrs.
Schwellenberg has been forced to town by ill-health; she
was very friendly, even affectionate, in going!' And
before the hour of parting arrived, the light cloud passed
away from her Majesty's face. It has been asked, Why
should she have grieved at losing an attendant, who, as
the Queen used to complain, could never tie the bow of
her royal necklace without tying her royal hair in with
it? But, in Miss Burney, Queen Charlotte was losing
much more than an unskilful tire-woman, or a nervous
reader, who, as we know on the same unimpeachable
authority, 'had the misfortune of reading rather low.' She
was losing one whom she declared to be 'true as gold,' and
who had a much larger share of mind than commonly fell to
the official lot; a familiar friend who was as far as possible
from being a learned lady, and yet capable of entertaining
her mistress with clever and stimulating talk such as her
Majesty loved. No retiring pension had been asked for
in the petition for leave to resign, and when the subject
was mentioned by the Queen, the petitioner hastened to
disavow all claim and expectation of that kind. She
found, however, that the question of what the occasion
demanded had been already considered and decided.
Though the term of service had been short, the character
of the servant, and the notorious failure of her health,
made it imperative that she should receive some provision. The Queen therefore announced her intention of
continuing to her second Robe-Keeper in retirement one-
half of the annual salary which had been paid to her in
office. 'It is but her due,' said the King. 'She has

given up five years of her pen.'* Two days after this matter was settled, Miss Burney took leave of the Royal Family. Emotional as one of her own heroines, she could not control her feelings in bidding farewell to the Queen, and was unable even to look at the King when he came to say 'Good-bye.' She quitted the Court on July 7, 1791, having been a member of the royal household for five years all but ten days. Burke recalled the satisfaction with which he had hailed her appointment; and, owning that he had never been more mistaken in his life, observed that the story of those five years would have furnished Johnson with another vivid illustration for his 'Vanity of Human Wishes.'

* Memoirs, iii. 118 n.

CHAPTER XI.

MISS BURNEY returned to her father, who, with his wife
and his youngest daughter Sarah, was then living in
Chelsea Hospital. The family at this time occupied
rooms on the ground-floor, which not long afterwards
were exchanged for others in the top story. After resting
three weeks at home, she set out on a tour to the south-
west of England, under the care of her friend Mrs. Ord.
The travellers journeyed by easy stages to Sidmouth,
taking Stonehenge on their way, and stopping at the
principal places which had been visited by the Court in
the summer of 1789. Having spent eight or nine days
on the coast of South Devon, they turned northwards,
and proceeded by the ruins of Glastonbury Abbey to
Bath. That most famous of English watering-places was
greatly altered from what it had been when Fanny passed
the season there with the Thrales eleven years before.
The circumference, she tells us, had trebled, though the
new buildings were scattered, and most of them un-

finished. "The hills are built up and down, and the vales so stocked with streets and houses, that, in some places, from the ground-floor on one side a street, you cross over to the attic of your opposite neighbour. It looks a town of hills, and a hill of towns." But the palaces of white stone rising up on every hand interested her less than the old haunts with which she was familiar —the North Parade, where she had lived with Mrs. Thrale; the houses in the Circus, where she had visited Mrs. Montagu and Mrs. Cholmley; the Belvedere, where she had talked with Mrs. Byron and Lord Mulgrave. Nearly a month slipped away in reviving old recollections, and in making some new acquaintances to replace the many that had disappeared. The retired official was much flattered by an introduction to the celebrated Duchess of Devonshire, and amused herself with the thought that her first visit after leaving the Queen should be paid to the greatest lady of the Opposition. Another month was divided between Mickleham and Norbury Park, and by the middle of October Miss Burney was again at Chelsea.

'We shall expect you here to dinner by four,' wrote her father. 'The great grubbery will be in nice order for you, as well as the little; both have lately had many accessions of new books. The ink is good, good pens in plenty, and the most pleasant and smooth paper in the world !

  ' " Come, Rosalind, oh, come and see
   What quires are in store for thee !' ' '

Are we wrong in thinking that these words express Dr. Burney's anxiety to see his daughter once more working as she had not worked since the last sheet of ' Cecilia ' was corrected for the press ? In the succeeding pages of the Diary we find more than one passage where the good man's eagerness for some new fruit of her talents is plainly confessed. Friends had united to persuade him that he had but to recall her from the royal dressing-room to her study, and fresh laurels, with abundant riches, would surely and speedily be hers. He was naturally impatient for some fulfilment of these prophecies. Rosalind appeared : she wore out the quills, and covered the quires ; but nothing came of her activity. Her health was now fairly restored, and, in the first ardour of com-position, she felt that she could employ two pens almost incessantly. Unhappily, her industry was devoted to a mistaken purpose. She had brought with her from Windsor the rough drafts of two tragedies, and without pausing to correct these, she occupied herself in writing a third. A less hopeful enterprise could not have been conceived. She had before her eyes the warning example of Mr. Crisp's failure. Had this old friend been living, he would doubtless have been wiser for his pupil than he was for himself. It is certain that Nature had not de-signed the Siddons for tragedy more distinctly than she intended Frances Burney for comedy. With the excep-tion of one or two powerful scenes, such as the death of Harrel, Fanny's chief successes had been won in the department of humorous writing. It was her misfortune that she had at this moment no literary adviser on whose judgment she could rely. Her acquaintance with Arthur Murphy seems to have ceased ; the Hastings trial, and the debates on the Regency, had cooled her relations with Sheridan and Burke. 'Mr. Sheridan,' she wrote, ' I have no longer any ambition to be noticed by.' Her regard for Burke continued ; but she had not yet met him since her deliverance from captivity. Dr. Burney was told only that she was engaged upon a play, and was made to understand that he must wait until it was

finished before he was indulged with a sight of the manuscript. Towards the end of 1791 she writes: 'I go on
with various writings, at different times, and just as the
humour strikes. I have promised my dear father a
Christmas-box and a New Year's gift; and therefore he
now kindly leaves me to my own devices.' We do not
find that the anxious parent received either of the
promised presents. The daughter's fit of application
seems to have soon died away: in the early part of 1792,
her father was ill and occupied with his ailments; and by
the time he was able to think of other things, Fanny had
ceased to prepare for coming before the public. Her
tragedies slept in her desk for three years: when, at the
end of that period, the earliest of them, which had been
begun at Kew and finished at Windsor, was put on the
stage, it was produced without revision, and failed—
as, no doubt, it would have done under any circumstances.

As Miss Burney's strength returned, she seems to have
fallen back into the indolent life of visiting and party-going
which she was leading when she joined the Royal Household. She saw once more the failing Sir Joshua, who
had worked at her deliverance as if she had been his own
daughter; though he passed from the scene before she
found an opportunity of thanking him for his exertions.
She attended a great public breakfast given by Mrs.
Montagu, whose famous Feather Room and dining-room
were thronged by hundreds of guests, and looked like a
full Ranelagh by daylight. At this entertainment she
met Mrs. Hastings, whose splendid dress, loaded with
ornaments, gave her the appearance of an Indian
princess. At another breakfast Fanny encountered Boswell, who had excited her displeasure by his revelation of
Johnson's infirmities, and who provoked her again by

telling anecdotes of the great Samuel, and acting them
with open buffoonery. During the Session, she spent
much of her time at the Hastings trial, listening to the
defence conducted by Law, Dallas, and Plomer, and
rallying Windham on the sarcasms aimed by Law at the
heated rhetoric of Burke. The great orator himself she
rarely encountered on these occasions. In June, 1792,
however, she spent a day with him at Mrs. Crewe's house
on Hampstead Hill.

"The villa at Hampstead is small, but commodious.
We were received by Mrs. Crewe with much kindness.
The room was rather dark, and she had a veil to her
bonnet, half down, and with this aid she looked still in a
full blaze of beauty . . . . She is certainly, in my eyes, the
most completely a beauty of any woman I ever saw. I
know not, even now, any female in her first youth who
could bear the comparison. She uglifies everything near
her. Her son was with her. He is just of age, and
looks like her elder brother! he is a heavy, old-looking
young man. He is going to China with Lord Macartney.*

"My former friend, young Burke, was also there. I
was glad to renew acquaintance with him; though I
could see some little strangeness in him: this, however,
completely wore off before the day was over. Soon after
entered Mrs. Burke, Miss French, a niece, and Mr.
Richard Burke, the comic, humorous, bold, queer brother
of *the* Mr. Burke . . . . Mrs. Burke was just what I have
always seen her, soft, gentle, reasonable, and obliging;
and we met, I think, upon as good terms as if so many
years had not parted us.

"At length Mr. Burke appeared, accompanied by Mr.
Elliot. He shook hands with my father as soon as he

* 1737-1806. Lord Macartney's mission to China was narrated in two interesting works, *Macartney's Journal*, and *Staunton's ' Account of the Embassy.'*

had paid his devoirs to Mrs. Crewe, but he returned my curtsey with so distant a bow, that I concluded myself quite lost with him, from my evident solicitude in poor Mr. Hastings's cause. I could not wish that less obvious, thinking as I think of it; but I felt infinitely grieved to lose the favour of a man whom, in all other articles, I so much venerate, and whom, indeed, I esteem and admire as the very first man of true genius now living in this country.

"Mrs. Crewe introduced me to Mr. Elliot: I am sure we were already personally known to each other, for I have seen him perpetually in the Managers' Box, whence, as often, he must have seen me in the Great Chamberlain's. He is a tall, thin young man, plain in face, dress, and manner, but sensible, and possibly much besides; he was reserved, however, and little else appeared.

" The moment I was named, to my great joy I found Mr. Burke had not recollected me. He is more near-sighted considerably than myself. 'Miss Burney!' he now exclaimed, coming forward, and quite kindly taking my hand, 'I did not see you;' and then he spoke very sweet words of the meeting, and of my looking far better than 'while I was a courtier,' and of how he rejoiced to see that I so little suited that station. 'You look,' cried he, 'quite renewed, revived, disengaged; you seemed, when I conversed with you last, at the trial, quite altered; I never saw such a change for the better as quitting a Court has brought about!'

"Ah! thought I, this is simply a mistake, from reasoning according to your own feelings. I only seemed altered for the worse at the trial, because I there looked coldly and distantly, from distaste and disaffection to your proceedings; and I here look changed for the better, only because I here meet you without the chill of disapprobation, and with the glow of my first admiration of you and your talents!

"Mrs. Crewe gave him her place, and he sat by me, and entered into a most animated conversation upon Lord Macartney and his Chinese expedition, and the two Chinese youths who were to accompany it. These last he described minutely, and spoke of the extent of the undertaking in high, and perhaps fanciful, terms, but with allusions and anecdotes intermixed, so full of general information and brilliant ideas, that I soon felt the whole of my first enthusiasm return, and with it a sensation of pleasure that made the day delicious to me.

"After this my father joined us, and politics took the lead. He spoke then with an eagerness and a vehemence that instantly banished the graces, though it redoubled the energies, of his discourse. 'The French Revolution,' he said, 'which began by authorizing and legalizing injustice, and which by rapid steps had proceeded to every species of despotism except owning a despot, was now menacing all the universe and all mankind with the most violent concussion of principle and order.' My father heartily joined, and I tacitly assented to his doctrines, though I feared not with his fears.

"One speech I must repeat, for it is explanatory of his conduct, and nobly explanatory. When he had expatiated upon the present dangers, even to English liberty and property, from the contagion of havoc and novelty, he earnestly exclaimed, 'This it is that has made ME an abettor and supporter of Kings! Kings are necessary, and, if we would preserve peace and prosperity, we must preserve THEM. We must all put our shoulders to the work! Ay, and stoutly, too!' . . .

"At dinner Mr. Burke sat next Mrs. Crewe, and I had the happiness to be seated next Mr. Burke; and my other neighbour was his amiable son.

" The dinner, and the dessert when the servants were removed, were delightful. How I wish my dear Susanna and Fredy* could meet this wonderful man when he is easy, happy, and with people he cordially likes! But politics, even on his own side, must always be excluded; his irritability is so terrible on that theme that it gives immediately to his face the expression of a man who is going to defend himself from murderers. . . .

" Charles Fox being mentioned, Mrs. Crewe told us that he had lately said, upon being shown some passage in Mr. Burke's book which he had warmly opposed, but which had, in the event, made its own justification, very candidly, ' Well! Burke is right—but Burke is often right, only he is right too soon.'

" ' Had Fox seen some things in that book,' answered Mr. Burke, ' as soon, he would at this moment, in all probability, be first minister of this country.'

" ' What!' cried Mrs. Crewe, ' with Pitt?—No!—no! —Pitt won't go out, and Charles Fox will never make a coalition with Pitt.'

" ' And why not?' said Mr. Burke dryly! ' why not this coalition as well as other coalitions?'

" Nobody tried to answer this.

" ' Charles Fox, however,' said Mr. Burke, afterwards, ' can never internally like the French Revolution. He is entangled; but, in himself, if he should find no other objection to it, he has at least too much taste for such a revolution.' . . .

" Mr. Richard Burke related, very comically, various censures cast upon his brother, accusing him of being the friend of despots, and the abettor of slavery, because he had been shocked at the imprisonment of the King of France, and was anxious to preserve our own limited

* Mrs. Locke.

monarchy in the same state in which it so long had flourished.

" Mr. Burke looked half alarmed at his brother's open-ing, but, when he had finished, he very good-humouredly poured out a glass of wine, and, turning to me, said, 'Come, then—here's slavery for ever!' This was well understood, and echoed round the table with hearty laughter.

" ' This would do for you completely, Mr. Burke,' said Mrs. Crewe, 'if it could get into a newspaper! Mr. Burke, they would say, has now spoken out; the truth has come to light unguardedly, and his real defection from the cause of true liberty is acknowledged. I should like to draw up the paragraph!'

" ' And add,' said Mr. Burke, 'the toast was ad-dressed to Miss Burney, in order to pay court to the Queen!' " . . . . After a stroll:

" The party returned with two very singular additions to its number—Lord Loughborough, and Mr. and Mrs. Erskine. They have villas at Hampstead, and were met in the walk; Mr. Erskine else would not, probably, have desired to meet Mr. Burke, who openly in the House of Commons asked him if he knew what friendship meant, when he pretended to call him, Mr. Burke, his friend?

" There was an evident disunion of the cordiality of the party from this time. My father, Mr. Richard Burke, his nephew, and Mr. Elliot entered into some general discourse; Mr. Burke took up a volume of Boileau, and read aloud, though to himself, and with a pleasure that soon made him seem to forget all intruders: Lord Lough-borough joined Mrs. Burke, and Mr. Erskine, seating himself next to Mrs. Crewe, engrossed her entirely, yet talked loud enough for all to hear who were not engaged themselves.

" For me, I sat next Mrs. Erskine, who seems much a woman of the world, for she spoke with me just as freely, and readily, and easily as if we had been old friends.

" Mr. Erskine enumerated all his avocations to Mrs. Crewe, and, amongst others, mentioned, very calmly, having to plead against Mr. Crewe upon a manor business in Cheshire. Mrs. Crewe hastily and alarmed, interrupted him, to inquire what he meant, and what might ensue to Mr. Crewe? ' Oh, nothing but the loss of the lordship upon that spot,' he coolly answered; ' but I don't know that it will be given against him : I only know I shall have three hundred pounds for it.'

" Mrs. Crewe looked thoughtful; and Mr. Erskine then began to speak of the new Association for Reform, by the friends of the people, headed by Messrs. Grey and Sheridan, and sustained by Mr. Fox, and openly opposed by Mr. Windham, as well as Mr. Burke. He said much of the use they had made of his name, though he had never yet been to the society; and I began to understand that he meant to disavow it; but presently he added, ' I don't know whether I shall ever attend—I have so much to do—so little time; however, the people must be supported.'

" ' Pray, will you tell me,' said Mrs. Crewe dryly, ' what you mean by the people? I never knew.'

" He looked surprised, but evaded any answer, and soon after took his leave, with his wife, who seems by no means to admire him as much as he admires himself, if I may judge by short odd speeches which dropped from her. The eminence of Mr. Erskine seems all for public life; in private, his excessive egotisms undo him.

" Lord Loughborough instantly took his seat next to Mrs. Crewe; and presently related a speech which Mr. Erskine has lately made at some public meeting, and which he opened to this effect:—'As to me, gentlemen, I have some title to give my opinions freely. Would you know what my title is derived from ? I challenge any man to inquire ! If he ask my birth,—its genealogy may dispute with kings ! If my wealth, it is all for which I have time to hold out my hand ! If my talents,—No ! of those, gentlemen, I leave you to judge for yourselves !'

"But I have now time for no more upon this day, except that Mr. and Mrs. Burke, in making their exit, gave my father and me the most cordial invitation to Beaconsfield in the course of the summer or autumn. And, indeed, I should delight to accept it."

The second half of this year was consumed by a round of visits, commencing in town, and ending in Norfolk. On leaving London, Miss Burney accompanied her eldest sister into Essex, where they spent some time together at Halstead Vicarage. From this place, Fanny went alone to stay at Bradfield Hall, near Bury St. Edmunds, with the family of the agriculturist, Arthur Young,* who had married a sister of the second Mrs. Burney.

All over the country, in the autumn of 1792, two subjects only were talked of, the Revolution in France, and the adventures of the emigrants to England. Little settlements of refugees had been, or were being, formed in various districts. One coterie had established themselves at Richmond, where they received much attention from Horace Walpole. Other unfortunates found their way to Bury. A third colony, and not the least important, sought retirement in the Vale of Mickleham. The fugitives, of course, were not only of different ranks, but of different political complexions. The Revolution had begun to

* Born in 1741, died in 1821 ; author of many works on agricultural and economical subjects. His " Travels in France " were published in this very year—1792.

devour its children; and some of the exiles had helped
to raise the passion which swept them away. Suffolk had
been visited in the spring by the celebrated Countess of
Genlis, governess to the children of Philip Egalité, Duke
of Orleans. This lady, who was now called Madame de
Sillery, or Brulard, hired a house at Bury for herself and
her party, which included an authentic Mademoiselle
d'Orléans, besides the Pamela who afterwards married
Lord Edward Fitzgerald, and another young girl. Her
establishment also comprised a number of men, who were
treated by the ladies sometimes as servants, sometimes as
equals. The vagaries of this curious household and its
mistress provoked comments which drove them from the
county before Miss Burney entered it. It was rumoured
that Madame Brulard's departure was hastened by the
arrival of the Duke de Liancourt, who warmly denounced
her influence over her infamous protector as a principal
cause of the French anarchy. Yet the nobleman just
named was himself known as a friend of the people. He
it was who, bursting into the King's closet to report the
fall of the Bastille, had been the first to utter the word
Revolution. Arthur Young, who, like most other well-to-do
Englishmen at that moment, was ready to forswear every
popular principle he had formerly professed, inveighed
against the Duke's folly, while he pitied the misfortunes of
a man to whom his travels had laid him under obligation.
Fanny met the new-comer at her host's table, and heard
from his own lips the story of his escape from France.
Being in command at Rouen when news of the bloody
Tenth of August reached that city, and finding a price set
on his head by the Jacobins, De Liancourt, with some
difficulty, made his way to the sea, where he embarked in
an open boat, and set sail, covered with faggots, for the
opposite coast. He entertained his friends at Bradfield

Hall with an account of his landing at Hastings, describing how he had walked to the nearest public-house, and, to seem English, had called for '*pot portère,*' and then, being extremely thirsty, for another; how, overcome by the strange liquor, he had been carried upstairs in a helpless state, and put to bed; how he had woke up before day-break in a miserable room, and fancied himself in a French *maison de force;* how, on creeping cautiously below, the sight of the kitchen, with its array of bright pewter plates and polished saucepans, had convinced him that he must be in a more cleanly country than his native land. What had brought the Duke to Bury we are not informed: he certainly would not have been at home with Walpole's friends, who seem to have been staunch adherents of the *ancien régime.*

Some, though not all, of the strangers at Mickleham had advanced several degrees beyond the timid consti-tutionalism of the Duke de Liancourt. The origin and early history of this settlement were communicated to Fanny by the journalizing letters of her sister, Mrs. Phillips. Two or three families had united to take a house near the village, called Juniper Hall, while another family hired a cottage at West Humble, which the owner let with great reluctance, 'upon the Christian-like supposi-tion that, being nothing but French papishes, they would never pay.' The party at the cottage were presided over by Madame de Broglie, daughter-in-law of the Maréchal who had commanded the Royalist troops near Paris. Among the first occupants of Juniper Hall were Narbonne, recently Constitutionalist Minister of War, and Mont-morency, *ci-devant duc,* from whom had proceeded the motion for suppressing titles of nobility in France. When Mrs. Phillips made the acquaintance of her new neigh-bours, they had been reinforced by fresh arrivals, including an officer of whom she had not yet heard. This was M. d'Arblay,* who, Susan was told, had been Adjutant-General to her favourite hero, Lafayette, when that leader surrendered himself to the Allies. On the chief being sent prisoner to Olmutz, the subordinate was permitted to withdraw into Holland, whence he was now come to join his intimate friend and patron, Count Louis de Narbonne. ' He is tall,' wrote Mrs. Phillips to her sister, ' and a good figure, with an open and manly countenance; about forty, I imagine.'

The letters from Mickleham were soon full of this General d'Arblay, who won the heart of good Mrs. Phillips by his amiable manners, and his attention to her children, while he fortified her in her French politics, which, to say the truth, were too advanced for Fanny's acceptance. Both the General and Narbonne were attached to their unfortunate master, but considered that they had been very badly treated by Louis, and that it was impossible to serve him, because he could not trust himself, and in consequence distrusted everybody else. D'Arblay had been the officer on guard at the Tuileries on the night of the famous Flight to Varennes. He had not been let into the secret of the plan, but was left, without warning, to run the risk of being denounced and murdered for having assisted the King's escape.

Miss Burney was now in Norfolk with her sister Charlotte. But this visit to her native county proved the reverse of joyful. Soon after her arrival at Aylsham, Mr. Francis, her brother-in-law, was seized with an attack of apoplexy, which ended in his death. During his illness, she interested herself in the accounts of Juniper Hall—

---

* Alexander d'Arblay was born at Joigny, near Paris. He entered the French artillery at thirteen years of age. He was commandant at Longwy, promoted into Narbonne's regiment, and in 1792 made *maréchal de camp*, or, as we should say, brigadier general.

she had already heard something of M. d'Arblay from the Duke de Liancourt—but her attention was mainly engrossed by the distress of those around her. When all was over, she remained to assist the widow in settling her affairs, and at the close of the year accompanied her and the children to London.

CHAPTER XII.

ON the opening of 1793, the French Constitutionalists were at the lowest point of depression and disgrace. They were reviled on all hands for having given weight and impetus to a movement which they were impotent to control. Norbury Park and Mickleham were eager that Miss Burney should see their new friends and judge them for herself. "Your French colonies," she wrote in reply to Mrs. Locke's pressing invitation, "are truly attractive: I am sure they must be so to have caught me—so substantially, fundamentally the foe of all their proceedings while in power." Having tarried long enough to pay her birthday duty to the Queen, she left London at the commencement of the season, and went down to Surrey. A day or two after her arrival came the news of the French King's execution. The excitement caused by this intelligence quickened the already frequent intercourse between the Lockes and Juniper Hall, and Fanny soon found herself on familiar terms with the refugees. Before the end of January, Madame de Staël appeared on the scene, and placed herself at the head of the little colony. Necker's daughter had earned the rage of the Commune by her exertions to save life during the massacres of August and September; nor was it at all clear that the privilege which she enjoyed as wife of the Swedish Ambassador would avail for her protection. She had, therefore, crossed the Channel, and now joined her Constitutionalist friends at Juniper Hall, whither she was soon followed by Talleyrand, who had come to England in her company. No other party of refugees could boast two names of equal distinction, though French titles had become plentiful as blackberries in several parts of England. Madame de Staël paid the most flattering attention to the author of 'Cecilia,' whose second novel had procured her considerable reputation in Paris. A warm but short-lived intimacy between the two ladies ensued. No two persons could be less suited to one another than our timid, prudish little Burney and the brilliant and audacious French *femme de lettres.* The public acts of the Bishop of Autun—'the viper that had cast his skin,' as Walpole called him—had not inclined Fanny in his favour; but his extraordinary powers conquered her admiration, and as she listened to the exchanges of wit, criticism, and raillery between him and Madame de Staël, she could see for the moment no blemishes in either, and looked on the little band of exiles, some of whom could almost vie with these leaders, as rare spirits from some brighter world. The group, consisting at different times of some dozen persons,*

---

* Among other names, we find, besides those already mentioned, the Marquise de la Châtre, M. de Jaucourt, M. Sicard, the Princesse d'Hénin, De Lally Tollendal, Dumont.

were all most agreeable; but one, perhaps the least dazzling of the whole constellation, proved more attractive than the rest :

"M. d'Arblay," wrote Fanny, "is one of the most singularly interesting characters that can ever have been formed. He has a sincerity, a frankness, an ingenuous openness of nature, that I have been unjust enough to think could not belong to a Frenchman. With all this, which is his military portion, he is passionately fond of literature, a most delicate critic in his own language, well versed in both Italian and German, and a very elegant poet. He has just undertaken to become my French master for pronunciation, and he gives me long daily lessons in reading. Pray expect wonderful improvements! In return, I hear him in English."

The natural consequences followed. In a few days we read : "I have been scholaring all day, and mastering too; for our lessons are mutual, and more entertaining than can easily be conceived." Our novelist, in short, was more romantic than any of her own creations : Evelina, Cecilia, and Camilla were prosaic women compared with Frances. On the verge of forty-one, she gave away her heart to an admirer, suitable to her in age, indeed, but possessing neither fortune, occupation, nor prospects of any kind. Whatever property d'Arblay could claim, the Convention had confiscated. Fanny herself had nothing but the small annuity which she enjoyed during the Queen's pleasure, and which might be discontinued if she married this Roman Catholic alien. Such a match, in any case, implied seclusion almost as complete as that from which she had recently escaped. This was anything but the issue that her father had been promised when he was pressed to sanction her resignation. It is not surprising, therefore, that he wrote her a remonstrance

stronger and more decided than he had been in the habit
of addressing to any of his children. But Dr. Burney
stood alone. The Lockes and Phillipses were as much
fascinated by their French neighbours as his enamoured
daughter. Susanna was in avowed league with the enemy.
Mr. Locke gave it as his opinion that two persons, with
one or more babies, might very well subsist on a hundred
a year. Thus assailed by opposing influences, Fanny went
to deliberate in solitude at Chesington, and sauntered
about the lanes where she had planned 'Cecilia,' wondering if the Muse would ever visit her again. The General's
pursuing letters convinced her that his grief at her hesitation was sincere and profound. He made a pilgrimage to
see her, which vouched his devotion, and gained him the
support of her simple hostesses, Mrs. Hamilton and
Kitty Cooke, who wept at his tale of misfortunes, and
learned for the first time what was meant by the French
Revolution. Finally, through the mediation of his favourite
Susanna, Dr. Burney was persuaded to give way and send
a reluctant consent. The wedding took place on the
31st of July, 1793, in Mickleham Church, in the presence
of Mr. and Mrs. Locke, Captain and Mrs. Phillips, M. de
Narbonne, and Captain Burney, who acted as proxy for
his father. On the following day, the ceremony was
repeated at the Sardinian Chapel in Lincoln's Inn Fields,
according to the rites of the Romish Church.

The marriage proved eminently happy. Dr. Burney,
though he shrank from giving away the bride, was a
respecter of accomplished facts, and soon became on
excellent terms with his new son-in-law. The late impetuous lovers proceeded to translate their romance into
the most sober prose. Love in a cottage had been the
goal of their ambition. Mr. Locke had promised a site
for the cottage; but as funds for building it were not

immediately forthcoming, the pair went first into farm
lodgings, afterwards into a hired house of two or three
rooms at Bookham, within two miles of Mickleham and
Norbury Park. D'Arblay, a man of real honour, would
have left his wife, almost in their honeymoon, to fight for
Louis XVII. at Toulon; but his offer of service was
declined by the English Government, and thenceforth the
General resigned himself to wait for better times. Like a
sensible man, *il cultivait son jardin.* Like a man of sense,
but not like a good husbandman. His wife, who, notwithstanding her happiness, seems to have lost her sense
of humour very soon after matrimony, enjoyed one of
her last hearty laughs at the expense of her lord:

"This sort of work is so totally new to him, that he
receives every now and then some of poor Merlin's*
'disagreeable compliments'; for when Mr. Locke's or
the Captain's gardeners favour our grounds with a visit,
they commonly make known that all has been done
wrong. Seeds are sowing in some parts when plants
ought to be reaping, and plants are running to seed while
they are thought not yet at maturity. Our garden, therefore, is not yet quite the most profitable thing in the
world; but M. d'A. assures me it is to be the staff of our
table and existence.

"A little, too, he has been unfortunate; for, after immense toil in planting and transplanting strawberries
round our hedge here at Bookham, he has just been
informed they will bear no fruit the first year, and the
second we may be 'over the hills and far away.'

"Another time, too, with great labour, he cleared a
considerable compartment of weeds; and when it looked
clean and well, and he showed his work to the gardener,
the man said he had demolished an asparagus bed!

* A French inventor whom Fanny had met at Streatham.

M. d'A. protested, however, nothing could look more like *des mauvaises herbes.*

" His greatest passion is for transplanting. Everything we possess he moves from one end of the garden to another to produce better effects. Roses take place of jessamines, jessamines of honeysuckles, and honeysuckles of lilacs, till they have all danced round as far as the space allows; but whether the effect may not be a general mortality, summer only can determine.

"Such is our horticultural history. But I must not omit that we have had for one week cabbages from our own cultivation every day! Oh, you have no idea how sweet they tasted! We agreed they had a freshness and a *goût* we had never met with before. We had them for too short a time to grow tired of them, because, as I have already hinted, they were beginning to run to seed before we knew they were eatable."

While the General was gardening, Madame plied her pen, using it once more, after the lapse of a dozen years, with a definite purpose of publication. Her first composition was for a charitable object. It was an address to the ladies of England on behalf of the emigrant French clergy, who, to the number of 6,000, were suffering terrible distress all over the country. This short paper is an early example of the stilted rhetoric which gradually ruined its author's style. Some months later we hear of a more important work being in progress. This tale, eventually published under the title of ' Camilla,' was commenced in the summer of 1794, though it did not see the light till July, 1796.

A son, their only child, was born on December 18, 1794, and was baptized Alexander Charles Louis Piochard, receiving the name of his father, with those of his two god-fathers, Dr. Charles Burney the younger, and the Count de Narbonne.

An illness, which retarded the mother's recovery, interrupted the progress of her novel, and perhaps counted for something in the failure of the tragedy with which, as we mentioned before, she tempted fortune on the stage. ' Edwy and Elgiva '—so this drama was called—was produced at Drury Lane on March 21, 1795. It says much for the author's repute that John Kemble warmly recommended her work to Sheridan, who seems to have accepted it without hesitation or criticism. The principal characters were undertaken by Kemble and Mrs. Siddons. At the close of the performance, it was announced that the piece was withdrawn for alterations. There was a little complaint that several of the actors were careless and unprepared ; but, on the whole, Madame d'Arblay bore her defeat with excellent temper. She consoled herself with the thought that her play had not been written for the theatre, nor even revised for the press ; that the manuscript had been obtained from her during her confinement ; and that she had been prevented by ill-health from attending rehearsals, and making the changes which, on the night of representation, even her unprofessional judgment perceived to be essential. Yet it is difficult to imagine that a tragedy by the author of ' Evelina' could, under any circumstances, have been successful ; and we are more surprised that Sheridan was so complaisant than that Dr. Burney had always shrugged his shoulders when the Saxon drama was mentioned in his hearing.

Three years sooner the dramatist would have felt her personal mishap more keenly, as she would have welcomed with far livelier pleasure an event of a public nature which occurred shortly afterwards. On April 23, 1795, Warren Hastings was triumphantly acquitted. The incident hardly stirred her at all. She was now experiencing that

detachment which is the portion of ladies even of social
and literary tastes, when they have accomplished the
great function of womanhood. Her father writes her a
pleasant account of his London life, relating some characteristic condolences which he had received from Cumberland on the fate of her play, mentioning his own visit of
congratulation to Hastings, and chatting about the doings
at the Literary Club. The blissful mother replies in a
letter, dated from the 'Hermitage, Bookham,' which is
principally occupied with praises of rural retirement and
the intelligent infant, though it ends with some words
about the tragedy, and a postscript expressing satisfaction
at the acquittal. Not long before, Frances Burney had
repined at living in what she rather inaptly called a
monastery: Frances d'Arblay is more than content with
the company of her gardener and their little 'perennial
plant.' At her marriage, she had counted on having the
constant society of Susanna and her Captain, as well as
the Lockes; but in June, 1795, the Phillipses remove to
town, and are not missed. The Bambino not only supplied all gaps, but made his willing slave work as hard at
'Camilla' as, long years before, she had worked at
'Cecilia' under the jealous eye of her Chesington
daddy.

She was now as keen as Crisp would have had her be
in calculating how she could make most money by her
pen. 'I determined,' she says, 'when I changed my
state, to set aside all my innate and original abhorrences,
and to regard and use as resources myself what had
always been considered as such by others. Without this
idea and this resolution, our hermitage must have been
madness.' She had formerly objected to a plan, suggested
for her by Burke, of publishing by subscription, with the
aid of ladies, instead of booksellers, to keep lists and

receive names of subscribers. She determined to adopt this plan in bringing out 'Camilla.' The Dowager Duchess of Leinster, Mrs. Boscawen, Mrs. Crewe, and Mrs. Locke, gave her the required assistance. In issuing her proposals, she was careful not to excite the prejudice which still prevailed against works of fiction.* She remembered that the word *novel* had long stood in the way of 'Cecilia' at Windsor, and that the Princesses had not been allowed to read it until it had been declared innocent by a bishop. 'Camilla,' she warned her friends, was 'not to be a romance, but sketches of characters and morals put in action.' It was, therefore, announced simply as 'a new work by the author of Evelina and Cecilia.' The manuscript was completed by the end of 1795; but, as in the case of 'Cecilia,' six months more elapsed before the day of publication arrived.

Meanwhile, the subscription-list filled up nobly. When Warren Hastings heard what was going forward, we are told that "he gave a great jump, and exclaimed, 'Well, then, now I can serve her, thank Heaven, and I will! I will write to Anderson to engage Scotland, and I will attack the East Indies myself!'" Nor was Edmund Burke less zealous than his old enemy. Protesting that for personal friends the subscription ought to be five guineas instead of one, he asked for but one copy of 'Camilla' in return for twenty guineas which he sent on behalf of himself, his wife, his dead brother Richard, and the son for whom he was in mourning. In the same spirit, three Misses Thrale order ten sets of the book. As we glance down the pages of the list, we meet with

---

* How strong this prejudice continued to be was shown not long afterwards in a notable instance. Jane Austen's father offered her 'Pride and Prejudice' to Cadell on November 1, 1797; the proposal was rejected by return of post, without an inspection of the manuscript, though Mr. Austen was willing to bear the risk of the publication.

most of the survivors of the old Blue Stockings, with
Mrs. Carter, Mrs. Chapone, Mrs. Montagu, and Hannah
Moore. There, too, are many literary women of other
types : Anna Barbauld, Amelia Alderson, afterwards Mrs.
Opie, Mary Berry, Maria Edgeworth, Sophia and
Harriet Lee.* There the incomparable Jane Austen,
then a girl of twenty, pays tribute to a passed mistress of
her future art. There also figure the names of many of
the writer's former colleagues in the royal household.
Even Mrs. Schwellenberg is on the list. Perhaps, as the
book was to be dedicated by permission to the Queen,
this was almost a matter of course. But the subscription was, in fact, a testimonial to a general favourite from
hundreds of attached friends, some of whom cared little
for literature ; as well as from a crowd of distant admirers,
who regarded her as the most eminent female writer of
her time.

The first parcel of ' Camilla ; or, A Picture of Youth,'
reached Bookham on an early day in July, 1796 ; and
Madame d'Arblay at once set off for Windsor to present
copies to the King and Queen. Immediately on her
arrival, she was admitted to an audience of the Queen,
during which the King entered to receive his share of the
offering. The excellent monarch was in one of his most
interrogative moods, and particularly curious to learn
who had corrected the proofs of the volumes before him.
His flattered subject confessed that she was her own
reader. ' Why, some authors have told me,' cried he,
' that they are the last to do that work for themselves !
They know so well by heart what ought to be, that they
run on without seeing what is. They have told me,
besides, that a mere plodding head is best and surest for
that work, and that the livelier the imagination, the less

* Author of the ' Canterbury Tales.'

it should be trusted to.' Madame had carried her husband with her to Windsor. They were detained there three days; and, as Walpole remarks with some emphasis, even M. d'Arblay was allowed to dine. Horace means, of course, that the General, who had the Cross of St. Louis, was invited to a place at Mdlle. Jacobi's table. Just before dinner, Madame d'Arblay was called aside by her entertainer, and presented, in the name of their Majesties, with a packet containing a hundred guineas, as a 'compliment' in acknowledgment of her dedication.

On the following day, the Chevalier and his wife repaired to the Terrace. "The evening was so raw and cold that there was very little company, and scarce any expectation of the Royal Family; and when we had been there about half an hour the musicians retreated, and everybody was preparing to follow, when a messenger suddenly came forward, helter-skelter, running after the horns and clarionets, and hallooing to them to return. This brought back the straggling parties, and the King, Duke of York, and six Princesses soon appeared . . . . The King stopped to speak to the Bishop of Norwich* and some others at the entrance, and then walked on towards us, who were at the further end. As he approached, the Princess Royal said, ' Madame d'Arblay, sir;' and instantly he came on a step, and then stopped and addressed me, and after a word or two of the weather, he said, ' Is that M. d'Arblay?' and most graciously bowed to him, and entered into a little conversation, demanding how long he had been in England, how long in the country, etc. Upon the King's bowing and leaving us, the Commander-in-Chief most courteously bowed also to M. d'Arblay; and the Princesses all came

---

* Dr. Manners Sutton, then also Dean of Windsor, and afterwards Archbishop of Canterbury.

up to speak to me, and to curtsey to him, and the Princess Elizabeth cried, ' I've got leave! and mamma says she won't wait to read it first!' "

The lively Princess, who was then twenty-six years of age, and had been concerned in bringing out a poem entitled the ' Birth of Love,' with engravings from designs by herself, intended to communicate that she had obtained permission to read ' Camilla,' though it had not yet been examined by her mother.

The subscribers to the new novel exceeded eleven hundred; but the number of copies printed was four thousand. Out of these only five hundred remained at the end of three months—a rate of sale considerably more rapid than that of ' Cecilia' had been. Macaulay mentions a rumour that the author cleared more than three thousand guineas by her work. This is not an improbable account; for Dr. Burney told Lord Orford within the first six weeks that about two thousand pounds had already been realized.* The material results were astonishing; yet ' Camilla' could not be considered a success. The ' Picture of Youth' had neither the freshness of ' Evelina,' nor the mature power of ' Cecilia.' It was wanting alike in simplicity and polish. By disuse of her art, the writer had lost touch with the public; by neglect of reading, she had gone back in literary culture. Hence it was generally felt that the charm which she had exercised was gone. The reviews were severe; new admirers appeared not; old friends found their faith a good deal tried. When the first demand was satisfied, there seems to have been no call for a fresh edition, though some years afterwards Miss Austen boldly coupled†

---

* Lord Orford to Miss Berry, Aug. 16, 1796.

† In ' Northanger Abbey,' which, though written in 1798, was not prepared for the press till 1863.

'Camilla' with 'Cecilia' as a 'work in which most thorough knowledge of human nature, the happiest delineation of its varieties, the liveliest effusions of wit and humour are conveyed to the world.' When its five volumes were most sharply handled, brother Charles could console the chagrined author with the distich:

> 'Now heed no more what critics thought 'em,
> Since this you know, all people bought 'em.'

The composition of 'Camilla' has been blamed for the opposite faults of affectation and slovenliness. 'Every passage,' says Macaulay, 'which the author meant to be fine is detestable; and the book has been saved from condemnation only by the admirable spirit and force of those scenes in which she was content to be familiar.' Other censors have observed that, while the rhetoric is inflated, the grammar is occasionally doubtful, and the diction sometimes barbarous. Now, it must be owned that the ordinary vocabulary of the Burneys was not remarkable for purity or elegance. In their talk and intimate letters, both the father and the daughters expressed themselves in the most colloquial forms, not seldom lapsing into downright slang. To give one instance only, the atrocious vulgarism of 'an invite' for 'an invitation' occurs in several parts of the Diary. When writing for the press, Dr. Burney guarded himself by the adoption of a wholly artificial style, that swelled, from time to time, into tedious magniloquence. Fanny was schooled for writing 'Cecilia' by the critical discussions of the Streatham circle, by much intercourse with Johnson, and by some study of style—chiefly the style of the 'Ramblers' and 'Lives of the Poets.' Having despatched her second novel, she ceased to be careful about literary questions. This indifference increased after her marriage. When describing the reception of 'Camilla' at Windsor, 'the Queen,' she writes, 'talked of some books and authors, but found me wholly in the clouds as to all that is new.' Her husband, insensible, of course, to the niceties of a foreign idiom, but apparently admiring pompous phraseology, conceived a relish for Dr. Burney's style; and Madame, delighting to think her 'dear father' perfect, was pleased to place his English in the very first class.* The eloquence of 'Camilla' seems to mingle faint Johnsonian echoes with the stilted movement of the music-master's prose; while too often the choice of words is left to chance. A recent editor of the two earlier novels has called attention to the numerous vulgarities of expression, not put into vulgar mouths, which occur in 'Camilla.' 'People "*stroam* the fields," or have "a depressing *feel*."' This editor suggests that Miss Burney's five years at Court may have done much to spoil her English, remarking that 'she lived at Windsor among hybrids.' By 'hybrids' we suppose we are to understand equerries. But the equerries, if not possessing great culture, were, at any rate, gentlemen of good position. If they used the incriminated phrases why not also the personages of the novel? We take it, however, that 'to stroam the fields' is not a low phrase acquired by Fanny at Court, but a provincialism which she learned in her native county, where the verb to 'stroam,' or to 'strome,' was certainly in use a hundred years ago,† and is, we are assured, familiarly employed at the present day. We believe that Madame d'Arblay's English was ruined, not by associating with Colonel Digby, or even Colonel Manners, but by neglect of reading, by retirement from lettered society, by fading recollections of Johnson, by untoward family influences, and by a strong hereditary tendency to run into fustian.

* Diary, iv. 3.   † Forby's 'Vocabulary of East Anglia,' p. 330.

In October, 1796, Dr. Burney lost his second wife, who, after a prolonged period of ill-health, died at Chelsea Hospital. To prevent him from brooding over his bereavement, Madame d'Arblay induced her father to resume a poetical history of astronomy which he had begun some time before. This occupation amused him for some time, though in the end the poem, which ran to a great length, was destroyed unfinished.

Out of the profits made by his wife's publication, M. d'Arblay built a small house on land leased to him by Mr. Locke at West Humble, near Dorking, and called it Camilla Cottage. If a family, as well as a nation, is happy that has no history, we must conclude that the d'Arblays lived very much at ease for some years after their removal to their new abode. When the excitement of planning, building, and taking possession is exhausted, Madame's pen finds little to record, beyond the details of occasional interviews with the Queen and Princesses at Buckingham House. She wisely declines a proposal of Mrs. Crewe to make her directress of a weekly paper, which was to have been started, under the name of *The Breakfast-Table*, to combat the progress of Jacobinical ideas. Later on she abandons unwillingly a venture of a different kind. Still thirsting for dramatic success, she had written a comedy called ' Love and Fashion;' and towards the close of 1799 was congratulating herself on having it accepted by the manager of Covent Garden Theatre.* The piece was put into rehearsal early in the following spring; but Dr. Burney was seized with such dread of another failure, that, to appease him, his daughter and her husband consented to its being withdrawn. The compliance cost some effort: Fanny com-

* According to her biographer, the manager had promised her £400 for the right of representation.

plained that she was treated as if she 'had been guilty of a crime, in doing what she had all her life been urged to, and all her life intended—writing a comedy.' 'The combinations,' she added, 'for another long work did not occur to me: incidents and effects for a drama did.'

This was only a transient disappointment. In the first days of 1800 came a lasting sorrow, in the loss of Mrs. Phillips, who, since the autumn of 1796, had been living with her husband in Ireland, and who died immediately after landing in England on her way to visit her father.* But, except by this grief, the peace of Camilla Cottage was never interrupted so long as the husband and wife remained together. In her old age, Madame d'Arblay looked back to the first eight years of her married life as to a period of unruffled happiness.

Then occurred a crisis. The d'Arblays had borne poverty cheerfully, even joyfully, so long as any stretch of economy would enable them to keep within their income. The cost of living and the burden of taxation had begun to increase almost from the day of their marriage. One of the motives for bringing out 'Camilla' was the rise of prices, which had doubled within the preceding eighteen months. Hardly was Camilla Cottage occupied, when an addition to the window-tax compelled the owners to block up four of their new windows. The expense of building so much exceeded calculation that, after all bills were settled, the balance remaining from the foundress's three thousand guineas produced only a few pounds of annual interest. In the spring of 1800, we read that the gardener has planted potatoes on every spot where they can grow, on account of the dreadful price of pro-

---

* Her death took place on January 6, 1800; she was buried in Neston churchyard, where Dr. Burney placed an epitaph to her memory.

visions. Towards the close of 1801, it is admitted that for some time previously they had been encroaching on their little capital, which was then nearly exhausted. As soon, therefore, as the preliminaries of peace were signed. M. d'Arblay determined to remove his family to France, hoping to recover something from the wreck of his fortune, and to obtain from the First Consul some allowance for half-pay as a retired officer. Crossing the Channel alone, in the first instance, the General involved himself in a double difficulty: he failed with the French Government by stipulating that he should not be required to serve against his wife's country, while he had cut off his retreat by pledging himself at the English Alien Office not to return within a year. In this dilemma, he wrote to his wife to join him in Paris with their child. Madame d'Arblay obeyed the summons, amidst the anxious forebodings of her father, but with the full approval of the Queen, who granted her a farewell audience, admitting that she was bound to follow her husband.

Dr. Burney's fears were more than justified by the event. His daughter left Dover a few days after the treaty was signed at Amiens. When she reached Paris, she found the city rejoicing at the conclusion of the war, yet worshipping Bonaparte, whose temper and attitude showed that the peace could not last. A reception by the First Consul, followed by a review, both of which Madame d'Arblay witnessed from an ante-chamber in the Tuileries, afforded striking evidence of the military spirit which animated everything:

" The scene, with regard to all that was present, was splendidly gay and highly animating. The room was full, but not crowded, with officers of rank in sumptuous rather than rich uniforms, and exhibiting a martial air that became their attire, which, however, generally speaking, was too gorgeous to be noble.

" Our window was that next to the consular apartment, in which Bonaparte was holding a levée, and it was close to the steps ascending to it ; by which means we saw all the forms of the various exits and entrances, and had opportunity to examine every dress and every countenance that passed and repassed. This was highly amusing, I might say historic, where the past history and the present office were known.

" Sundry footmen of the First Consul, in very fine liveries, were attending to bring or arrange chairs for whoever required them ; various peace-officers, superbly begilt, paraded occasionally up and down the chamber, to keep the ladies to their windows and the gentlemen to their ranks, so as to preserve the passage or lane, through which the First Consul was to walk upon his entrance, clear and open ; and several gentlemanlike-looking persons, whom in former times I should have supposed pages of the back-stairs, dressed in black, with gold chains hanging round their necks, and medallions pending from them, seemed to have the charge of the door itself, leading immediately to the audience chamber of the First Consul.

" But what was most prominent in commanding notice, was the array of the aides-de-camp of Bonaparte, which was so almost furiously striking, that all other vestments, even the most gaudy, appeared suddenly under a gloomy cloud when contrasted with its brightness . . . .

" The last object for whom the way was cleared was the Second Consul, Cambacérès, who advanced with a stately and solemn pace, slow, regular, and consequential; dressed richly in scarlet and gold, and never looking to the right or left, but wearing a mien of fixed gravity and importance. He had several persons in his suite, who, I think, but am not sure, were ministers of state.

"At length the two human hedges were finally formed, the door of the audience chamber was thrown wide open with a commanding crash, and a vivacious officer—sentinel—or I know not what, nimbly descended the three steps into our apartment, and placing himself at the side of the door, with one hand spread as high as possible above his head, and the other extended horizontally, called out in a loud and authoritative voice, 'Le Premier Consul!'

"You will easily believe nothing more was necessary to obtain attention; not a soul either spoke or stirred as he and his suite passed along, which was so quickly that, had I not been placed so near the door, and had not all about me facilitated my standing foremost, and being least crowd-obstructed, I could hardly have seen him. As it was, I had a view so near, though so brief, of his face, as to be very much struck by it. It is of a deeply impressive cast, pale even to sallowness, while not only in the eye, but in every feature—care, thought, melancholy, and meditation are strongly marked, with so much of character, nay, genius, and so penetrating a seriousness, or rather sadness, as powerfully to sink into an observer's mind. . . .

"The review I shall attempt no description of. I have no knowledge of the subject, and no fondness for its object. It was far more superb than anything I had ever beheld; but while all the pomp and circumstance of war animated others, it only saddened me; and all of past reflection, all of future dread, made the whole grandeur of the martial scene, and all the delusive seduction of martial music, fill my eyes frequently with tears, but not regale my poor muscles with one single smile.

" Bonaparte, mounting a beautiful and spirited white horse, closely encircled by his glittering aides-de-camp, and accompanied by his generals, rode round the ranks, holding his bridle indifferently in either hand, and seem-ing utterly careless of the prancing, rearing, or other freaks of his horse, insomuch as to strike some who were near me with a notion of his being a bad horseman."

Having introduced his wife to old friends in Paris, and paid a visit with her to his relations at Joigny, the General settled his family in a small house at Passy. Instead of being seen at Chelsea again within eighteen months, as her father had been led to expect, she was detained in France more than ten years. From the moment when Lord Whitworth quitted Paris in May, 1803, her oppor-tunities of communicating with England were few and far between. All remittances thence, including her annuity, ended with the peace. The claims to property on which her husband had built proved delusive. Apparently they would have been without means of any kind, but that, just as war was declared, the influence of General Lauris-ton procured for his old comrade the *retraite*, or retiring allowance, for which the latter had been petitioning. Yet this only amounted to £62 10s. yearly, so that the luckless pair would have been far better off in their cottage at West Humble. Moreover, the receipt of half-pay made it impossible for them to risk any attempt at escape while the war continued. At length, in 1805, M. d'Arblay ob-tained employment in the Civil Department of the Office of Public Buildings. He became, in fact, a Government clerk, plodding daily between his desk and a poorly-furnished home at suburban Passy. He seems to have been eventually promoted to the rank of *sous-chef* in his department.

We learn, however, from the scanty notices belonging to this period, that the Chevalier was treated with consideration by the heads of his office, and that he and Madame kept their footing in Parisian society. 'The society in which I mix,' writes the lady, 'when I can prevail with myself to quit my yet dearer fireside, is all that can be wished, whether for wit, wisdom, intelligence, gaiety, or politeness.' She would resume, she adds, her old descriptions if she could only write more frequently, or with more security that she was not writing to the winds and the waves. Her worst distress was the rarity with which letters could be despatched, or travel either way, with anything like safety. At another time she tells her father : 'I have never heard whether the last six letters I have written have as yet been received. Two of them were antiques that had waited three or four years some opportunity . . . . the two last were to reach you through a voyage by America.' The very letter in which this is said lost its chance of being sent, and was not finished till a year later. Dr. Burney, in his fear of a miscarriage, finally gave up writing, and charged his family and friends to follow his example. Fanny had nothing to regret in her husband, except his being overworked and in poor health : her heart shrank from leaving him ; yet her longing for England increased from year to year. Her visionary castles, she said, were not in the air, but on the sea.

In 1810 she had prepared everything for flight, when fresh rigours of the police obliged her to relinquish her design. In 1811 she had a dangerous illness, and was operated upon by the famous surgeon, Baron de Larrey, for a supposed cancer. In the summer of 1812, when Napoleon had set out on his Russian campaign, she obtained a passport for America, took ship with her son at Dunkirk, and landed at Deal. During the interval between her first and second attempts at crossing, all correspondence with England was prohibited on pain of death. One letter alone reached her, announcing in brief terms the death of the Princess Amelia, the renewed and hopeless derangement of the King, and the death of Mr. Locke.

CHAPTER XIII.

Madame d'Arblay's Plans for her Son—Landing in England—Arrival at Chelsea—Saddening Change in Dr. Burney—Alexander d'Arblay at Cambridge—Publication of the 'Wanderer'—Death of Dr. Burney—Madame d'Arblay presented to Louis XVIII.—M. d'Arblay appointed to the Corps de Gardes du Roi—Arrives in England and Carries Madame back to France—Madame d'Arblay presented to the Duchess d'Angoulême—The Hundred Days—Panic at Brussels—M. d'Arblay invalided—Settles in England—His Death—Remaining Days of Madame d'Arblay—Visit from Sir Walter Scott—The Memoirs of Dr. Burney—Tributes to their Value—Death of Alexander d'Arblay—Death of Madame d'Arblay—Conclusion.

MADAME D'ARBLAY had other reasons for wishing to return to England besides the mere desire to see her father and kindred. The longer her only child remained in France, the greater risk he ran of being caught by the conscription, which continually increased its demands. The young Alexander was now of an age to be prepared for a profession, and it cannot be doubted that his mother was anxious to make provision for this purpose. Before leaving Paris, she had begun a treaty in London for the publication of her fourth story. Through what channel this was done we do not learn, but as early as December, 1811, Lord Byron* had heard that a thousand guineas were being asked for a new novel by Madame d'Arblay. She brought the manuscript over with her in a half-finished state.

The travellers did not escape the perils of the time, though happily they were taken prisoners by their own

---

* Moore's 'Life of Byron,' Letters 78, 80.

countrymen.   They and several others had engaged berths on board an American vessel, the astute captain of which delayed his departure so long, in order to obtain more passengers, that when at length he entered British waters, he found himself a prize to the coastguard, news having just arrived that the United States had declared war against England.

It was the middle of August when mother and son found themselves again on English ground.   'I can hardly believe it,' writes the former to her sister Charlotte, now Mrs. Broome; 'I look around me in constant inquiry and doubt; I speak French to every soul, and I whisper still if I utter a word that breathes private opinion.' She goes on to describe her meeting with her father : ' I found him in his library by himself—but, oh ! my dearest, very much altered indeed—weak, weak and changed—his head almost always hanging down, and his hearing most cruelly impaired.   I was terribly affected, but most grateful to God for my arrival.'   During the separation, Dr. Burney had not been unfortunate until the infirmities of age overcame him : the pension which he ought to have received from Mr. Pitt had been procured for him by Mr. Fox.   He had been happily employed in writing for Rees's Encyclopædia; had received flattering notice from the Prince of Wales ; had heard his Royal Highness quote Homer in Greek and imitate Dr. Parr's lisp, and talked familiarly with him at the opera ; had been a courted guest in many great houses ; and had enjoyed the meetings of the Club till his sight and hearing both began to fail.   When he could no longer go abroad, he spent most of his time in reading in his bedroom.   Madame d'Arblay employed herself during this visit to England in nursing her father in his last days, in settling her son at Cambridge, and in bringing out her new book.

Having obtained the Tancred scholarship, Alexander d'Arblay commenced residence at Christ's College, Cambridge, in October, 1813. He eventually graduated as tenth Wrangler, and became Fellow of his college. 'But,' says Macaulay, who had mixed with his fellow-students, 'his reputation at the University was higher than might be inferred from his success in academical contests. His French education had not fitted him for the examinations of the Senate House;* but in pure mathematics we have been assured by some of his competitors that he had very few equals.'

'The Wanderer; or, Female Difficulties' appeared in the beginning of 1814. Notwithstanding the falling-off which had been observed in 'Camilla,' the whole edition of the new work was bespoken before it was published. In six months, 3,600 copies were sold at two guineas a copy. But it may be doubted whether the most conscientious reader persevered to the end of the fifth volume. Ten years of exile had destroyed all trace of the qualities which made 'Evelina' popular.

Dr. Burney lived to his eighty-eighth birthday, and died at Chelsea on the 12th of April, 1814, in the presence of his recovered daughter, who had tended his last hours. A tablet to his memory, bearing an inscription from her pen, was placed in Westminster Abbey.

A few days after his death, Madame d'Arblay was presented to Louis XVIII. By desire of Queen Charlotte, she attended a reception held by the restored King in London on the day preceding his departure for France. Her sovereign—for it must be remembered that she was now a French subject—paid her the most courteous

* He had studied mathematics in Paris according to the analytical method instead of the geometrical, which was at that time exclusively taught at Cambridge.

attention. Addressing her 'in very pretty English,' he told her that he had known her long, for he had been charmed with her books, and 'read them very often.' He bade her farewell in French, with the words 'Bonjour, Madame la Comtesse.'

M. d'Arblay had no further reason to complain of Bourbon ingratitude. Within a few weeks he received a commission in the King's Corps de Gardes, and soon afterwards he was restored to his former rank of Maréchal de Camp. He obtained leave of absence towards the close of the year, and came to England for a few weeks ; after which Madame d'Arblay returned with him to Paris, leaving their son to pursue his studies at Cambridge.

In the early weeks of 1815, Madame d'Arblay was admitted to an audience of the Duchesse d'Angoulême, the King's niece ; close on which followed the return of Bonaparte from Elba, and the Hundred Days. Neither the General nor his wife seems to have felt any alarm till the Corsican reached Lyons. Then a passport was obtained for Madame, that she might be able to leave France in case of need, while her husband remained fixed to his post in the capital. In the night between the 19th and 20th of March, after the King had left Paris, and not many hours before Napoleon entered it, Madame d'Arblay took her departure, accompanied by the Princesse d'Hénin. After many difficulties and misadventures, the fugitives reached Brussels. In that city Madame d'Arblay was presently joined by her husband, who had followed Louis XVIII. to Ghent with the rest of the royal body-guard. She remained in Brussels till the close of the campaign, and for some weeks longer. At a later date she wrote from memory a narrative of what befell her during this period. It includes a description of the scenes that occurred in the Belgian capital while the armies were facing each other within cannon-sound of its streets. The account is graphic, though too diffuse to be quoted at length; evidently it furnished Thackeray with much of the material for the famous chapters in ' Vanity Fair.' We give some abridged extracts :

" What a day of confusion and alarm did we all spend on the 17th ! . . . That day, and June 18th, I passed in hearing the cannon ! Good Heaven ! what indescribable horror to be so near the field of slaughter ! such I call it, for the preparation to the ear by the tremendous sound was soon followed by its fullest effect, in the view of the wounded. . . . And hardly more afflicting was this disabled return from the battle, than the sight of the continually pouring forth victims that marched past my windows to meet similar destruction. . . . .

" Accounts from the field of battle arrived hourly ; sometimes directly from the Duke of Wellington to Lady Charlotte Greville, and to some other ladies who had near relations in the combat, and which, by their means, were circulated in Brussels ; and in other times from such as conveyed those amongst the wounded Belgians, whose misfortunes were inflicted near enough to the skirts of the spots of action, to allow of their being dragged away by their hovering countrymen to the city. . . .

." During this period, I spent my whole time in seeking intelligence. . . .

" Ten times, at least, I crossed over to Madame d'Hénin, discussing plans and probabilities, and interchanging hopes and fears. . . .

" Madame d'Hénin and Madame de la Tour du Pin projected retreating to Gand, should the approach of the enemy be unchecked ; to avail themselves of such protection as might be obtained from seeking it under the wing of Louis XVIII. M. de la Tour du Pin had, I believe, remained there with his Majesty.

" M. de Lally and the Boyds inclined to Antwerp, where they might safely await the fate of Brussels, near enough for returning, should it weather the storm, yet within reach of vessels to waft them to the British shores should it be lost.

" Should this last be the fatal termination, I, of course, had agreed to join the party of the voyage, and resolved to secure my passport, that, while I waited to the last moment, I might yet be prepared for a hasty retreat.

" I applied for a passport to Colonel Jones, to whom the Duke of Wellington had deputed the military command of Brussels in his absence; but he was unwilling to sanction an evacuation of Brussels, which he deemed premature. It was not, he said, for *us*, the English, to spread alarm, or prepare for an overthrow: he had not sent away his own wife or children, and he had no doubt but victory would repay his confidence. . . .

" I found upon again going my rounds for information, that though news was arriving incessantly from the scene of action, and with details always varying, Bonaparte was always advancing. All the people of Brussels lived in the streets. Doors seemed of no use, for they were never shut. The individuals, when they re-entered their houses, only resided at the windows: so that the whole population of the city seemed constantly in public view. Not only business as well as society was annihilated, but even every species of occupation. All of which we seemed capable was, to inquire or to relate, to speak or to hear. Yet no clamour, no wrangling, nor even debate was intermixed with either question or answer; curiosity, though incessant, was serene; the faces were all monotony, though the tidings were all variety. I could attribute this only to the length of time during which the inhabitants had been habituated to change both of masters and measures, and to their finding that, upon an average, they neither lost nor gained by such successive revolutions . . . .

"But what a day was the next—*June 18th*—the greatest, perhaps, in its results, in the annals of Great Britain ! . . .

"I was calmly reposing, when I was awakened by the sound of feet abruptly entering my drawing-room. I started, and had but just time to see by my watch that it was only six o'clock, when a rapping at my bedroom door . . . made me slip on a long kind of domino, . . . and demand what was the matter. "Open your door ! there is not a moment to lose !" was the answer, in the voice of Miss Ann Boyd. I obeyed, in great alarm, and saw that pretty and pleasing young woman, with her mother, Mrs. Boyd. . . . They both eagerly told me that all their new hopes had been overthrown by better authenticated news, and that I must be with them by eight o'clock, to proceed to the wharf, and set sail for Antwerp, whence we must sail on for England, should the taking of Brussels by Bonaparte endanger Antwerp also. . . .

"My host and my maid carried my small package, and I arrived before eight in the Rue d'Assault. We set off for the wharf on foot, not a fiacre or chaise being procurable. Mr. and Mrs. Boyd, five or six of their family, a governess, and I believe some servants, with bearers of our baggage, made our party. . . . When we had got about a third part of the way, a heavy rumbling sound made us stop to listen. It was approaching nearer and nearer, and we soon found that we were followed by innumerable carriages, and a multitude of persons. . . .

"Arrived at the wharf, Mr. Boyd pointed out to us our barge, which seemed fully ready for departure ; but the

crowd, already come and still coming, so incommoded us,
that Mr. Boyd desired we would enter a large inn, and
wait till he could speak with the master, and arrange our
luggage and places. We went, therefore, into a spacious
room and ordered breakfast, when the room was entered
by a body of military men of all sorts; but we were
suffered to keep our ground till Mr. Boyd came to inform
us that we must all decamp ! . . .

"He conducted us not to the barge, not to the wharf,
but to the road back to Brussels; telling us, in an accent
of depression, that he feared all was lost—that Bonaparte
was advancing—that his point was decidedly Brussels—
and that the Duke of Wellington had sent orders that all
the magazines, the artillery, and the warlike stores of
every description, and all the wounded, the maimed, and
the sick, should be immediately removed to Antwerp.
For this purpose he had issued directions that every
barge, every boat, should be seized for the use of the
army; and that everything of value should be conveyed
away, the hospitals emptied, and Brussels evacuated.

"If this intelligence filled us with the most fearful
alarm, how much more affrighting still was the sound of
cannon which next assailed our ears! The dread rever-
beration became louder and louder as we proceeded. . . .

"Yet, strange to relate! on re-entering the city, all
seemed quiet and tranquil as usual! and though it was in
this imminent and immediate danger of being invested,
and perhaps pillaged, I saw no outward mark of distress
or disturbance, or even of hurry or curiosity.

"Having re-lodged us in the Rue d'Assault, Mr. Boyd
tried to find some land carriage for our removal. But
not only every chaise had been taken, and every diligence
secured; the cabriolets, the calèches, nay, the waggons
and the carts, and every species of caravan, had been

seized for military service. And, after the utmost efforts he could make, in every kind of way, he told us we must wait the chances of the day, for that there was no possibility of escape from Brussels, either by land or water. . . .

"I was seated at my bureau and writing, when a loud 'hurrah!' reached my ears from some distance, while the daughter of my host, a girl of about eighteen, gently opening my door, said the fortune of the day had suddenly turned, and that Bonaparte was taken prisoner.

"At the same time the 'hurrah!' came nearer. I flew to the window; my host and hostess came also, crying, *' Bonaparte est pris ! le voilà ! le voilà !'*

"I then saw, on a noble war-horse in full equipment, a general in the splendid uniform of France; but visibly disarmed, and, to all appearance, tied to his horse, or, at least, held on, so as to disable him from making any effort to gallop it off, and surrounded, preceded, and followed by a crew of roaring wretches, who seemed eager for the moment when he should be lodged where they had orders to conduct him, that they might unhorse, strip, pillage him, and divide the spoil.

"His high, feathered, glittering helmet he had pressed down as low as he could on his forehead, and I could not discern his face; but I was instantly certain he was not Bonaparte, on finding the whole commotion produced by the rifling crew above-mentioned, which, though it might be guided, probably, by some subaltern officer, who might have the captive in charge, had left the field of battle at a moment when none other could be spared, as all the attendant throng were evidently amongst the refuse of the army followers.

"I was afterwards informed that this unfortunate general was the Count Lobau. . . .

"The delusion of victory vanished into a merely passing advantage, as I gathered from the earnest researches into which it led me; and evil only met all ensuing investigation; retreat and defeat were the words in every mouth around me! The Prussians, it was asserted, were completely vanquished on the 15th, and the English on the 16th, while on the day just passed, the 17th, a day of continual fighting and bloodshed, drawn battles on both sides left each party proclaiming what neither party could prove—success.

"It was Sunday; but Church service was out of the question, though never were prayers more frequent, more fervent. Form, indeed, they could not have, nor union, while constantly expecting the enemy with fire and sword at the gates. Who could enter a place of worship, at the risk of making it a scene of slaughter? But who, also, in circumstances so awful, could require the exhortation of a priest, or the example of a congregation, to stimulate devotion? No! in those fearful exigencies, where, in the full vigour of health, strength, and life's freshest resources, we seem destined to abruptly quit this mortal coil, we need no spur—all is spontaneous; and the soul is unshackled.

"Not above a quarter of an hour had I been restored to my sole occupation of solace, before I was again interrupted and startled; but not as on the preceding occasion by riotous shouts; the sound was a howl, violent, loud, affrighting, and issuing from many voices. I ran to the window, and saw the *Marché aux Bois* suddenly filling with a populace, pouring in from all its avenues, and hurrying on rapidly, and yet as if unconscious in what direction; while women with children in their arms, or clinging to their clothes, ran screaming out of doors; and cries, though not a word was ejaculated, filled the air, and from every house, I saw windows closing, and shutters fastening; all this, though long in writing, was presented to my eyes in a single moment, and was followed in another by a burst into my apartment, to announce that *the French were come!*

" I know not even who made this declaration; my head was out of the window, and the person who made it scarcely entered the room and was gone.

" How terrific was this moment! My perilous situation urged me to instant flight; and, without waiting to speak to the people of the house, I crammed my papers and money into a basket, and throwing on a shawl and bonnet, I flew downstairs and out of doors.

" My intention was to go to the Boyds, to partake, as I had engaged, their fate; but the crowd were all issuing from the way I must have turned to have gained the Rue d'Assault, and I thought, therefore, I might be safer with Madame de Maurville, who, also, not being English, might be less obnoxious to the Bonapartists. . . .

" What a dreadful day did I pass! dreadful in the midst of its glory! for it was not during those operations that sent details partially to our ears that we could judge of the positive state of affairs, or build upon any permanency of success. Yet here I soon recovered from all alarm for personal safety, and lost the horrible apprehension of being in the midst of a city that was taken, sword in hand, by an enemy. . . .

" The *alerte* which had produced this effect, I afterwards learnt, though not till the next day, was utterly false; but whether it had been produced by mistake or by deceit I never knew. The French, indeed, were coming; but not triumphantly; they were prisoners, surprised and taken suddenly, and brought in, being disarmed, by an escort; and, as they were numerous, and their French uniform was discernible from afar, the almost universal belief at Brussels that Bonaparte was invincible, might perhaps, without any intended deception, have raised the report that they were advancing as conquerors.

"I attempt no description of this day, the grandeur of which was unknown, or unbelieved, in Brussels till it had taken its flight, and could only be named as time past."

The writer's pleasure at the success of the Allies was saddened by an accident which happened to General d'Arblay, who, while employed in raising a force of refugees at Trèves, had received a severe wound in the calf of his leg from the kick of a restive horse. This misfortune impaired still further a constitution already weakened. Being for the time disabled for service, and having passed his sixtieth year, the General found himself placed on the retired list, and obtained leave to settle with his wife in England. When sent on a mission to Blucher, he had been honoured by his master with the title of Comte, which, as being conferred only *par une sorte d'usage de l'ancien régime*, and being neither established by patent, nor connected with the ownership of an estate, he never used after the occasion on which it was given. He died at Bath on May 3, 1818.

Little remains to be told of the life of Madame d'Arblay. During her residence at Bath she renewed her acquaintance with Mrs. Piozzi. We have a long and entertaining account from her pen of an escape from drowning which she met with while staying at Ilfracombe. But with this exception, her last diaries and letters contain little of interest. Soon after the death of her husband she removed to No. 11, Bolton Street, Piccadilly. Her latter days she spent chiefly in retirement, seeing few persons but her own relations, and a small circle of established friends. Among the latter were Mrs. Locke and the poet Rogers, with the latter of whom she had made acquaintance on her first return from France. She was delighted, however, by a visit from Sir Walter Scott, who was brought to her by Rogers. Sir Walter, in his Diary for November 18, 1826, thus records the interview: "Introduced to Madame d'Arblay, the celebrated authoress of 'Evelina' and 'Cecilia,' an elderly lady with no remains of personal beauty, but with a simple and gentle manner, and pleasing expression of countenance, and apparently quick feelings. She told me she had wished to see two persons—myself, of course, being one, the other George Canning. This was really a compliment to be pleased with—a nice little handsome pat of butter made up by a neat-handed Phillis of a dairy-maid, instead of the grease fit only for cart-wheels which one is dosed with by the pound. I trust I shall see this lady again."

From the year 1828 to 1832, she occupied herself in compiling the Memoirs of Dr. Burney. This book, published in her eightieth year, has all the faults of her later style, in their most aggravated form. But her friend Bishop Jebb, while gently hinting at these defects, could honestly congratulate her on the merit of her work. "Much as we already know of the last age, you have brought many scenes of it, not less animated than new, graphically before our eyes; whilst I now seem familiar with many departed worthies, who were not before known to me, even so much as by name." Southey also wrote to her son: "'Evelina' did not give me more pleasure, when I was a schoolboy, than these Memoirs have given me now; and this is saying a great deal. Except Boswell's, there is no other work in our language which carries us into such society, and makes us fancy that we are acquainted with the persons to whom we are there introduced."

In January, 1837, she lost the last prop of her old age. Alexander d'Arblay, having taken Orders soon after his degree, became minister of Ely Chapel in 1836, and was about to marry, when he was carried off by an attack of influenza. His mother survived him nearly three years: she had a severe illness, attended by spectral illusions, in November, 1839; and died in London on January 6, 1840—a day which she had observed from the beginning of the century in memory of the death of her sister Susanna. She was buried at Walcot, near Bath, by the side of her husband and their only child.

Except for the production of the "Memoirs," the last quarter of a century in Madame d'Arblay's life was barren both of incident and employment. The details of her experience during the preceding fifteen years could not fail to interest us, if we had them related as she would have told them in her prime. Especially, we should like to know something more about that long detention in France, when chafing under police restrictions, and fretting for news from home, her heart vibrated to the continual echoes of cannon announcing Napoleon's victories. But Fanny married, and growing elderly, was quite a different person from the Fanny of St. Martin's Street and Chesington, of Streatham and Bath, of Windsor and Kew. Her Diary proper came to a final stop with the death of Mrs. Phillips in 1800. She will always be remembered as Frances Burney of the eighteenth century. Deriving her inspiration in part from Richardson, she heads the roll of those female novelists whose works form a considerable part of English literature. The purity of her writings first made the circulating library respectable. "We owe to her," says

Macaulay very justly, "not only 'Evelina,' 'Cecilia,' and 'Camilla,' but 'Mansfield Park,' and the 'Absentee.' Yet great as was her influence on her successors,* it was exhausted before the present century began. Indeed, it has been suggested, with some reason, that the excessive sensibility of her heroines is answerable for a reaction in Miss Edgeworth and Miss Austen; for the too great amount of bright and cold good sense of the first; for the over-sobriety of feeling of the second.† Fanny's genius for expressing character in dialogue, aided by touches of description, placed her among the first memoir-writers of that journalizing age. A little more power of compression would have made her diaries equal to the best of Boswell's sketches.

"The author herself," says Mr. Leslie Stephen, "with her insatiable delight in compliments—certainly such as might well turn her head—her quick observation and lively garrulity, her effusion of sentiment rather lively than deep, but never insincere, her vehement prejudices corrected by flashes of humour, is always amusing." We may assent to every word of this sentence, and yet feel that it does its subject something less than justice. We trust that our readers have found Fanny amusing; we trust also that they have recognised in her the possession of some higher qualities. If she was vain, her egotism was of the most innocent kind. It was more harmless than Goldsmith's, for we cannot recall in her utterances a single envious or jealous remark. Of how many self-conscious authors can the like be said? The simple love of praise which led her to entertain her acquaintance with what was said about herself, has assisted to render her

---

* Miss Austen took the title of 'Pride and Prejudice' from some words on the last page of 'Cecilia.'
† Introduction to 'Evelina' by Annie Raine Ellis.

interesting to a wider circle. " Vain glory," says Bacon
quaintly, " helpeth to perpetuate a man's memory: like
unto varnish that makes ceilings not only shine, but last."
If she had strong prejudices, they were free from every
taint of personal malevolence. Her dislike of the Opposition resembled Johnson's professed hatred of the Scotch,
at which the doctor himself used to laugh. She goes to
the trial of Hastings, full of zeal for his cause, and spends
her time there chiefly in conversing with his prosecutors.
And however prejudiced on some points, she was far
from narrow-minded on many matters of controversy.
Though brought up a strict Protestant, she married a
Roman Catholic. Though to the end of her days an
attached daughter of the English Church, she expresses
unqualified esteem for the piety of those very pronounced
dissenters, Mr. and Mrs. Barbauld. The sympathy
between herself and her own family was at all times perfect. There were no rivalries among them. " I am sure,"
she wrote modestly in 1800, " my dear father will not
think I mean to parallel our works." She was extremely
pleased when Queen Charlotte declared a tale published
by her half-sister Sarah to be " very pretty." Her
faithfulness to duty and her friends was celebrated by her
royal mistress in the saying that Miss Burney was " true
as gold." When she had cast in her lot with her Chevalier,
no isolation, no privation, no anxiety for the future could
make her repine. " I never forget," she wrote in her
poverty, " Dr. Johnson's words. When somebody said
that a certain person had no turn for economy, he
answered, ' Sir, you might as well say that he has no
turn for honesty.' " Whatever cavils have been raised
by Croker and one or two like-minded detractors, no
artifice or indirect dealing can be laid to her charge, even
in literary matters, in regard to which such manœuvres

are too often deemed excusable. We are not holding her up as a pattern of elevated or extraordinary virtue. She was simply the best representative of a worthy and amiable family who had been trained in the school of Samuel Johnson. That type of character has passed away. The rugged old dictator's political creed is unintelligible to the present age; his devotion is taken for superstition or formalism; his canons of criticism are obsolete. His disciples felt nothing of what was stirring in the air. They were but little accessible to fresh ideas. The cause of popular freedom, the Evangelical movement in religion, the romantic spirit in poetry appealed to them with the smallest effect. They were zealous for authority; they were not in the least introspective; when they wanted a line or two of verse, they nearly always went to Pope for it. The speculations, the problems of the modern world were all unknown to them. They were far less inclined to embrace new dogmas of faith or agnosticism than to observe old rules of action. Yet when we read the annals of the Burneys—the accomplished, the genial, self-respecting, conscientious, pious Burneys—may we not be pardoned for thinking that there was a good deal, after all, in those antiquated Johnsonian principles?

THE END.

BILLING AND SONS, PRINTERS, GUILDFORD.

LITERARY AND SOCIAL LIFE.

LADY MARY WORTLEY MONTAGU.

By ARTHUR R. ROPES, M.A., Sometime Fellow of King's College, Cambridge. With Nine Portraits after Sir Godfrey Kneller. Cloth extra, $2.50.

MRS. THRALE (afterwards Mrs. PIOZZI).

By L. B. SEELEY, M.A., Sometime Fellow of Trinity College, Cambridge. With Nine Copper Plates after Hogarth, etc. Cloth, $2.50.

FANNY BURNEY AND HER FRIENDS.

By L. B. SEELEY, M.A., Sometime Fellow of Trinity College, Cambridge. With Nine Copper Plates after Gainsborough, etc. Cloth, $2.50.

HORACE WALPOLE AND HIS WORLD.

By L. B. SEELEY, M.A., Sometime Fellow of Trinity College, Cambridge. With Eight Copper Plates after Reynolds, etc. Cloth, $2.50.

GLIMPSES OF ITALIAN SOCIETY IN THE EIGHTEENTH CENTURY.

From the "Journey" of Mrs. PIOZZI. With an Introduction by the Countess MARTINENGO CESARESCO, and several Illustrations. Cloth, $1.75.

NEW YORK: CHARLES SCRIBNERS' SONS.